The Family Circle Book of
429 Great Gifts-to-Make
all year around
for just
10¢ to $10

by Anna Marie Doherty
and the Editors of Family Circle Magazine

RAWSON ASSOCIATES PUBLISHERS, INC., NEW YORK

•

Editorial Director / **Arthur Hettich**
Creative Director / **Joseph Taveroni**
Art Director / **Carol Ceraldi**
Associate Editor / **Margaret Wiener**
Illustrations / **William J. Meyerriecks**
Cover Design / **Cosgrove Associates**

Library of Congress Cataloging in Publication Data

Doherty, Anna Marie.
The Family circle book of 429 great gifts-to-make all
year around for just 10¢ to $10.

Includes index.
1. Handicraft. 2. Gifts. I. Family circle.
II. Title.
TT157.D618   745.5   77–76991
ISBN 0–89256–022–3

foreword

Year after year the feature most popular with the readers of Family Circle Magazine is the catalog of quick gifts-to-make for less than $10 which appears in our November issue. Because everybody likes to save time and money, it's a sell-out almost as soon as it hits the supermarkets.

Thanks to the creativity and good taste of our editors, and the excellent how-to directions that back up the designs they select, readers have come to rely on Family Circle as *the* source for beautiful and functional gifts they are proud to make and give.

Because of reader demand we decided to do this book—the most comprehensive and varied collection of gifts-to-make ever published—all at prices you can afford.

Arthur M. Hettich
Editor
Family Circle Magazine

contents

introduction

We have divided the 429 gifts in this book into 10 chapters to help you zero in on just the right gift for the person or occasion you have in mind.

In order to be included, each item had to meet the following guidelines:

$10 OR UNDER PRICE TAG

The price of an item includes only those materials you would have to purchase especially to make the gift. It does not include the tools, household items and needlework notions you would normally have on hand—such things as hammers, saws, glue, sewing threads, knitting needles, brown paper, cardboard, string, etc.

Only a few of our gifts cost over $10, and they are not counted in the 429 figure on the cover. But we included them anyway because their value far exceeds the few extra dollars it costs to make them. It is our sincere hope that inflation doesn't push borderline prices over the $10 limit by the time this book reaches you.

MADE OF READILY AVAILABLE MATERIALS

We have been scrupulous about using only those materials that are easily available to readers at normal retail outlets such as dime stores, lumberyards, home improvement centers, hobby and craft shops, pharmacies, and fabric stores. A large percentage of our gifts make thrifty use of leftovers. As a matter of fact, you'll be able to put together many of them for virtually nothing, as they can be made from the things you were never able to throw away—fabric scraps and remnants, odds and ends of yarn and embroidery floss, the pieces of lumber, dowelling and plywood you tossed into your wood bin, small amounts of paint and varnish, plus food and household containers that can easily be turned into useful and attractive gifts anyone would be glad to receive.

EASY TO MAKE

Quite a few of our gifts are so easy to make that only a few sentences are needed to tell you "how-to." Where necessary, fuller directions are given, many with illustrations, so that you will have all the information you need to complete a project. Any additional helps are included in METHODS (chapter 11). All directions are written in the same familiar FAMILY CIRCLE style that you have come to know and trust over the years.

Anna Marie Doherty
Director/Editorial Services Department
Family Circle Magazine

*Great gifts you'll be
proud to give at
make-them-yourself savings*

People go to gift shops because they stock the kind of unusual but reasonably-priced items that show you care, without costing a fortune. The same kind of "something for every occasion" selection is represented by the 49 gifts in this chapter. It doesn't matter that a lot of them cost next to nothing to make—because they sure don't look like it. You keep the price way down by the ingenious use of on-hand household items, easily recycled into really great-looking gifts that will express your creativity, as well as your thoughtfulness.

directions for items shown above appear on following page

1

CHAPTER 1

FRUIT-SHAPED VINYL PLACEMATS—Three of these fruit-shaped placemats can be made in minutes from ½-yard heavy-weight knit-backed vinyl. Draw free-hand patterns inside 16″ diameter circles and cut out. Trace on fabric side; cut out with X-acto knife.

SENSATIONAL APOTHECARY JARS—Buy dime store apothecary jars in various sizes and shapes. Wash and dry thoroughly. Using enamel paints and a stick, dribble two strong colors on the *inside* surfaces, then spray on white enamel. The colors will mingle in a marble-like pattern. When paint is dry, spray again.

STRIPED AND BASKETWEAVE RIBBON PLACEMATS—Our ribbon placemats are a striped or basketweave pattern on a muslin backing. Washable ribbon can be used, or the mats sprayed with protective coating to prevent staining.
MATERIALS (*for each mat*): Muslin backing, 1 piece 12″x20″; 1½″-wide ribbon for border, about 2 yds.; ribbon of various widths and patterns for center, eight or nine 18″ lengths for either mat, *plus* 12 or 13 ten-inch lengths for woven mats; transparent nylon thread.
DIRECTIONS: Narrowly hem muslin backing. Press hem. *For striped mat:* On backing wrong side, lay 18″ ribbons in a pleasing arrangement of widths and patterns, overlapping ribbon edges ⅛″ and leaving 1″ of backing uncovered on all edges. Edgestitch ribbons to backing. For *woven mat,* lay 18″ ribbons across backing and 10″ ribbons up and down. Weave ribbons. Edgestitch outer edge of woven arrangement 1″ from muslin edges all around.
    Pin border ribbon in place, mitering corners. Edgestitch inner edge; outer edge will extend about ½″ beyond backing. *Optional:* Line placemat with cotton fabric cut to finished mat measurements, turning edges under ¼″; stitch in place.

WINE-LABELED TRAY AND BOOKENDS—A tray and bookends that make wonderful use of wine labels saved from prize vintages, show how much you care.
GENERAL MATERIALS: Paper wine labels; red spray lacquer; black self-adhesive plastic tape; clear plastic coating; makeup sponge; paper towels; gold gift wrap.
GENERAL DIRECTIONS: Soak wine bottles in warm soapy water until glue softens. Starting at a corner, peel off labels and place printed side down on a wet surface; smooth out flat. Allow to dry, then trim edges if necessary.
To affix labels: Brush a thin layer of white glue on prepared surface and smooth labels over it, one at a time, working from center to edges to press out bubbles. Tamp down with a damp sponge, then with a wadded paper towel until label is flat. When dry, follow label directions for applying clear plastic coating.
Tray: We used an unfinished wood picture frame (12″x16″, inside dimensions) and cut a piece of hardboard the same size to fit inside it. For "feet" we nailed four 1″ diameter wooden cabinet knobs at the corners. Sand all surfaces smooth and spray with several coats of red lacquer. Border top of hardboard with ¼″ strips of black tape. Position labels on board to best advantage, then affix following GENERAL DIRECTIONS, one at a time. When dry, cover with plastic coating and allow to cure for a week. Glue board into frame to complete tray.
Bookends: Sand wooden bookends. Spray with several coats of red lacquer. Select and prepare large labels and cut a "lining" for each (¼″ larger than label) from gold gift wrap. On bookend, draw outline ⅛″ larger than label lining. Affix ⅛″ strips of black tape flush inside outline. Glue lining to bookend inside tape, then affix label over lining, following GENERAL DIRECTIONS. (Reverse arrangement of black border and gift wrap for smaller label at top.) Dry, coat, cure, *as above.*

BUTTON-TRIMMED BUTTON TIN—A button tin is made from an empty cold-water detergent can. Sides and lid are sanded, painted with white paint, and the buttons glued on with white glue. When dry, surface is sprayed with varnish.

MATCHSTICK TRIVET AND COASTER SET—Use burned kitchen matches that are even and straight (not warped). On waxed paper, arrange the matches in the designs, as shown. The trivet is approximately 6½″ square, and the coasters, 3¼″ square. In a slow, steady stream, drip rubber cement onto the matches, holding them in shape and pushing them together gently so they adhere firmly to each other. When the cement has dried thoroughly, apply a coat of shellac to the glued surface. Let dry. Turn over. Shellac top. Let dry. Shellac twice more.

TURPENTINE CAN DESK ORGANIZERS—Remove tops of four pint-size and three quart-size turpentine cans. Turn upside down. Spray each with paint three times; dry between coats. Hold cans together with double-stick foam tape strips.

CUTTING BOARD CHESSBOARDS—Chessboards are made from dime-store cutting boards. At left, a solid sheet of white self-adhesive vinyl topped with yellow squares. At right, squares are cut from self-adhesive vinyl tape, applied to cardboard and then to the cutting board.

RECYCLED CAN SPOON HOLDERS—These colorful spoon holders are made from empty cans, 6″ high x 2½″ in diameter. They are covered with strips of self-adhesive cloth tape strips, slightly overlapped. Widths of the tapes are as follows: black, 2″; blue and yellow, 1½″; red and yellow, 1½″; red and orange, ¾″. Each strip must be cut 9″ long to fit around the can with an overlapping seam.

FLUTED ALUMINUM CANDLE HOLDER—One 6″ quiche pan, one 4″ scal-

4

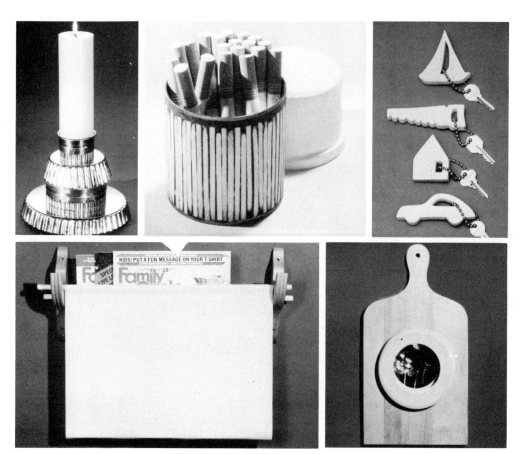

loped cookie cutter, one 3″ quiche pan and one 2″ cutter are soldered one on top of the other to form a holder for a hefty candle.

MATCH-COVERED CIGARETTE CAN—A cigarette can is made from a small-size vegetable can (beans, mushrooms). Burned-out kitchen matches are glued to the sides. Plastic wood filler is pressed around the matches to fill the whole surface. Allowed to dry, the surface is sanded with fine sandpaper to expose matches, then sealed with spray varnish.

KEY TAGS—Boat, workshop, house and car-key tags are easily cut from ½″ scrap pine with saber or jig saw; sand edges.

VINYL MAGAZINE RACK—Fold the short ends of a 14″x54″ piece of vinyl in thirds so ends overlap 2″ at back. Move overlap 1″ off exact center back; sew through all thicknesses. For dowel casings, stitch ¾″ from each fold. Drill holes in drapery brackets for ⅜″ dowel. Place 17″ dowels in casings. Set back dowel in holes; hang front over bracket.

BREADBOARD MIRROR—There's nothing handier than a mirror placed right next to the kitchen door for a fast look-see before you leave the house. On a standard-size breadboard, center a dime-store mirror (5½″ in diameter) and set in place with white glue. Over it, glue 1½″ wide molding (5¾″ outer diameter). The molding is a stock size, available in lumberyards. Dry flat overnight before hanging. Needs no finish.

5

YARN BOWLS FOR DRIED FLOWERS—Yarn Bowls are made with different types of colored yarn dipped in a glue glaze and wound around an inflated balloon. When completely dry, the balloon is popped and peeled away. Base is a separate, straight-sided coil of yarn applied to bottom of bowl.

FABRIC COVERED TISSUE BOXES—Folded fabric scraps become decorative box covers when starched and ironed.

MATERIALS: 3/8 yd. fabric; white glue; spray starch.

DIRECTIONS: *Large box:* Spray-starch and iron (follow label directions) two pieces of fabric, each 13½"x18". Fold in half lengthwise. Center the folded edge on the slit top of box; finger-press the fabric ends into an apothecary fold. Fold the excess fabric into a hem along bottom edge. Spray-starch and iron again, pressing all folds into the fabric. Glue pieces together at ends with the folded edges adjoining along the top center. *For small box:* Spray-starch and iron two 13¼"x10½" pieces. *For boutique-size:* Use two 13½"x16" pieces and follow directions for making the large box.

PHOTOGRAPHER'S LIGHT BOX—Any photo enthusiast would welcome a light box for viewing slides. Ours is made with a half-circle-shaped fluorescent light bracket. Trace fixture's end curve on edge of two 7" pieces 1x4 pine; cut away curves. Glue/screw ½"x7" fixture support strips along cut edge. Glue fixture in place on support strips. Screw ⅛" translucent sheet acrylic on top.

TOWEL RACK—Drill a ¼" hole at each end of four 9" lengths of ½" square doweling. With dowels 3½" apart, thread about 4 feet of ¼" nylon rope through holes; tie knots under the holes. Hanging loop measures about 14". Vary size according to towel size.

PINE ACCENT PIECES—If you have a saber saw, you can make our 22" **accessory shelf** and 8" **plant bracket** in no time.

Accessory Shelf—MATERIALS: 38" of 1x8 pine; 18" of 1x2 pine; 6d finishing nails; two 2" #10 flathead wood screws; wood putty; white glue; polyurethane finish.

DIRECTIONS: Following the directions in the METHODS chapter, enlarge the pattern in Fig. 1 and cut out. With a saber saw or jig saw, cut two brackets. Cut 1x8 shelf 22" long. Glue/nail shelf to brackets, with brackets 1¼" in from ends of shelf. Glue/nail 1x2 between brackets, flush with back of shelf. Countersink all nails and fill holes with wood putty. Sand smooth; sand front shelf corners to ease sharp points. Drill pilot holes 16" apart through 1x2 and drive screws through 1x2 into wall studs. Countersink screws and fill holes. Apply finish.

Plant Bracket—MATERIALS: 16" of 1x8 pine; two 1¼" #7 flathead wood screws; two 12d finishing nails; polyurethane finish.

DIRECTIONS: Following the directions in the METHODS chapter, enlarge the pattern in FIG. 2 and cut out. With a saber saw or jig saw, cut bracket. Drill two ⅛" angled blind holes in back of bracket (*see* FIG. 2). Cut 8"-long shelf; round front edges (use small jar or similar object as a template for marking). Drill pilot holes through shelf and attach to bracket with screws, driving screw heads slightly below surface. Apply finish. Drive nails part way into wall stud at intervals and angles to align with holes in bracket. Hang bracket.

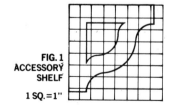

FIG. 1
ACCESSORY SHELF

1 SQ.=1"

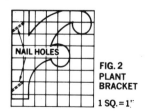

NAIL HOLES

FIG. 2
PLANT BRACKET

1 SQ.=1"

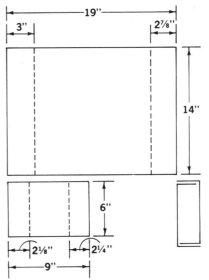

CARTRIDGE AND RECORD ORGANIZERS—You will need cardboard, self-adhesive vinyl; glue; razor blade and mat knife to make these storage cases.

MATERIALS: Quantities needed for Cartridge Holders are given first, followed by quantities in parentheses for Record Holders: 28-ply cardboard, enough to make two pieces 6″x9″(14″x19″) for each *section;* black and colored self-adhesive vinyl, enough to make two pieces 6″x7½″(14″x16½″) for each section; black plastic binding strips (stationery store) 48″(26″) for *entire unit;* razor blades; vinyl cement or contact cement; black felt marker.

DIRECTIONS: Cut cardboard to dimensions given in MATERIALS. Mark off the measurements, shown in the diagrams on one side. Using a ruler and a razor blade, score the board on the marked line; *do not go through the board.* Line up the scored line with the table edge and bend the board down at a right angle. Cover the unscored side with black self-adhesive vinyl, leaving 2½″ uncovered at one end. Color edges with black felt marker. Cover the outer surface with colored self-adhesive vinyl, leaving uncovered 2½″ at end opposite to uncovered end of the black side. Glue two folded cardboards together, as shown. Stack the sections as shown in photo; slip plastic binding strips over edges to hold sections together.

PERPETUAL CALENDAR MADE WITH BLOCKS—One set of alphabet blocks and one set of numbered blocks from dime store are enough to spell out month, day and date for whole year. Box is wood-lattice stripping glued with white glue.

MATERIALS: Four feet 1½″ lattice; one foot ⅞″ lattice; 1 set alphabet blocks; 1 set number blocks; white glue; medium and fine sandpaper; rubber bands.

DIRECTIONS: Pick out alphabet blocks to be used. Letters should include all combinations of abbreviations of months *(days of week optional)* and numbers 1 to 31 for days. We used 21 blocks and found that all but a few days of the week (in some months) could be abbreviated (otherwise, a shorter abbreviation was used). Sand blocks with medium-grade sandpaper until all printed designs disappear. Make the back for the calendar box by gluing together two lengths of 1½″ lattice and two lengths of ⅞″ lattice (rough edges sanded with fine-grade sandpaper). Place three rows of 7 blocks on top of back, aligning edges and slip rubber bands over both until back glue dries (about 30 minutes). Remove rubber bands. Cut four side pieces from 1½″ lattice (sand rough edges) and butt-join the corners around the blocks, gluing where the pieces meet. Place rubber bands around sides until glue dries.

SEWING CADDY—This handy helper is made from an icing or baking powder can. With white glue, secure pincushion to lid; cover can with tape measure strips, slightly overlapping tape at the ends.

PINE ORGANIZERS—Everyone loves to receive gifts that organize their paperwork, and these good-looking pine accessories would enhance anyone's desk.
In and Out trays keep track of 8½"x11" papers. For sides, cut two pieces 1" pine, 2½"x11½"; sand corners round. Draw lengthwise center line on each. With router set for ⅜" depth, cut groove on line with ⅛" straight-face cutter. Run a bead of glue in slots. Slip 9⅜"x11½" painted hardboard into grooves.
Peg appointment board: Sand corners round on 1x8x1' pine. Position page on board; mark holes for pages and for pencil pegs. Drill holes for ¼" pegs and glue in place.
Globe Light: Sand corners round on 1½"x6"x6". Drill hole in top and into side for ceiling receptacle wires; chisel clearance for wire screws. Assemble as shown.

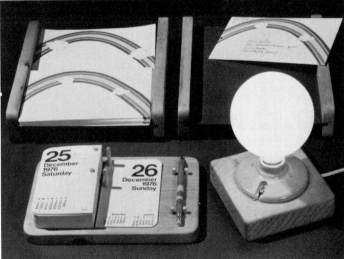

9

directions for these items start on following page

SEE-THROUGH TRAY—See-through serving tray is
two sheets of sheet acrylic with fringed linen
fabric sandwiched in between. Handles are wood doweling.

continued

11

SEE-THROUGH TRAY—MATERIALS: $\frac{1}{4}''$ Plexiglas® acrylic plastic, 2 sheets 12″x 18″; $\frac{3}{4}''$ doweling, four $1\frac{1}{2}''$ lengths and four 1″ lengths; $\frac{1}{4}''$ doweling, two 12″ lengths; four flathead screws, $1\frac{3}{4}''$ long; drill with $\frac{1}{4}''$,⋅$\frac{3}{8}''$, $\frac{5}{32}''$ and $\frac{3}{16}''$ bits; razor blade; 1 fringed placemat 12″x18″.
DIRECTIONS:
1. Smooth edges of the plastic sheets by scraping with a razor blade. On both sheets, drill a $\frac{3}{16}''$ hole $\frac{5}{8}''$ from each corner.
2. In $1\frac{1}{2}''$ dowels, drill a $\frac{1}{4}''$ hole all the way through, $\frac{1}{2}''$ from one end. In the center of the other end, drill a hole $\frac{3}{8}''$ deep with the $\frac{5}{32}''$ bit.
3. In 1″ dowels, with $\frac{5}{32}''$ bit, drill a hole through from end to end. In one end, with $\frac{3}{8}''$ bit, drill a hole $\frac{1}{8}''$ deep. In this hole, insert the flathead screw, through the dowel, through the plastic sheets (with placemat between) up into the $1\frac{1}{2}''$ dowels on top. Tighten and countersink screw in bottom dowel. Insert $\frac{1}{4}''$ dowels through holes in top dowels, as shown.

JIGSAW PUZZLE TRAY AND COASTERS—The cork-surfaced puzzle tray obligingly breaks apart into coasters when needed.
MATERIALS: Two pieces of Homasote® cork-faced bulletin board, each $8\frac{3}{4}''$x12″; wrapping paper; carbon paper; fine sandpaper; saber saw with non-serrated blade; shoe polish.
DIRECTIONS: Following the directions in the METHODS chapter, enlarge pattern. Using carbon paper, trace the pattern onto both boards. Cut first across the center line, then cut each half into individual sections. Lightly sand the cut edges to remove rough spots. Wash off carbon marks. Darken edges with shoe polish.

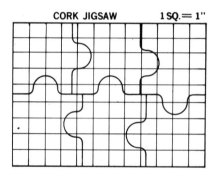

CORK JIGSAW   **1 SQ.= 1″**

PLYWOOD ALBUM COVER—For each cover, cut $\frac{1}{4}''$ plywood $11\frac{1}{4}''$x$13\frac{1}{2}''$ and 11″x$13\frac{1}{2}''$; glue $\frac{1}{4}''$ apart to canvas strip $2\frac{3}{4}''$x$13\frac{1}{4}''$. Glue paper inside of cover over canvas. Bolt album paper between covers. Varnish.

PLYWOOD FRAME AND BOX—Frame: Cut two $11\frac{1}{4}''$x$13\frac{1}{4}''$ pieces of $\frac{1}{4}''$ plywood. Saw $7\frac{1}{4}''$x$9\frac{1}{4}''$ opening from middle of one. Glue both together with strips of $\frac{1}{4}''$x$1\frac{5}{8}''$ lattice flush with bottom and side edges; leave top open for glass and photo.
Cigarette box: Cut two $7\frac{1}{4}''$x$9\frac{1}{4}''$ pieces of $\frac{3}{4}''$ plywood. Saw $3\frac{1}{2}''$x5″ opening from middle of one; glue on $\frac{1}{4}''$ plywood bottom cut to fit. In center of top, glue $3\frac{1}{2}''$x5″ inset of $\frac{1}{4}''$ plywood. Round corners, then varnish.

PIPE-JOINT DECOR—Candelabra: Glue (epoxy) two $\frac{1}{2}''$ elbow joints in "S" shape; make four. Glue into holes in two 4″ and two 5″ lengths $1\frac{1}{2}''$ dowel; glue.
Holder: Glue one $\frac{1}{2}''$ elbow joint in each end of two $\frac{1}{2}''$ "T" joints, glued to one $\frac{1}{2}''$ coupling.
Napkin rings: 1″ couplings.

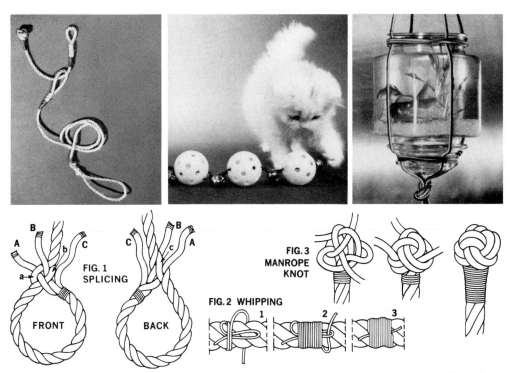

FIG. 1 SPLICING
FRONT
BACK

FIG. 3 MANROPE KNOT

FIG. 2 WHIPPING
1 2 3

MANILA DOG LEASH (*for a neck size up to 14"*)—Using splicing directions and Fig. 1 as a guide, make one 6" loop (*for handle*) and one 3" loop at ends of 6' length of ¼" Manila or sisal rope. *For collar*—splice a 2" loop at one end of a 33" length of ¼" manila. About 14" from the top of the eye, whip the rope with twine (*see* Fig. 2), then unravel the rest of the rope to the end. Using Fig. 3 as a guide, work a Manrope Knot. First work each strand around and *under* its neighbor on the right (counter clockwise). The ends will emerge from the top. *Do not pull taut.* Repeat, this time crossing each strand *over* instead of under its neighbor strand to the right. All the strands will emerge from the bottom. Do not pull taut. Now repeat both steps from the beginning. Place the second strand parallel to the first. Now slowly pull all the strands taut. All ends will emerge from the bottom. Cut ends off fairly short and whip to the rope with carpet thread or twine to hide the raw ends. Pass knot through small eye of leash, and through small eye of collar when worn by dog.

How to Splice Rope: Unravel about 6" of rope. Where the unravelled end meets the rope, twist open the strands in the rope. Start the splice by tucking end B under *strand b,* then tuck end A under *strand a.* Turn work over to back and tuck end C under the *strand c.* Pull strands up tight and repeat the whole process.

JINGLE BALLS—Our cat toy is made of three toy-store whiffle balls and six bells strung on satin macrame twine. Knot at each end and between each ball and bell.

GOLDFISH BOWL SLING—Rawhide shoelaces are tied in a simple knot around a dime-store apothecary jar.
MATERIALS: 1 apothecary jar with cover; six 36" leather shoelaces or thongs.
DIRECTIONS: Tie 4 laces in three places (beneath jar lid with a single knot, 10" above jar and again 15" above this knot). Wrap one lace twice around neck and tie; wrap and tie 24" length of lace twice around groove of lid, to hold the 4 upright laces in place.

13

ARMCHAIR LAPBOARD—A piece of ¼″ plywood (22″x32″) is rounded at corners and a semicircle, approximately 7″ deep and 18½″ wide, is cut on one side. Board is sanded, spray-painted and waxed. Water-resistant Con-Tact® foil is cut and applied to top.

REVERSIBLE COMFORTER—A puffy comforter made from two sheets—one solid, one print. Sandwich layers of fiberfill in the middle, sew around edges and tuft with grosgrain bows, stitched in place with sewing thread through all layers.

CANE DESK ACCESSORIES—Cup: Wrap 3¼″x10″ cane around sanded 2½″ sq. ¼″ plywood base with rounded corners. Tack and glue to base. Lap and glue ends.
Basket: 7¾″ square base; 11¼″x31″ cane. Glue ¾″-wide ⅛″ plywood strips inside top edges.
Holder: 3″ sq. base and top; 3¼″x12″ cane. Drill holes of correct size for pencils in top piece.

YELLOW PILLOW TOP—A combination of Garter Stitch and Stockinette Stitch knitted on the diagonal.
MATERIALS: Bear Brand, Fleisher's or Botony Twin-Pak Knitting Worsted or Machine-Washable Win-Knit (4 oz. pak); or Bucilla Machine-Washable Softex (4 oz. ball); or Bucilla Machine-Washable Superwash Knitting Worsted (2 oz. ball): 6 oz. of any color; knitting needles, 1 pair No. 10, OR ANY SIZE NEEDLES WHICH WILL OBTAIN THE STITCH GAUGE BELOW; a 14″ fabric-covered, knife-edge pillow.
GAUGE: 3½ sts = 1″.
Note: Use 2 strands of yarn held together throughout.
Starting at a corner with 2 strands of yarn held together, cast on 3 sts. Work in garter stitch as follows: *Row 1:* K each st across. *Row 2:* Inc in first st; inc in next st, k last st. There are 5 sts on needle. *Row 3:* K each st across. *Row 4:* Inc as before in first st, k 2, inc in next st, k 1—7 sts on needle. *Row 5:* K each st across. *Row 6:* Inc in first st, k each st across until 2 sts rem on left-hand needle, inc in next st, k last st—9 sts on needle. *Rows 7 through 38:* Rpt Rows 5 and 6 alternately 16 times more—at end of 38th row there are 41 sts on needle. Keeping 2 sts at each end in garter st, work rem sts in stockinette stitch as follows: *Row 39 (wrong side of work):* K 2, p in each st across until 2 sts rem on left-hand needle, k 2. *Row 40:* Inc in first st, k each st across until 2 sts rem on left-hand needle, inc in next st, k last st—2 sts increased. *Rows 41 through 54:* Rpt Rows 39 and 40 alternately 7 times more—at end of 54th row there are 57 sts on needle. Work in garter st as follows: *Row 55:* K across. *Row 56:* Rpt Row 40. *Rows 57 and 58:* Rpt Rows 55 and 40—61 sts on needle. *Rows 59 and 60:* K each st on each row—61 sts. This is center of pillow top, diagonally from corner to corner. *Row 61:* K across. *Row 62:* K 1, decrease by k 2 tog; k each st across until 3 sts rem on left-hand needle, k 2 tog, k 1—2 sts decreased. *Rows 63 and 64:* Rpt Rows 61 and 62—57 sts rem on needle. Work in stockinette stitch as follows: *Row 65 (wrong side):* K 2, p in each st across until 2 sts rem on left-hand needle, k 2. *Row 66:* K 1, k 2 tog, k each st across until 3 sts rem on left-hand needle, k 2 tog, k 1—2 sts decreased. *Rows 67 through 78:* Rpt Rows 65 and 66 alternately 7 times more—43 sts rem on needle. Work in garter stitch as follows: *Rows 79 through 116:* Rpt Rows 61 and 62 alternately 19 times—5 sts rem. *Last Row:* K 1, sl 1 st; k 2 tog, psso; k 1. Bind off rem 3 sts.
Finishing: Block to measure 14″x14″. Matching knitted edges to seams on pillow, sew pillow top in place, catching each st along edges.

RIBBON-LATTICED PILLOWS—To sew a lattice pillow edgestitch ribbons, as shown, to two 13″ squares quilted cotton. Sew front to back around three sides and four corners. Turn and stuff firmly. Whipstitch opening.

CALICO PLACEMAT/NAPKIN SET—Line 14″x17″ print **placemats** with blue fabric; stitch edges with 1″ wide seam binding. Use ½″ binding on 14″-square **napkins**. Make a red, lined 7″ **ring** ¾″ wide; press flat. Sew bottom layer to mat in two rows, 1″ apart. On top layer, sew 5″ lined heart made from a freehand pattern. Fold napkins and insert in rings.

ROUND EMBROIDERED PURSE MIRROR AND SQUARE NEEDLE-POINT WALL MIRROR—Embroidery and needlepoint change round dime-store mirrors into important decorative accents.

Embroidered Mirror—MATERIALS: Craft mirror, 2″ in diameter; white felt; scraps of yarn in assorted colors; fabric glue; cardboard.

DIRECTIONS: Cut two 5″ white felt circles and one 4″ cardboard circle. In the center of one felt circle, trace the 2″ mirror. Just outside the traced line, embroider a circle of Blanket Stitches. Add flowers, as shown, embroidered with Fly stitch, Lazy Daisy Stitch, and French Knots (*see* METHODS chapter). With cardboard circle in between, sew the felt circles together, using a Buttonhole Stitch edging and making a loop at top, as shown. Glue mirror in place.

Needlepoint Mirror—MATERIALS: Knitting worsted: 2-oz. forest green for background and 4 yds. pale lime green for leaves; approximately 6″ of pastel yarn scraps for each bud; 13″ square of #10 Penelope canvas; 10″ square of firm ⅛″ backing such as Masonite; 5″ round dime store makeup mirror; small jar of heavy duty glue; picture hanger; 10″ square piece of felt to match green yarn for backing; masking tape; neutral color waterproof felt tip marker.

DIRECTIONS: With masking tape, bind the canvas edges. With a waterproof felt marker, draw a 10″ square in the center of the canvas; trace the 5″ mirror in the center of this square and draw in small buds, as shown. With Half Cross Stitch, or Continental, work the background in forest green knitting worsted up to the bud outlines, one stitch inside the mirror outline and two rows *beyond* the square outline, leaving an empty 4x4 mesh square at each corner to facilitate mitering. Work the buds. Block canvas; trim edges ¾″ from worked area. With heavy duty glue, attach stitched canvas to a 10″ square of firm backing by applying a thin layer of the glue to the wood backing and then pressing stitched canvas in place, mitering the corners. Glue down the sides of canvas, removing tape and trimming excess. When dry, glue 10″ felt square to back; secure hanger in place. Glue mirror to front of the square.

*Sturdy and beautiful toys that are
really made to last through a childhood*

Small children will have fun playing with the 25 toys shown in this chapter. And you will have fun making them because they cost little more than the love, time and patience it takes to put them together. There are puzzles and pillow-toys made from scraps, dolls to hug in all sizes from pompon to big sister, and a "free" dollhouse made from a cardboard shipping box. You'll like the wooden toys made from lumberyard scrap, so sturdy that they'll become cherished heirlooms when your children pass them along to their children.

directions for item shown above appear on following page

17

CHAPTER 2

TODDLER'S PATCHWORK TREE PUZZLE—Every child loves a puzzle! This one is 12"x12" and is made of fabric stiffened with iron-on interfacing or backing material and cut into shapes, as shown.

MATERIALS: One 12" square each of solid color blue calico, unbleached muslin for lining and thin polyester batting; scraps of two different green calicoes and of green polka dot fabric; 2" belt backing, 1 yd.; fusible webbing, ¼ yd.; red calico bias foldover tape, 1 package; round self-adhering Velcro® fasteners.

DIRECTIONS:

1. Following the directions in the METHODS chapter, enlarge the pattern and cut out.
2. Make a cardboard template of the shaded diamond shape; trace five times on one green calico, ten on the other and 15 each on backing and webbing. Cut out.
3. Layer fusible webbing between diamond fabric and backing; fuse.
4. Trace the tree trunk pattern pieces onto polka dot fabric, backing and webbing; cut out. Layer and fuse.

(*Optional:* In steps 1 and 2, the fabrics can be fused to the backing *before* the shapes are cut; this method is easier but more wasteful of materials.)

5. Pin blue calico square over batting square; pin at edges. Pin tree pattern to center of blue square, ⅜" above bottom edge. Trace. Cut out tree design; discard.
6. Place remaining shape on muslin lining square, matching edges. Baste the irregular inner area to hold in place. Work close machine zigzag stitch on all inner and outer edges. Remove basting. Bind edges, mitering corners.
7. Fasten Velcro® to backs of puzzle pieces and in matching positions on muslin.

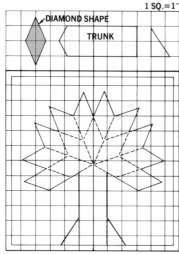

1 SQ.=1"

DIAMOND SHAPE

TRUNK

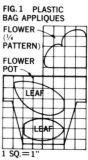

FIG. 1 PLASTIC
BAG APPLIQUES

FLOWER
(¼ PATTERN)

FLOWER POT

LEAF

LEAF

1 SQ.=1"

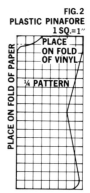

FIG. 2
PLASTIC PINAFORE
1 SQ.=1"

PLACE ON FOLD OF VINYL

PLACE ON FOLD OF PAPER

¼ PATTERN

ESPECIALLY FOR THE KIDS—From the beginning of time children have been told about the alleged benefits of a "place for everything and everything in its place." If your kids persist in reveling in the mess they make, you might try enticing them to neat-up with this see-through **plastic bag** for toys. Its companion is a **plastic pinafore,** which hangs neatly on a **child-height costumer.** After loving **Teddy,** he, too, can be popped into the toy bag.

Plastic Toy Bag—MATERIALS: 1½ yds. 38″ clear vinyl; 10 yds. orange double fold bias tape; 9″x12″ felt pieces (two pink and one each green, yellow and orange); 12 café-curtain rings; string.

DIRECTIONS: Following the directions in METHODS chapter, enlarge motifs in FIG. 1 and cut out. Trace ¼ flower, turning clockwise to complete shape; cut out.

Cutting: *Vinyl:* One piece 18″x36½″ (sides) and 12″ diameter circle (bottom). *Felt:* One pink flower, 3″ yellow center, green 4½″x1″ stem; leaves, 1 each.

Sewing: Edgestitch center to flower. At equal distance from each short end, tape stem to bag with end at bottom edge. Center and tape flower over stem, edges touching, then leaves. Edgestitch. Appliqués are on wrong side of vinyl. With wrong sides together stitch ¼″ center back seam and bind. Baste bottom to sides, wrong sides together and bind. Bind top edge. Fold 1¼″ hem to outside. Stitch over binding. Evenly space 12 rings over binding and sew on by hand. Cut two pieces, each 30″ of double fold tape and household string. Fold tape lengthwise over strings and stitch edges together. Run both drawstrings through rings. Pull each drawstring at opposite sides to draw up.

Plastic Pinafore—MATERIALS: Remainder of materials left from Plastic Toy Bag.

DIRECTIONS: Use FIG. 1 appliqués. Following directions in METHODS chapter, enlarge pattern in FIG. 2 for pinafore on folded brown paper. Cut back neck edge curved and front neck edge straight across (*see dotted line*). Cut 6″ opening along center back from top edge.

Cutting—*Vinyl:* Place opened pinafore pattern shoulder edges at fold of vinyl and cut out; curve back neckline and cut 6″ slash. *Felt:* One pink flower, yellow center, green 3″x1″ stem and leaves in both sizes; orange pot.

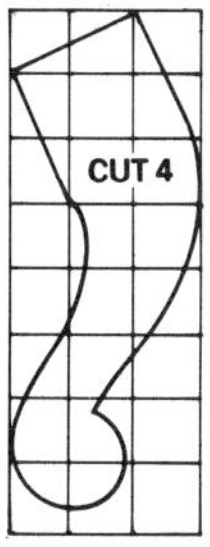

Sewing: With centers matching and pot touching lower edge, stitch appliqués same as Plastic Toy Bag. Starting at end of back opening, turn under tape ¼″ and bind neckline. Bind outside edges in same way, lapping turned-under end. Cut four 12″ bias strips for ties. Fold in half lengthwise and edgestitch. Stitch one to each side at waistline. Wear pinafore with appliqués on the inside.

Child's Costumer (*30″*)—MATERIALS: 27½″ of 2x2 lumber; 3′ of ½x4 pine; white glue; 4d finishing nails; paint, as desired; polyurethane finish; four coat hooks with ¾″ flathead wood screws.

DIRECTIONS: Following the directions in METHODS chapter, enlarge the pattern in FIG. 3 and cut out. Trace onto ½″ pine four times. Use a saber saw, jig saw or coping saw to cut out. Glue/nail the legs flush with the bottom of the 2x2, with each leg overlapping and concealing the end of the adjacent one. Countersink nails and fill holes with wood putty. Sand smooth. Paint legs. Apply polyurethane finish to entire unit. Paint hooks. Attach with screws 2½″ from top of 2x2 post.

Furry Teddy (*15″*)—MATERIALS: Two pieces furcloth, each 18″ long by 16″; scraps of felt; stuffing.

DIRECTIONS: Following directions in METHODS chapter, enlarge the pattern in FIG. 4 and cut out.

Sewing:

1. Center and trace around pattern on wrong side of a furcloth piece, nap running downward. Lap over second piece, right sides together, naps and edges matching. Pin and stitch on traced lines, *except between ears.* Stitch again at crotch. Cut away outer fabric, leaving ½″ seam allowance all around. Turn.

2. Place pattern over bear and mark with pins the stitching lines at ears and with basting at arms and legs. Stitch across ears.

3. Trace features onto felt and cut out. Cut 5″ piece of dark string. Glue string mouth on felt and sew eyes and nose to felt face. Hand appliqué face, ears and paws to front.

4. Stuff legs and arms to ½″ from basting. Stitch. Stuff body and head. Turn in edges between ears and slipstitch. Remove basting.

FIG. 3
CHILD'S COSTUMER
BASE PIECE

CUT 4

1 SQ.= 1″

¼″ BLACK FELT
FUSCHIA FELT
ORANGE FELT
RED FELT
NAVY BLUE THREAD

CENTER LINE
CUT TWO

FUSCHIA FELT

FIG. 4
TEDDY BEAR
HALF PATTERN
AND
PLACEMENT
DIAGRAM
1 SQ.=1″

19

WOOD TOYS MADE TO LAST—With little more than wood, glue, a saw and a couple of dollars, you can make your own toys. More important, when your child's flashy, battery-operated robot rests in the dump awaiting burial, your lovingly made toy will still be around.

For this reason, the toys are all made of hardwoods—cherry, walnut, maple, oak —which are both durable and rich-looking. You need only small quantities for these projects and may be able to find enough in the scrap pile of a local cabinet-maker. Softwoods, such as fir and pine, can be used instead. These are less expensive and easier to work with, but they will not be as handsome, nor will they stand up as well.

If you cannot find pieces of wood that are thick enough for some of the toys, it is a simple matter to glue together two pieces (as on the wheeled pig) or even three (the trailer). Use white glue for this purpose, as well as for all glued assemblies, and clamp pieces together until dry. To finish the toys, sand thoroughly with medium, then fine and very fine, sandpaper. Rub in linseed oil to bring out the richness of the wood grain. Use paint only for such details as faces.

Wheeled Toys—GENERAL DIRECTIONS (for CAR-AND-TRAILER AND PIG)—*Making the Shapes:* Sizes and shapes of such fanciful wheeled toys as the car and trailer and

20

the pig are less important than your child's imagination, which will make them out to be whatever he or she wishes them to be. Cut the body shapes to a rough outline with a band saw, saber saw or keyhole saw. Sand curved shapes and

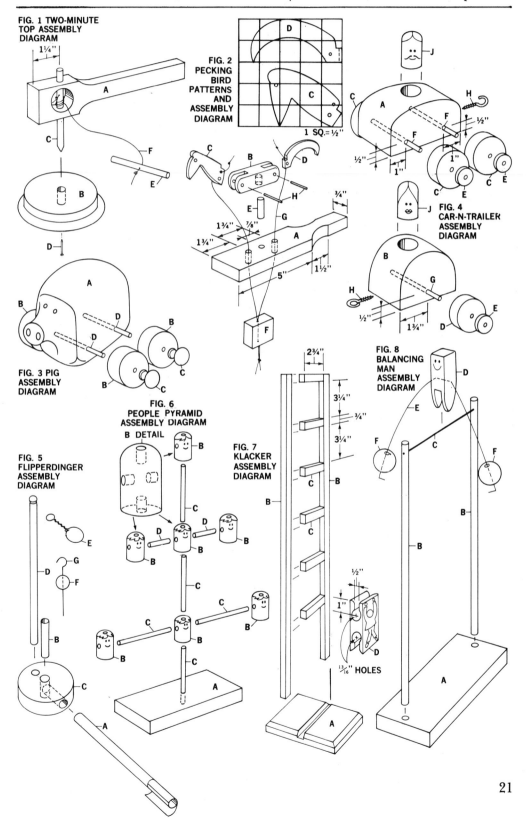

FIG. 1 TWO-MINUTE TOP ASSEMBLY DIAGRAM

FIG. 2 PECKING BIRD PATTERNS AND ASSEMBLY DIAGRAM

1 SQ.=½"

FIG. 4 CAR-N-TRAILER ASSEMBLY DIAGRAM

FIG. 3 PIG ASSEMBLY DIAGRAM

FIG. 6 PEOPLE PYRAMID ASSEMBLY DIAGRAM

B DETAIL

FIG. 5 FLIPPERDINGER ASSEMBLY DIAGRAM

FIG. 7 KLACKER ASSEMBLY DIAGRAM

FIG. 8 BALANCING MAN ASSEMBLY DIAGRAM

¹³⁄₁₆" HOLES

rounded corners with coarse sandpaper, then medium and fine. A sanding drum will be a big help on this job.

Wheels and Axles: Use a hole saw, available wherever tools are sold, to cut the various-sized wheels. It is important to drill axle holes in the toy body as closely parallel to the bottom of the body as possible, so that all wheels are even. This is best done on a drill press, but if none is available, use a power hand drill, with a pre-drilled scrap piece of hardwood as a guide; clamp the guide to the side of the toy body.

Assembling: Drive $\frac{1}{4}''$ dowels through the axle holes; these should fit snugly without gluing. Drill $\frac{9}{16}''$ holes in the centers of the wheels and place them over the axles. Then glue hubcaps, cut with the hole saw and pre-drilled, over the axles, allowing enough clearance for the wheels to turn freely. Or you can substitute drawer pulls for the hubcaps (as on the pig) by drilling $\frac{1}{4}''$-deep blind holes in the pulls and gluing them on the axle ends.

1. Two-Minute Top—MATERIALS: $\frac{3}{4}''$x$1\frac{3}{4}''$x$8''$ handle (A); $\frac{3}{4}''$x$3''$-diameter spinner (B); $\frac{3}{8}''$ dowel x $4\frac{1}{2}''$ shaft (C); small roundhead escutcheon pin or finishing nail (D); $\frac{3}{8}''$ dowel x $3''$ pull-string handle (E); $36''$ heavy wrapping string (F).

DIRECTIONS: Cut handle A to shape shown (*see* FIG. 1). Drill a $1''$-diameter hole through side and $\frac{7}{16}''$-diameter hole through top to bottom, centering both holes $1\frac{1}{4}''$ from end of A. Sand lower end of shaft C to taper and drive in escutcheon pin or nail so that top will spin on a slick surface. Drill hole, large enough for pull string to pass through, $1\frac{1}{2}''$ from top of shaft C. Drill $\frac{3}{8}''$ hole through center of spinner B. Insert Shaft C through hole and glue so that bottom of shaft is $1\frac{1}{4}''$ below bottom spinner B. Drill small hole through center of E, pass string through hole and knot end.

To spin top, slide shaft up through smaller holes in handle, pass string through large hole and hole in shaft, wind it around shaft; hold handle and pull string.

2. Pecking Bird—MATERIALS: $\frac{3}{4}''$x$1\frac{3}{4}''$x$8''$ base (A); $1''$x$1''$x$2\frac{1}{4}''$ body (B); $\frac{1}{4}''$x$1\frac{1}{2}''$x$2''$ head (C); $\frac{1}{4}''$x$1\frac{1}{2}''$x$2''$ tail (D); $\frac{1}{4}''$ dowel x $1''$ leg (E); $\frac{3}{4}''$x$1\frac{1}{4}''$x$1\frac{1}{4}''$ weight (F); two $12''$ lengths of mono filament fishing line or heavy thread (G); two $1''$ lengths of coat hanger wire (H).

DIRECTIONS: Cut handle A as shown in FIG. 2. Drill two $\frac{1}{4}''$ holes spaced as indicated. Drill a $\frac{1}{4}''$ blind hole $\frac{1}{4}''$ deep between these two holes. Use multiple saw cuts to make channels $\frac{9}{32}''$ wide and $\frac{1}{2}''$ deep in each end of body B. Drill holes in each end of B the same size as wire pieces H. Drill a $\frac{1}{4}''$ blind hole $\frac{1}{4}''$ deep in the bottom of the body. Round off all corners of the body with sandpaper.

Cut head C and tail D according to pattern (*see* FIG. 2) and drill holes where shown, slightly larger than wire pieces H. Drill $\frac{1}{16}''$ holes through narrow dimensions of C and D as shown. Insert fishing line or thread through these holes and knot at top. Insert head and tail into body channels and secure with wires H. Mount body on handle with dowel leg E. Pass fishing line or thread ends through holes in base. Drill $\frac{1}{16}''$ hole through weight F. Pass strings through hole and tie together below weight.

Move the handle in a circular motion to see the bird peck the handle while moving its tail up and down.

3. Pig—MATERIALS: $3\frac{1}{2}''$x$6\frac{1}{4}''$x$4\frac{1}{4}''$ body (A); four $\frac{7}{8}''$x$2\frac{1}{2}''$-diameter wheels (B); four $1''$ drawer pull hubcaps (C); two $\frac{1}{4}''$ dowel x $5\frac{1}{4}''$ axles (D).

Note: Shape body so that snout is approximately $1\frac{1}{4}''$ diameter. Drill $\frac{3}{16}''$ holes for eyes, $\frac{5}{16}''$ for nostrils (*see* FIG. 3).

4. Car-and-Trailer—MATERIALS: $2\frac{1}{2}''$x$4\frac{1}{2}''$x$2\frac{1}{2}''$ car body (A); $2\frac{1}{4}''$x$3\frac{1}{2}''$x$3''$ trailer body (B); four $\frac{7}{8}''$x$2''$-diameter car wheels (C); two $\frac{3}{4}''$x$1\frac{1}{2}''$-diameter trailer wheels (D); six $\frac{3}{16}''$x$\frac{7}{8}''$-diameter hubcaps (E); two $\frac{1}{4}''$ dowel x $5''$ car axles (F); $\frac{1}{4}''$ dowel x $4\frac{1}{2}''$ trailer axle (G); screw hook and screw eye (H); two $1''$ dowel x $2''$ people (J).

Note: After car and trailer bodies are assembled, drill $1''$-diameter blind holes $\frac{3}{4}''$

deep in the top of each. Sand dowels J so that they fit easily into these holes. Round off tops of dowels by sanding and paint simple faces on them (see Fig. 4).

5. Flipperdinger—MATERIALS: 5/8″ dowel* x 7″ blow tube (A); 3/8″ dowel* x 13/4″ jet tube (B); 1″x23/4″-diameter base (C); 3/8″ dowel x 71/4″ post (D); wire coat hanger basket (E); 3/4″-square balsa wood (F); paper clip (G); self-adhering vinyl. *Note: A 7/16″ hole must be drilled the length of the blow tube, a 1/4″ hole the length of the jet tube; this is best done on a drill press. If you find that you cannot drill these holes, you can substitute plastic tubing for these two parts. DIRECTIONS: Drill a 5/8″ hole from the edge to the center of base C. Drill a 3/8″ hole through the center of the top of base C to meet the 5/8″ hole. Glue the blow tube and jet tube in place, creating an unobstructed air passage. Wrap the end of the blow tube with protective self-adhesive vinyl (see Fig. 5).

Drill a 3/8″ blind hole 1/4″ deep in the top of the base at the edge opposite the blow tube; glue post D in this hole. Cut a shallow notch around post D 1/4″ below the top. Make a wire "basket" 1″ in diameter centered over the jet tube, wrapping the wire around the notched post and twisting it as securely as you are able.

Cut off all corners of the balsa square with a sharp knife, then sand it to the shape of a ball. Straighten the paper clip and bend the top to a hook. Force the paper clip through the center of the ball, with hooked end protruding 1/2″ at top.

To operate the flipperdinger, insert the straight end of the paper clip into the jet tube and blow into the blow tube. The force of your breath will suspend the ball in mid-air and, with a bit of luck and/or skill, you will be able to hook the ball onto the basket rim.

6. People Pyramid—MATERIALS: 3/4″x21/2″x6″ base (A); seven 1″ dowel x 13/4″ people (B); four 1/4″ dowel x 31/4″ arms, legs (C); two 1/4″ dowel x 11/2″ arms, legs (D). DIRECTIONS: Drill 1/4″-diameter, 1/4″-deep blind holes in center of base (A) and in top, bottom and two sides of each dowel (B). Round off tops of dowel people with sandpaper and paint on simple faces (see Fig. 6). Children can assemble the people in any configuration they wish by linking them with dowel arms and legs.

7. Klacker—MATERIALS: 3/4″x43/4″x61/2″ base (A); two 1/2″x3/4″x251/2″ posts (B); six 1/2″x3/4″x23/4″ rungs (C); 11/4″x13/4″x4″ "acrobat" (D). DIRECTIONS: Use multiple saw cuts to make a 1/2″-wide, 3/8″-deep groove across center of long side of base A. Bevel edges of base. Assemble ladder by gluing rungs C (wide faces vertical) between posts B, flush with the top and at 31/4″ intervals. Glue ladder posts B into base groove. In the narrow edge of piece D, drill 13/16″ holes centered 1″ from each end. From each end, cut down to the holes to make a channel slightly wider than 1/2″. Round the edges of D with sandpaper. Paint a figure on piece D (see Fig. 7).

Place the acrobat on the top rung of the ladder and watch him tumble head-over-heels until he reaches the base.

8. Balancing Man—MATERIALS: 1″x3″x6″ base (A); two 1/4″ dowel x 133/4″ posts (B), 51/2″ length of coat hanger "high wire" (C); 3/4″x3/4″x3″ tightrope walker (D); 16″ thin, stiff wire "balancing bar" (E); two 1″-diameter wooden balls (F), available at hobby shops, wood craft shops, jewelry stores. DIRECTIONS: Drill holes the same diameter as the hanger wire (C), 3/8″ from one end of each post (B); insert high wire into holes. Drill 1/4″-diameter blind holes 1/4″ deep, 3/8″ in from each end of base; glue in posts. Make 1″-deep multiple saw cuts in the bottom of piece D to form legs; clean out with a rasp. Taper legs and round edges of D with sandpaper (see Fig. 8). Drill 1/32″ hole 11/4″ from bottom of legs. Thread wire E through hole, centering it and bending it slightly at each side of D to hold it in place. Drill 1/32″ holes through centers of wooden balls F. Thread ends of wire E through balls; bend over ends so they can't pull out. Paint a face on tightrope walker.

The "daredevil" will rock back and forth on the high wire or teeter precariously on one leg on top of the posts. He can balance on your finger, too.

EASY-TO-MAKE CARDBOARD DOLLHOUSE—A dollhouse under the tree on Christmas morning is hard to beat as a child-pleaser, but the prices of the beautiful ones in the stores make most of us turn pale. Here's a dream of a dollhouse you can make of corrugated cardboard in one day's pleasurable work—and all it will cost you is the price of some spray paint. Corrugated cardboard, as you know, is the stuff cartons are made of, so lay your hands on some big ones and cut them up for the walls, floors and roof. You'll need a utility knife, glue and our diagrams. You can even make the wallpaper—white paper decorated with a felt-tip pen.

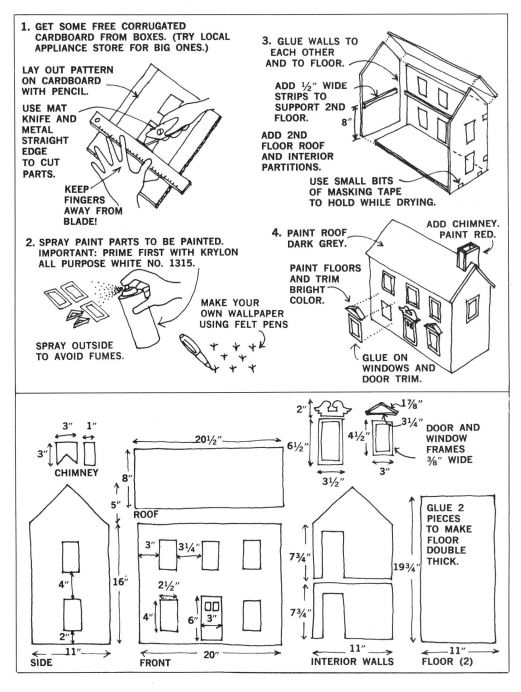

24

25

CAR AND BUS PILLOW TOYS—Draw freehand car 11″x19″; bus 13″x25″; appliqués. Cut pieces needed from scraps. Zigzag appliqués to front and back. Stitch; turn; stuff.

FELT DOLL FAMILY—The members of this doll family vary in size from 10″ to 20″, including legs. They are made entirely from scraps of felt, braid, dress trim and yarn. Using our photo as a guide, cut two pieces of felt for the head-body pattern. Cut out felt hair and decorative facial and floral shapes. Cut felt sections for arms and legs, in two layers, if you wish. Arrange in place. For sewing, use a small running stitch (becomes a part of the design). Sew features and trim in place on top layer of felt body section. *Optional:* Decorate back layer. Sew two body sections together, inserting arms and legs. Stitch arms and legs into the seams or on body, leaving opening at bottom. Lightly stuff body section and close the opening with a running stitch. Add yarn or pompon hair and ribbon trim.

FELT PISTOL, HOLSTER AND SHERIFF'S BADGE—Your little sheriff can keep the peace with toys made of felt scraps. For patterns, trace a toy pistol, holster and star. Cut pattern sections by color, two pieces each for holster back and front, two pieces each for pistol parts . Whipstitch edges to join pieces. Stuff gun with

fiberfill before sewing top edge. Cover one of your child's belts with felt. Cut slits in the holster and whipstitch edges. Cut three stars and one lining star. Stuff and whipstitch; add safety pin on back.

FELT TOOLS AND TOOL BAG—Use permanent-press fabric from your scrap bag to make the tool bag. Stitch two 15"x19" pieces with right sides together, making a 2" deep casing-hem at top. Whipstitch 3" and 4" letters to bag front. With Dad's help, trace tools for patterns. Cut pattern sections by color, adding ¼" for seam allowance. Stitch and stuff.

27

BIG AND LITTLE SISTER RAG DOLLS—Every little girl loves rag dolls, and these are especially appealing and huggable. Big Sister is 29″ tall; Little Sister, 22″. Comparable dolls in the stores would cost up to $23.95. You can make these for only a few dollars a pair, using leftovers—polyester knits and permanent-press cottons. All you probably need to buy is one pound of polyester fiberfill.

Notes on Selection of Materials: For the doll body, polyester double knit is recommended because it stretches, is long-wearing and washable. Select a flesh-tone for the head, torso and arms, a stripe for the legs (stockings) and black for the feet (shoes). Permanent press polyester/cotton blends in checks and small prints are recommended for the clothes. Lace, ruffling, felt, other trims, stuffing material and yarn should also be of synthetic fibers so that the entire doll is completely washable—obviously an asset in a huggable rag doll.

MATERIALS—*for Doll Bodies:* Figures given first are for one Big Sister; those for one Little Sister follow in parentheses. Fabric for head, torso, and arms, one piece 24″x36″ (17″x24″); striped fabric for legs, one piece 12″x20″ (8″x14″); black fabric for feet, one piece 12″ square (8″x8″); ⅜″ doweling, one 10″ (7″) length; white fabric glue; 4-ply acrylic yarn, one 4-oz. skein (enough for both dolls); polyester fiberfill (one lb. is enough for both dolls); red, blue, pink and black felt scraps for facial features; dressmaker's carbon and tracing wheel.

MATERIALS—*for clothes (one Big- and one Little-Sister Doll):* Dress fabric, one piece 24″x36″ (18″x24″); for the trimmings measure the area to be covered to determine yardage; bloomer fabric, one piece 12″x40″ (9″x28″); ¼″ elastic, one piece 14″ (10″) for waist, two pieces, each 6″ (4″) for legs; dressmaker's carbon and tracing wheel.

DIRECTIONS—*Enlarging the Patterns:* Following the directions in the METHODS chapter, enlarge the patterns for the doll bodies (*see* FIGS. 1 *and* 2) *and* for the clothes (*see* FIGS. 3 *and* 4) on the following pages. Be sure to include the directional arrows and other pattern markings. Cut out patterns; label each.

Cutting and Marking: Pin patterns to the fabrics with the directional arrows on the lengthwise grain. Trace darts, fold lines and gathering lines on the fabric. Cut out; leave pattern pinned to each piece until ready to sew. Trace the facial features from the head pattern to felt of the colors indicated. Cut out.

Sewing and Stuffing Doll Bodies—GENERAL DIRECTIONS:

1. When stitching doll sections together, leave an opening for stuffing as shown on pattern pieces.

2. Use a pencil or spoon handle to push in the stuffing—firmly and completely fill each body section.

3. When joining stuffed body sections, take tiny hand stitches with an occasional back stitch for reinforcement.

Making The Dolls

Sewing: Seams are ⅜″, unless otherwise indicated. Stitch seams with fabric right sides together. Press seams open.

1. *Torso:* Stitch two sections together. Turn right side out and stuff.

2. *Arms:* Stitch two sections together. Reinforce the seam at the thumb with a second row of shorter (20 per inch) stitches; clip seam as shown on pattern. Repeat with other two arm sections. Turn right side out and stuff both arms.

3. *Legs and feet:* Stitch bottom edge of leg to top edge of foot. Stitch together two each of the joined sections on their long edges for leg front and back seams. Stitch soles to feet. Turn right side out and stuff legs and feet.

4. *Face:* Glue felt facial features in place on one of the head pieces. Stitch darts on tracing lines. Stitch darts on other head piece.

5. *Hair:* For *braids,* cut yarn into about 116 30″ lengths for Big Sister and into about 90 24″ lengths for Little Sister. Stitch through the center of the yarn lengths along the center line of the head section as shown (*see* FIG. 5). Do not braid hair

FIG. 1 BIG SISTER DOLL PATTERN
HEAD–CUT 2–FEATURES ON ONE ONLY

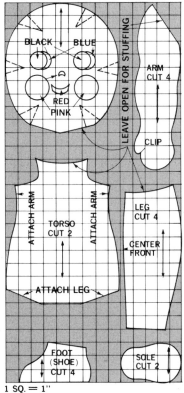

1 SQ. = 1"

FIG. 2 LITTLE SISTER DOLL PATTERN
HEAD–CUT 2–FEATURES ON ONE ONLY

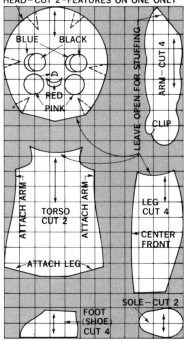

yet. For *shaggy hair,* cut about half a skein of yarn into 8" lengths for Big Sister and 6" lengths for Little Sister. Stitch to the head piece in circles as shown (*see* FIG. 6). Cut and stitch more yarn if needed for additional fullness.

6. *Head:* Stitch head sections together, being careful to keep yarn out of the seam. Turn right side out. Stuff head.

7. Insert a dowel halfway into the head and halfway into the torso, in the center of the stuffing. Stitch the head to the neck.

8. Stitch the arms and legs in place, making sure the thumbs point upward and the toes forward.

9. *For braided hair:* Tie ends with yarn or ribbon. Trim yarn ends evenly. Tack braids with a few stitches to the head at about ear position. *For shaggy hair:* Finger-comb hair, bringing it down over the forehead and around the face.

Making the Doll Clothes

Sewing: Seams are ⅜", unless otherwise indicated. Stitch seams with fabric right sides together. Press seams open.

Dress:

1. *Bodice:* Stitch shoulder and underarm seams. *Style with collar:* Stitch two pairs of collar sections together; clip seam. Turn right side out, press. Topstitch trim of your choice on the seamed edge. Stitch raw edge, with seam binding, to neck edge.

Style without collar: Turn neck edge ⅛" to *right* side; topstitch trim over raw

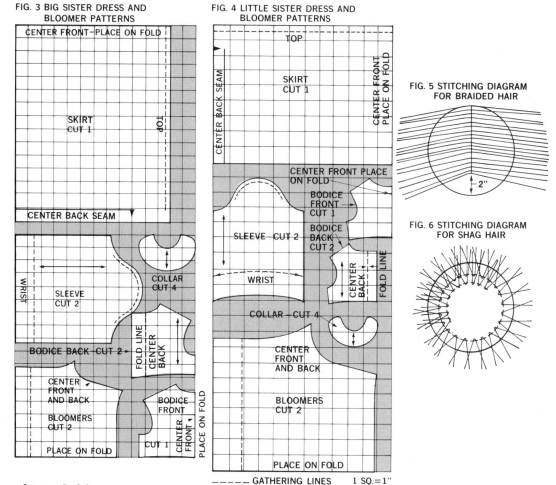

FIG. 3 BIG SISTER DRESS AND
BLOOMER PATTERNS

CENTER FRONT—PLACE ON FOLD

SKIRT
CUT 1

TOP

CENTER BACK SEAM

WRIST

SLEEVE
CUT 2

COLLAR
CUT 4

BODICE BACK—CUT 2

FOLD LINE

CENTER
BACK

CENTER
FRONT
AND BACK

BLOOMERS
CUT 2

BODICE
FRONT

PLACE ON FOLD

CUT 1

CENTER
FRONT

PLACE ON FOLD

FIG. 4 LITTLE SISTER DRESS AND
BLOOMER PATTERNS

TOP

SKIRT
CUT 1

CENTER BACK SEAM

CENTER FRONT
PLACE ON FOLD

CENTER FRONT PLACE
ON FOLD

BODICE
FRONT
CUT 1

SLEEVE — CUT 2

BODICE
BACK
CUT 2

FOLD LINE

CENTER
BACK

WRIST

COLLAR — CUT 4

CENTER
FRONT
AND BACK

BLOOMERS
CUT 2

PLACE ON FOLD

PLACE ON FOLD

- - - - - GATHERING LINES   1 SQ.=1"

FIG. 5 STITCHING DIAGRAM
FOR BRAIDED HAIR

2"

FIG. 6 STITCHING DIAGRAM
FOR SHAG HAIR

edge to finish.

2. *Sleeves:* Narrowly hem the bottom edge and gather to fit doll's arm. Over the gathers, topstitch trim to match neck or collar trim. Stitch sleeve seam. Pin and stitch sleeves in bodice armholes, pulling up gathers to fit.

3. *Skirt:* Stitch the center back seam on the line indicated on the pattern, leaving seam open above the notches. Gather skirt top edge (*see Gathering line on pattern*) to fit the bodice bottom edge. Pin and stitch skirt to bodice.

4. *Back Opening:* Fold under the back edges of the joined bodice and skirt ⅛", then fold again on the lines indicated on patterns; topstitch edges. Sew snap fastener at each side of opening.

Bloomers:

1. Stitch center front and back seams.

2. Turn waist raw edge ¼" to wrong side; pin. Stitch elastic over raw edge, stretching elastic as you stitch.

3. Double-turn the bloomer leg bottom edges ⅛" to wrong side; pin. Topstitch trim over folded edge. Stitch elastic to wrong side of bloomer legs on marked gathering line, stretching elastic as you stitch.

4. Stitch inner leg seam.

Finishing: Dress doll and turn up a hem deep enough to allow bloomers to show.
Optional: To make an apron, gather a square of white fabric onto a waistband; trim edges as desired. Add a bib to make a pinafore.

31

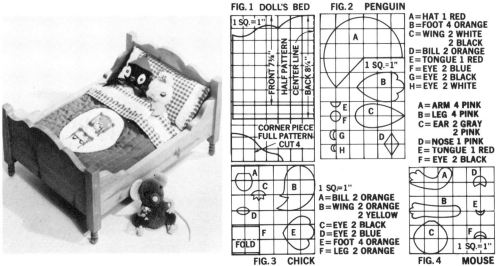

FIG. 1 DOLL'S BED   FIG. 2   PENGUIN

1 SQ.=1"

A=HAT 1 RED
B=FOOT 4 ORANGE
C=WING 2 WHITE
      2 BLACK
D=BILL 2 ORANGE
E=TONGUE 1 RED
F=EYE 2 BLUE
G=EYE 2 BLACK
H=EYE 2 WHITE

1 SQ.=1"

A=ARM 4 PINK
B=LEG 4 PINK
C=EAR 2 GRAY
     2 PINK
D=NOSE 1 PINK
E=TONGUE 1 RED
F=EYE 2 BLACK

1 SQ=1"
A=BILL 2 ORANGE
B=WING 2 ORANGE
      2 YELLOW
C=EYE 2 BLACK
D=EYE 2 BLUE
E=FOOT 4 ORANGE
F=LEG 2 ORANGE

1 SQ.=1"

FIG. 3 CHICK   FIG. 4   MOUSE

HOME DEC FOR DOLLS—It's very important to have the proper-size bed for one's dolls. This 15"x22" pine bedstead is obviously just the right "double" size for a chick and a penguin, and the perfect "single" size for a 12" baby doll. The happy bedfellows and the guardian mouse are made from pompons.

Doll's Pine Bedstead—MATERIALS (*bed*): 28" of 1x10 pine; 40" of 1x4 pine; 20" of 1x3 pine; 36" of 5/4 x 5/4 pine; 40" of 1x1; four decorative finials, 3/4"-diameter x 2" long; 1/4" hardboard, 13 7/8"x19 7/8"; 6d, 4d finishing nails; white glue; wood putty; clear varnish.

DIRECTIONS: Following the directions in METHODS chapter, enlarge the one-half patterns in FIG. 1 and cut out. Trace onto a larger piece of paper, turning pattern over to make complete pattern pieces. Trace onto 1x10 and cut headboard and footboard with a saber saw, jig saw or compass saw. Cut two 9 1/4" corner posts from 5/4x5/4; glue/nail headboard between posts, centering it 3/4" below tops of posts. Cut two 8 1/4" corner posts and similarly fasten footboard.

Rip 1x4 to 3" width. Cut two 19 1/2" side rails and glue/nail between corner posts, with bottoms of rails even with bottoms of headboard and footboard. Cut four corner pieces from 1x3 (FIG. 1). Glue/nail to side rails and corner posts. Cut two 19 1/2" lengths of 1x1 and glue/nail to insides of side rails, flush with the bottom, using 4d nails. Notch corners of hardboard to fit around corner posts and glue hardboard to 1x1s. Glue finials to bottoms of legs. Countersink all visible nails and fill holes with wood putty. Sand smooth, easing edges and corners of posts. Apply varnish.

Pompon Dolls—Directions are given for *each* animal measuring approximately 7" high.

MATERIALS: Coats & Clark's Red Heart Wintuk (4-ply, 4 oz. skeins): For **Penguin**— 1 skein each of No. 1 White and No. 12 Black; For **Chick**—1 skein of No. 230 Yellow; two cardboard rings, 4"-diameter with 2" center, two rings 3"-diameter with 1 1/2" center, and two rings 2 1/4"-diameter with 1 1/4" center; small scraps of felt in pink, grey, white, black, red, yellow, orange and blue; small length of ribbon; artificial flowers; small amount of cotton stuffing; 2 small buttons; 2 pipecleaners, 10" long.

GENERAL DIRECTIONS—*Note:* Do not stretch yarn when measuring strands. After cutting strands for pompon, divide into bundles as directed.

Place 2 equal size rings together and wind bundles around the double rings, drawing yarn through center opening and over edge until all stands are used. Cut yarn around outer edge between rings. Double a 2-yard length of yarn. Slip between the rings and tie securely around strands of pompon. Do not cut off ties. Remove rings after tying, pushing cut ends of pompon through rings one side at a time. Trim pompon evenly.

When fastening pompons together, sew tie ends through center of other pompon and knot securely. Cut tie ends. Following directions in METHODS chapter, enlarge the patterns in FIGS. 2, 3 and 4 and cut out of felt pieces.

Penguin—Body: Cut 40 strands of White, each 2 yards long. Divide strands into eight bundles of 4 strands each. Wind all bundles around 4″ rings. Cut, tie and trim following GENERAL DIRECTIONS.

Head: Cut 25 strands of Black, each 2 yards long. Divide into 5-strand bundles and wind all bundles around 3″ rings. Finish same as Body.

Tail: Wind Black 60 times around 3 fingers. Slip off fingers and tie center with a 1-yd. length of yarn. Cut loops open; roll pompon between hands and trim.

Attach head and tail to body as directed. Whipstitch 1 Black and 1 White felt section together for each wing. Sew broad end of wing to each end of a 1½″ long felt strip; place strip around back of neck and sew wings in place through neck. Whipstitch parts for bill together and attach tongue. Sew bill to head at foldline. Paste White and Black eye pieces to Blue pieces and Blue pieces to large White pieces. Paste eye sections on head. Whipstitch felt sections together, stuffing before closing heel. Sew feet to body. Fringe the narrow ends of a 1″x9″ strip of Blue felt and tie around neck. Whipstitch straight edges of hat together; sew a fringed piece of Blue felt 1″x1½″ to top for tassel and sew entire hat to head.

Chick—Using Yellow only, work Body, Head and Tail same as Penguin.

Top Tuft: Wind Yellow yarn 25 times around 3 fingers. Slip off fingers and tie center with a 1-yard length of yarn. Cut loops open; roll pompon between hands and trim. Sew tuft to top of head.

Attach head and tail to body as directed. Whipstitch 1 Yellow and 1 Orange felt piece together for each wing. Sew a small tuck in broad end of each wing; sew to neck same as Penguin. Place 2 pieces for bill together. Fold along dotted line and sew to head. Paste Blue eyes over Black so that only lashes show; paste eyes to head. Whipstitch straight edges of leg together to form a cylinder. Close one short end and stuff. Whipstitch feet sections together, stuffing before closing heel. Sew open end of leg to foot; sew other end of leg to body. Rpt for other leg. Tie ribbon and flowers around tuft.

Guardian Mouse—Directions are given for mouse measuring about 7″ high.

MATERIALS: Coats & Clark's Red Heart Wintuk (4-ply, 4 oz. skeins): 1 skein of No. 404 Grey; two cardboard rings 4″-diameter with 2″ center, and two rings 2¼″-diameter with 1¼″ center; small felt scraps of pink, black, and red; small amount of cotton stuffing; artificial flowers.

GENERAL DIRECTIONS: See GENERAL DIRECTIONS for Pompon Dolls.

Following the directions in METHODS chapter, enlarge the pattern in FIG. 4 and cut out of felt pieces.

DIRECTIONS: Using Grey only, work Body and Head same as Penguin.

Legs: (*make 2*): Cut 4 strands of Grey, each 2 yds. long. Divide into 2-strand bundles and wind all bundles around 2¼″ rings. Finish same as Body.

Nose: Wind Grey 30 times around 2 fingers. Slip off fingers and tie center with a 1-yd. length of yarn. Cut loops open, roll pompon between hands and trim to a point. Sew to head. Attach head and legs to body as directed. Whipstitch 1 Pink and 1 Grey felt piece together for each ear. Sew to head. Whipstitch together 2 pieces for each foot and arm, stuffing before closing. Sew arms to body. Bend feet up at heel and tack into position. Sew feet under legs having ends flush with edge of pompon. Cut a strip of pink ½″x8″ for tail, fold lengthwise and trim one end to a point. Whipstitch edges closed. Sew to body. Sew straight edges of felt nose together and paste on pompon nose. Paste tongue and eyes on head; tack flowers to hand.

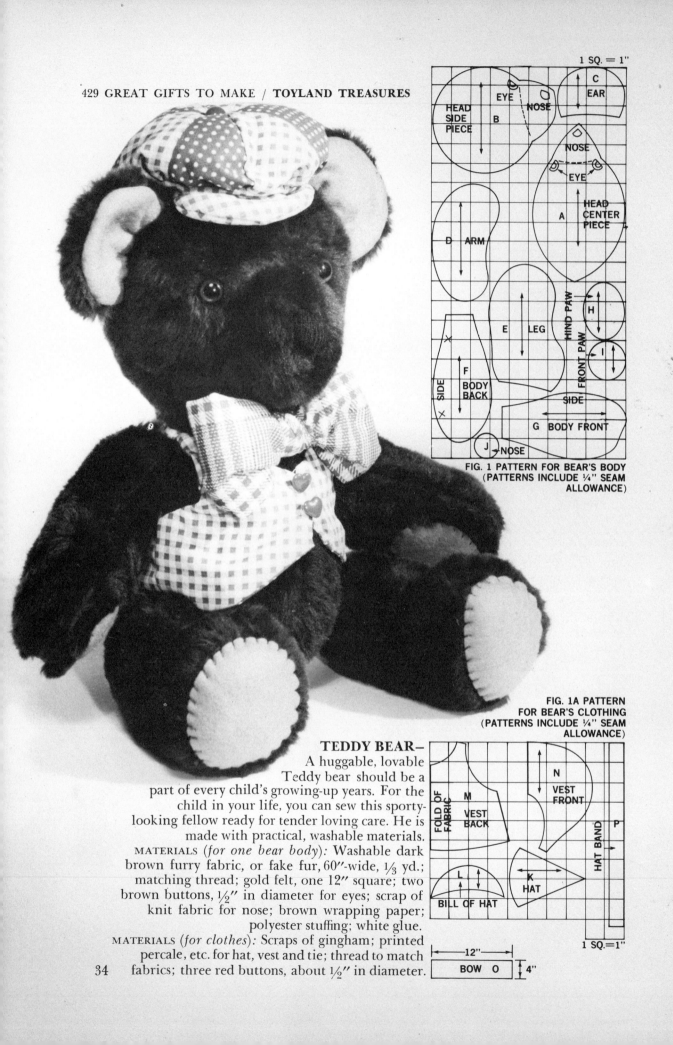

1 SQ. = 1"

**FIG. 1 PATTERN FOR BEAR'S BODY
(PATTERNS INCLUDE ¼" SEAM
ALLOWANCE)**

**FIG. 1A PATTERN
FOR BEAR'S CLOTHING
(PATTERNS INCLUDE ¼" SEAM
ALLOWANCE)**

TEDDY BEAR—

A huggable, lovable Teddy bear should be a part of every child's growing-up years. For the child in your life, you can sew this sporty-looking fellow ready for tender loving care. He is made with practical, washable materials.

MATERIALS (*for one bear body*): Washable dark brown furry fabric, or fake fur, 60"-wide, ⅓ yd.; matching thread; gold felt, one 12" square; two brown buttons, ½" in diameter for eyes; scrap of knit fabric for nose; brown wrapping paper; polyester stuffing; white glue.

MATERIALS (*for clothes*): Scraps of gingham; printed percale, etc. for hat, vest and tie; thread to match fabrics; three red buttons, about ½" in diameter.

34

DIRECTIONS—*Enlarging the Patterns:* Following the directions in the METHODS chapter, enlarge the bear body and clothing patterns (*see* FIGS. 1 and 1A). Be sure to include the directional grain arrow and other markings. Cut out patterns; label each. Seam allowance of 1/4″ is included on all pieces.

Cutting and Making Bear Body: With the directional arrow on the lengthwise

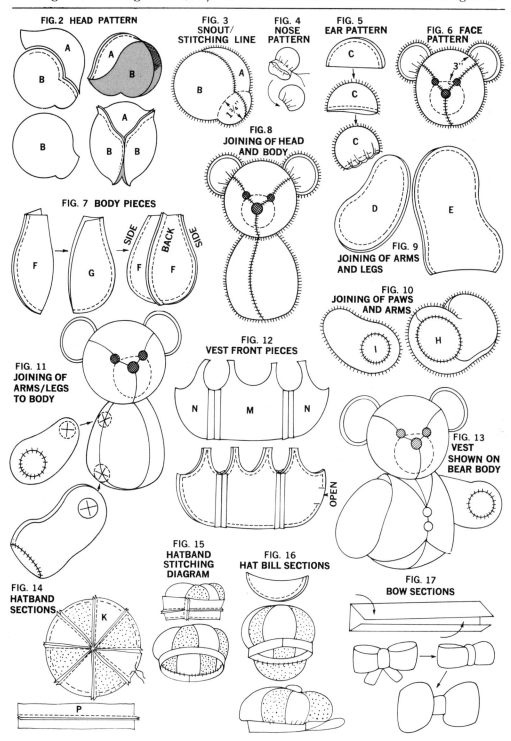

FIG. 2 HEAD PATTERN

FIG. 3 SNOUT/ STITCHING LINE

FIG. 4 NOSE PATTERN

FIG. 5 EAR PATTERN

FIG. 6 FACE PATTERN

FIG. 8 JOINING OF HEAD AND BODY

FIG. 7 BODY PIECES

FIG. 9 JOINING OF ARMS AND LEGS

FIG. 10 JOINING OF PAWS AND ARMS

FIG. 11 JOINING OF ARMS/LEGS TO BODY

FIG. 12 VEST FRONT PIECES

FIG. 13 VEST SHOWN ON BEAR BODY

FIG. 14 HATBAND SECTIONS

FIG. 15 HATBAND STITCHING DIAGRAM

FIG. 16 HAT BILL SECTIONS

FIG. 17 BOW SECTIONS

grain of the fabric, pin or trace the pattern pieces on the *wrong side* of a single layer of fabric as many times as needed to cut pieces as follows: A—cut one. B, F and G—cut one; reverse pattern and cut one more. C—cut two; also cut two from *felt*. D and E—cut two; reverse pattern and cut two more. H and I—cut two of *felt only*. J—cut one of knit fabric.

With tailor tacks, on fabric right side, mark position of eyes, nose and hand-stitching line on head; mark position of arms and legs on body back.

Sewing Bear Body: Seam allowance is ¼″ throughout. Stitch seams with fabric right sides together. With a crochet hook pull from seam any fur caught there.

1. To make the *head,* stitch A to B sections (*see* FIG. 2), leaving opening at bottom. Turn right side out; stuff. Turn in edges of opening; slipstitch.

2. To form the *snout,* hand-stitch around the face two or three times, on the tacked stitching line (*see* FIG. 3); use a doubled thread and pull it tightly to create a definite indentation.

3. Hand-gather edge of *nose* (J) piece (*see* FIG. 4). Tuck in the raw edge. Stitch nose to face at tacks where the three seams meet (*see* FIG. 6). Sew on button-eyes.

4. To make each *ear,* stitch together one fur and one felt ear (C) piece (*see* FIG. 5). Turn right side out but do not stuff. Tuck in the raw edges. Hand-gather bottom edge. Sew ears to head (*see* FIG. 6), measuring 3″ along face seamline to center of the ear.

5. To make the *body,* stitch two body back pieces (F) together (*see* FIG. 7); stitch two body front pieces (G) toegther. Stitch front to back. Turn right side out; stuff. Using a double thread, join head and body at neck (*see* FIG. 8), hand-stitching around three or four times.

6. Make arms and legs by stitching together twc D and two E sections, leaving opening, as shown in FIG. 9. Turn right side out; stuff.

7. Turn in raw edges of opening in arms; slipstitch. Sew felt paws (I) on palm sections of arms (*see* FIG. 10). On legs, sew felt paws (H) over opening as shown.

8. Using a double thread, hand-stitch arms and legs to body at marked positions (*see* FIG. 11) with arm paw pads facing inward. Stitch around three or four times, in a circle as shown, to ensure that the limbs are very firmly attached. Secure thread ends.

Directions for Bear's Clothing-Cutting: Using the enlarged patterns, cut clothing pieces as follows. Seam allowance of ¼″ is included on all pieces: K—cut four of one print and four of another. L, M and P—cut two. N—cut two of one print and two of another. O—cut one.

Sewing: Seam allowance is ¼″ throughout. Stitch seams with fabric right sides together. Press seams open.

1. To make the vest, stitch back (M) to two front (N) pieces (*see* FIG 12). Make vest lining the same way. Stitch vest to lining all around, leaving small opening on one side, as shown. Clip seam on curved edges. Turn vest right side out through opening; slipstitch opening. Press vest.

2. Put vest on bear, lapping front shoulder over back shoulder; slipstitch shoulder seam. Slightly overlap front edges; sew on buttons through all layers (*see* FIG. 13).

3. Stitch together hat (K) sections and hatband (P) sections (*see* FIG. 14). Gather hat bottom edge to fit hatband, minus ¼″ at each end of band for seaming. Using FIG. 15 as a guide, stitch hatband seam; then stitch hat gathered edge to one band edge, as shown. Turn under other edge of band ¼″ and stitch to inside of hat, as shown.

4. Stitch together hat bill (L) sections (*see* FIG. 16). Turn right side out. Turn raw edges in ¼″; press. Stitch to hatband, as shown. Lightly stuff hat. Sew button to center top through stuffing. Sew bill to hat center front with a few stitches, as shown. Sew hat to bear's head.

5. Fold bow piece (O) in thirds, lengthwise (*see* FIG. 17). Make bow. Tuck ends in; fluff out the sides, as shown. Sew to bear's chest.

*Unique yet inexpensive gifts
destined to become
treasured family keepsakes*

Collector's items are gifts made by loving hands that cost a little more—not in money but in time and skill. Among the 75 gifts shown here are semi-precious items on which you'd spend a fortune at a boutique—little treasure boxes paved with sequins, glorious gilded Easter eggs and personalized gifts of every kind. For Christmas there are appliquéd stockings. Different tree ornaments? See the tiny stuffed dolls the kids can paint, or the felt decorations, or the delicate stars made with toothpicks, barley and crochet cotton.

directions for items shown above appear on following page

RUFFLED CROCHETED PILLOWS—Crochet then embroider these lovely pillows.
Round Crocheted Pillow—Pillow measures 8½″ in diameter, plus ruffle.
MATERIALS: J.&P. Coats "Knit-Cro-Sheen": 2 balls of #37 Dk. Lavender (A); 1 ball
each of #35-C Tango (B), #10-A Canary Yellow (C), #76 Robinette (D), #1 White
(E), #43 Dk. Yellow (F) and #25 Crystal Blue (G); J.&P. Coats deluxe six-strand
floss: 1 sk each of Yellow, White, Red, Purple, Rose, Green and Blue; steel crochet
hook, No. 1/0 (zero), OR ANY SIZE HOOK WHICH WILL OBTAIN THE STITCH GAUGE
BELOW; 1 pillow 8½″ in diameter; about 48″ of eyelet lace of desired width.
GAUGE: 11 sc=2″; 6 rnds=1″.
Note: Use 2 strands of same color held tog throughout. Wind each single ball of
cotton into 2 equals parts.
Back: Start at center with 2 strands of A held tog, ch 5. Join with sl st to form ring.
Rnd 1: 7 sc in ring. Do not join rnds; carry a contrasting strand between first and
last sc of each rnd to indicate beg of rnds. *Rnd 2:* 2 sc in each sc around. *Rnd 3:*
(Sc in next sc, 2 sc in next sc) 7 times—21 sc. *Rnd 4:* (Sc in each of next 2 sc, 2 sc
in next sc) 7 times—7 sc inc. *Rnd 5:* (Sc in next 3 sc, 2 sc in next sc) 7 times—35 sc.
Continue to inc 7 sc evenly spd on every rnd until there are 91 sc in rnd; then,
being careful not to have incs fall directly above previous incs, inc 7 sc evenly
spaced around every other rnd 6 times—133 sc. Work 2 rnds even. At end last rnd,
sl st each of next 3 sc. Break off; fasten.
Front: Work same as Back until 3 rnds have been made; break off A; using 2
strands held tog, attach B Continuing to work incs same as for Back, work 3 rnds
of each color in sequence: B,C,D,E,F,A,B,G. At end of last rnd, sl st in next 3 sts.
Break off; fasten.
Embroidery (*see* METHODS chapter): Using a darning needle and 3 strands of Floss,
embroider small motifs evenly spaced on each color circle as follows: 1. 4 small
Yellow daisies in Lazy Daisy Sts with Satin St centers. 2. Groups of 2, 3 or 4
White French Knots. 3. A star of 7 Red Straight Sts. 4. A Cross of Purple Chain
Sts. 5. 3 Rose Lazy Daisy Sts close tog for rosette and 3 Green single sts for leaves.
6. Group of 3 Red French Knots with Green Straight Sts for stem and leaves. 7. 2
Blue Cross Sts in a diagonal line. Rpt same motifs on same color circles.
Finishing: Press pieces on wrong side through a damp cloth. Gather lace to fit
along outer edge of pillow. Sew ends together. Sew gathered edge to back of last
rnd of front, allowing tog edge of crochet to rem free. Hold back and front tog
with wrong sides tog; taking sts through back of sts and catching lace, sew pieces
tog, leaving a large opening. Insert pillow, sew opening.
Square Crocheted Pillow—Pillow measures 8″ square, plus ruffle.
MATERIALS: J.&P. Coats "Knit-Cro-Sheen": 2 balls of #37 Dk. Lavender (MC); 1
ball each of #25 Crystal Blue, #43 Dk. Yellow, #46-A Mid Rose, #76 Robinette,
#1 White, #135-C Tango and #10-A Canary Yellow; J.&P. Coats deluxe six-strand
floss: 1 sk each of Royal Blue, Red, Green, Yellow, White, Mid Rose, Dk. Rose,
Lt. Aquatone, Purple; steel crochet hook, No. 1/0 (zero), OR ANY SIZE HOOK WHICH
WILL OBTAIN THE STITCH GAUGE BELOW; 1 pillow 8″ square; about 56″ of eyelet
lace of desired width.
GAUGE: 11 sc=2″; 6 rows=1″.
Note: Work with 2 strands of same color held tog throughout. Wind each single
ball of cotton into 2 equal parts.
Back: With 2 strands of MC held tog, ch 48. *Row 1:* Sc in 2nd ch from hook and
in each ch across—47 sc. Mark this row for right side. Ch 1, turn. *Row 2:* Sc in
each sc across. Ch 1, turn. Rpt last row until length is about 8½″. Fasten off.
Front Squares (Make 2 of each color; 16 in all): With 2 strands held tog, ch 13.
Row 1: Sc in 2nd ch from hook and in each ch across—12 sc. Ch 1, turn. *Rows 2
through 13:* Sc in each sc across. Ch 1, turn. At end of last row, omit ch 1. Break
off and fasten.

To Join: Arranging colors as desired, with a single strand of matching color, sew squares in 4 rows of 4 in each row, matching sts.

Embroidery (*see* METHODS chapter): Rpt same motif on squares of same color. Using a darning needle and 3 strands of Floss, embroider a different motif on each square, using contrasting colors: 1. A small circle of Chain Sts at center, with French Knots around circle in a different color. 2. Small flowers in Straight Sts, with Green long and short stems also in Straight St, and small French Knot at tip of some stems for buds. 3. Three rosettes each formed by 3 Lazy Daisy Sts worked close tog and 3 single sts around each rosette for leaves. 4. About 5 groups of 2 Cross Sts each placed at random. 5. Lattice in Chain St. 6. Groups of 2, 3 or 4 French Knots. 7. Four small daisies in Lazy Daisy Sts with Satin St centers. 8. Four evenly spaced flowers of 3 French Knots with Green Straight St stems.

Finishing: Same as for Round Pillow.

GIANT MONOGRAM TOWEL HOLDERS—Make personal towel holders from 7″ wooden initial and rubber-tipped doorstops. Drill hole and screw in doorstop. Drill two holes for the type of screw or bolt required by the wall construction. Fill; sand; stain.

RIBBON-TRIMMED GIFT MATCHES—Create boutique matches with ribbons (the same width as matchbooks and boxes) simply glued in place.

WOODEN FINIAL CANDLESTICKS—Quick candlesticks are made from wood drapery rod finials used in different combinations.

MATERIALS: Large and small finials for drapery rods; ½″ doweling; Minwax in desired colors; drill; hacksaw.

DIRECTIONS: For all candlesticks remove pointed ends of finials. For taper holder, saw off screw from bottom with hacksaw and place candle in resultant hole. For single-tier holders, press candle onto the screw. For double-tier holders, saw off screw from one end and connect rounded ends with a ½″ dowel; press candle onto remaining screw. For tall candlestick, remove double screw from flat end and drill holes into small ends large enough to accept the screws. Screw finials together and press candle onto the top screw. *Finishing:* Sand and apply two coats of wax.

CLOTHESPIN CHESS SET—Kings, queens, bishops, knights, rooks and pawns are made from round clothespins. Half are dyed black with liquid shoe dye, the others left natural. Fold-up chess board of wood-lattice stripping becomes storage box.

MATERIALS: Six feet of $7/8''$ lattice; four feet of $3/4''$ lattice; 1 package round wooden clothespins; $1\frac{1}{2}''$-width black cloth tape; black shoe dye; matte varnish; fine hobby saw; small triangular file.

DIRECTIONS: Cut pieces from clothespins with hobby saw. From the head end, cut Queen ($1\frac{3}{4}''$ tall), King ($1''$) and Rook ($5/8''$). From the middle of the clothespin where wood forks, cut Bishop ($1\frac{3}{8}''$), Knight ($1\frac{1}{4}''$) and Pawn ($7/8''$). To the King, glue a crown ($1\frac{1}{4}''$ from head end of clothespin). To the Knight add a "nose" in the fork of the shape. Use small triangular file to notch top of Queen and King pieces to make crown effect. With a long pin, dip half the pieces in black shoe dye (1 King, 1 Queen, 2 Bishops. 2 Knights, 2 Rooks and 8 Pawns). *Note:* Areas and pieces not colored black can be kept clean by spraying with matte varnish.

To make fold-up board: For one side cut two lengths from each width of lattice, each $7''$ long. Glue long sides together to form box top. Repeat for bottom. Cut $7/8''$ lattice into sixty-four $7/8''$ pieces to form chess squares for playing surface. Dye 32 squares black. Frame glued sections on three sides with $7/8''$ lattice ($3\frac{3}{4}''$ for sides; $7''$ for front); butt-join at corners and glue. Glue squares to top and bottom box sections alternating colors. On fourth (back) side, butt $\frac{1}{2}''$ lattice into frame, where it will fit snugly under the slightly extending chessboard top. Repeat for other half of box. When glue is dry, place box top on bottom; "hinge" the back with $7\frac{1}{2}''$ of tape.

PILLOWS FOR CAT LOVERS—The **10″ cat** shape is repeated again on an appliquéd pillow. A **"fraidy" cat** is stitched to the third **pillow**.

MATERIALS: 12″x14″ fabric: Two each pink, turquoise and green, one gold; scraps orange and purple fabric; six $3/8''$ buttons; stuffing.

DIRECTIONS: Following the directions in METHODS chapter, enlarge and cut out patterns.

Pillow A. Cut pink front and back 1″ larger than cat shape. Pin gold cat and green eyes to front.

40

Pillow B. Cut 12″x14″ green back. Lap green over pink to make same size front. Pin two 2″ green stripes, then yellow zigzag shape. Pin orange cat, green eyes.

Pillow C. Cut 12″x14″ blue back and front. Pin wavy green grass at bottom, navy and purple stripes, gold sun at top; pink cat, green eyes.

To Appliqué: Edgestitch along raw edges; cover with wide machine satin stitch in contrasting color. Sew buttons in center of eyes.

To Make Pillows: With right sides together, stitch front to back with ½″ seam, leaving 5″ opening on one side. Turn. Stuff. Slipstitch opening.

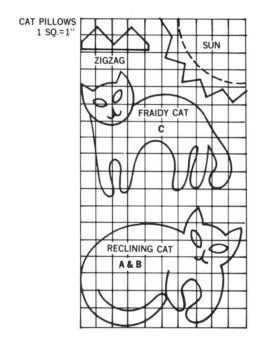

CAT PILLOWS
1 SQ.=1″

ZIGZAG

SUN

FRAIDY CAT
C

RECLINING CAT
A & B

CROSS-STITCH CHRISTMAS CARDS—Just a few, for very special people to save, maybe even frame, as keepsakes. They're easy—you do them all in Cross Stitch on even-weave fabrics. After you have completed each design, you fray the fabric to form a fringe all around. Then mount the fabric on lightweight cardboard and use a tasseled cord to attach a sheet of paper inside for your message.

MATERIALS: Even-weave linen or other evenly-woven fabric, 10"x12" in colors of your choice; 6-strand embroidery floss, 1 skein each in the colors of your choice; metal-edge ruler; white and colored tailor's chalk; masking tape; large sheet of 6-ply mounting board; paper clip; safety razor; white fabric glue; dressmaker's carbon; 32" silk cords with tassels; liner paper for inside greeting.

DIRECTIONS: Divide floss and use two or three strands, as specified.

1. Tape edges of fabric rectangle with masking tape to prevent fraying.

2. With tailor's chalk, draw a 5¾"x8¼" rectangle in the center of the fabric. Covering 2 by 2 squares of the weave at a time, cross stitch (*see* METHODS chapter) over this line with *two* strands matching floss to form an outer almost invisible line of stitching as a frame for the design.

Note: Do not pull the floss hard as tight stitches will distort the weave. To get the proper tension, practice on a scrap of fabric first, then work the frame.

3. Within this frame, work one of the decorative borders in FIG. 2, covering the 2 by 2 squares with *three* strands of floss.

4. Following the directions in the METHODS chapter, enlarge the card designs of your choice (*see* FIGS. 3 to 7).

5. Using dressmaker's carbon, trace enlarged design onto fabric, inside border.

6. Using *three* strands of floss, fill in the areas with cross stitch, again covering 2 by 2 squares with each stitch.

7. Cut off excess fabric to within ¼" of the frame stitches. Gently pull away the cross threads to ravel the edges and form fringe.

8. It is possible to cut three 9"x12" cards from one sheet of 6-ply board (use a sharp razor and ruler for an even cut). To fold each piece in half to make a 6"x9" card: Place ruler crosswise on the board at exact center as a guide; make a deep ridge in the board with the curved edge of a paper clip (do not cut board). With the ruler held firmly in place, gently bring the board up *slowly* so it doesn't crack. Remove ruler and bend completely to form the folded card shape.

9. Turn embroidery right side down on work surface; run a bead of glue on the back near the inside of the frame stitching. Position on front of folded card and smooth in place.

10. Add cord and tie to secure. Fold a piece of card-size paper; slip under cord.

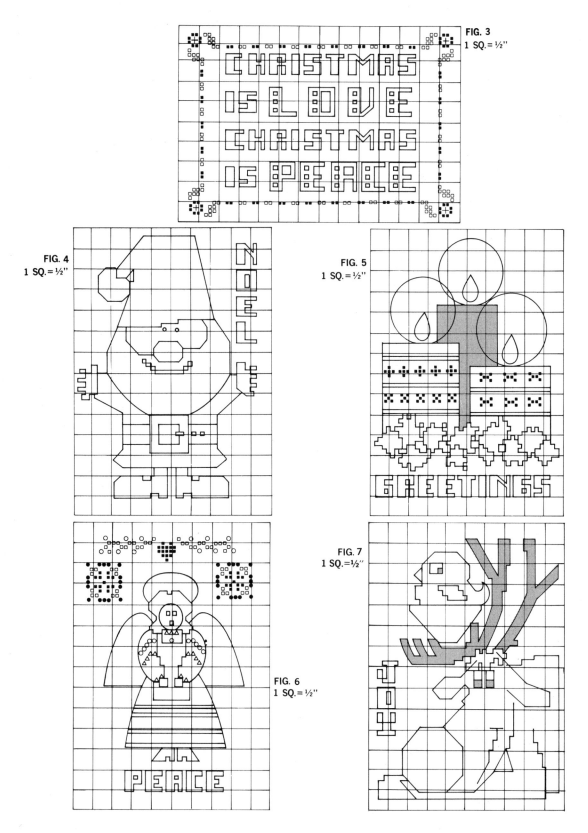

FIG. 3
1 SQ. = ½"

FIG. 4
1 SQ. = ½"

FIG. 5
1 SQ. = ½"

FIG. 6
1 SQ. = ½"

FIG. 7
1 SQ. = ½"

43

GOLD-TRIMMED EASTER EGGS—Pantyhose containers, can you believe it? That's what these beautiful big eggs are—decorated with pieces of gift wrap, then coated with shiny varnish. Add lace, gold braid, fill with Easter candy, tie with a ribbon. The others are real, regular eggs, made to look like porcelain treasures. To empty: Make a pinhole in each end, stir contents with toothpick to break yolk, blow through hole at one end to empty, rinse shells, drain, let dry. Glue on gold gift-wrap cord, dividing eggs into geometric sections. Paint sections with glossy enamel. These gorgeous eggs are not just for the children's Easter baskets—make them for your true love, for your friends and for yourself.

MATERIALS: Gift-wrap paper; white glue; clear liquid varnish; egg-shaped plastic containers; one tube of clear flexible cement; masking tape; for one egg, about ½ yd. each of gold braid, ½"-wide white eyelet ruffling and green grosgrain ribbon.

DIRECTIONS:

1. Cut small bumps from edge of larger egg section; cover lip edge with masking tape.

2. On the outside of both sections, glue on paper pieces, 1" square or smaller.

3. Apply four very thin coats of clear liquid varnish to paper-covered surfaces; let dry thoroughly after each coat. Remove masking tape.

4. On both egg sections, use cement to glue gold braid to outside edges; add ruffling to inside edges with white glue.

FABRIC-APPLIQUÉD DESK ACCESSORIES—With a half yard of chintz, white glue, spray paint and ribbon, you can make a stunning assortment of gifts that would cost a fortune at a bed/bath boutique. As you can see, a small-flowered print with a stripe is best. For wood **tissue boxes** and **frame**, spray and sand repeatedly until perfectly smooth. Cut out flowers and stripes with nail scissors and spread back evenly with white arts-and-crafts glue; position and smooth in place. Trim frame with velvet and grosgrain. More ribbon is used on a **pencil cup** (recycled baking-powder can) and **tin basket**. These should be sprayed-dried-sprayed until color is even; glue trim as shown. Stitch **towel** appliqués by hand or machine. Cover the **album** and **stationery box** with fabric first, then trim. We even appliquéd the **note paper!**

FABULOUS FELT TREE ORNAMENTS—Never mind that sophisticated silver and shine, you may say—what most kids like in Christmas decorations is color and lots of it, and toylike, childlike ornaments. Since felt comes in knockout shades of every color, use it for these appealing and fanciful decorations—and a white tree to set off the felt snowman, Santa, angel, teddy, soldier, tree and stars.

MATERIALS: 72″ wide felt in about 10 colors, or packaged felt pieces sold in two sizes—6″x9″ and 9″x12″; for felt amounts required, see *Note* below. White fabric glue; brown paper and lightweight cardboard for patterns; ruler and compass; thread to match felt; large needle; green yarn (to attach felt ornaments to tree).

Note: How much felt to buy depends on how many of each item you make.

GENERAL DIRECTIONS: All of our felt decorations are quickly and easily "appliquéd" with glue. On the background felt the appliqués are built up in layers, each one glued to the one beneath and overlapped *as shown in the photo.*

Enlarging the Patterns: Following the directions in the METHODS chapter, enlarge the designs in FIG. 1 on brown wrapping paper, in the grid sizes indicated below.

Tree-size Ornaments: 1 sq.=⅜″.

Treetop Star: 1 sq.=¾″.

Cutting:

1. Trace the full outline of each enlarged pattern onto felt. This is the background piece on which the appliqués are glued in layers. Cut out.

2. For items that have a front and a back (treetop star) cut another piece of felt to match the first.

3. Now trace the background pattern and the appliqué parts of each pattern onto cardboard; cut out.

4. Trace patterns onto felt in appropriate colors of your choice. Cut out appliqués. (*Note:* If your tracing lines show, use the reverse side of all pieces.)

Gluing: Glue the appliqués in layers to the background piece, overlapping the appliqués as shown in the photo.

Tree Ornaments: Using needle, pull two 7″ lengths of green yarn through top of ornament. Knot ends to form a loop hanger. (We also tied these ornaments to gift-wrapped packages.)

Treetop Star: With matching thread, use a machine straight stitch to sew star back and assembled front piece together, ¼″ from edges, leaving one V-shaped segment open to insert treetop branch.

FIG. 1 FELT APPLIQUÉ DESIGNS   1 SQ. = ⅜"

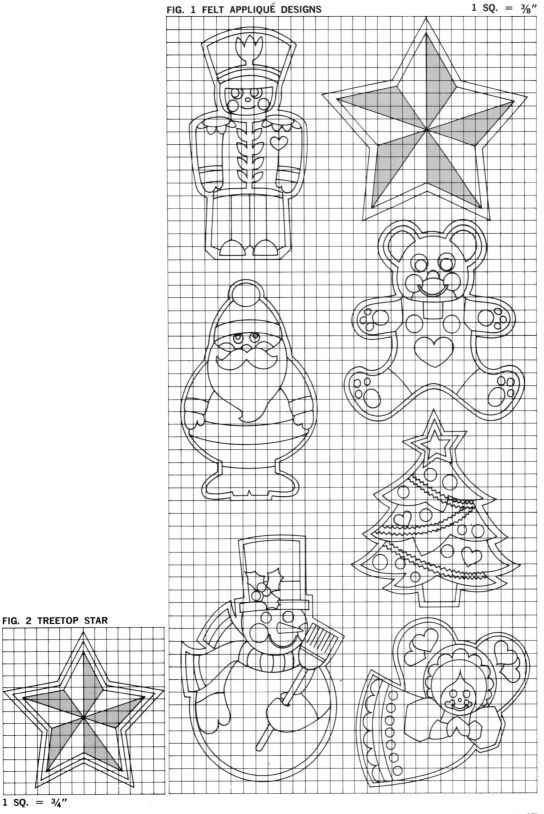

FIG. 2 TREETOP STAR

1 SQ. = ¾"

STUFFED DOLL TREE ORNAMENTS

1 SQ. = 1"

STUFFED DOLL TREE ORNAMENTS—Tree ornaments (pincushions or cuddly toys) are identical on front and back. Sew and stuff; decorate with colorful felt-tip markers.

MATERIALS (*for one ornament*): White cotton fabric, two pieces approximately 7″x9″; felt tip pens in various colors; carbon paper and pencil or tracing wheel; kapok or other stuffing.

DIRECTIONS: Following the directions in METHODS chapter, copy and enlarge the patterns. Trace each enlarged pattern onto two pieces of white fabric. Color the areas inside the traced lines on *both* pieces (this is a job children love to do). Trim away excess fabric ¼″ from outer edge of the design. With right sides together, stitch around ¼″ from the edge, leaving 2″ open at bottom. Turn right side out. Stuff. Whipstitch opening. Attach hanger.

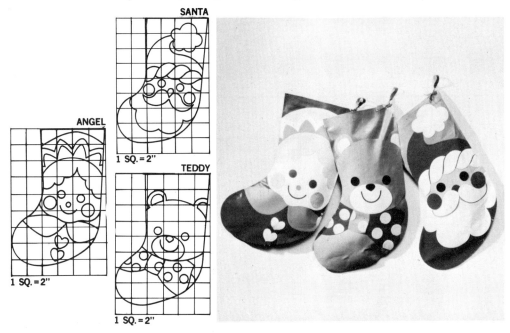

VINYL CHRISTMAS STOCKINGS—Hung up and waiting for Santa Claus are three cute vinyl stockings—an angel, teddy and Santa himself; you can make these 17″-long stockings in a flash with a little stitching and glue.

MATERIALS: ½ yd. knit-backed vinyl for stocking shapes; scraps of vinyl in assorted colors for appliqués; white fabric glue; thread to match stocking vinyl colors; X-acto knife; wooden board or stacks of newspapers to protect work surface when cutting; light and dark carbon paper.

DIRECTIONS: Following the directions in METHODS chapter, enlarge the stocking designs and cut out. Re-trace 1″ of stocking top edge two times and cut out for "facings."

1. From vinyl yardage cut out two entire stocking shapes for each stocking.

2. Using carbon paper, trace appliqué shapes onto vinyl scraps in appropriate colors and cut out.

3. Glue stocking facings to wrong sides of stocking top edges. With wrong sides facing, glue stocking pieces together around all edges except top.

4. Cut ⅜″-wide strip of vinyl, 7″ long, from scrap. Cut a ⅜″ slash through all layers ⅜″ from top edge and ½″ from back edge of stocking. Insert doubled strip from back to front and knot over the top edge to form a loop for hanging.

5. Glue appliqués in place on stocking front.

49

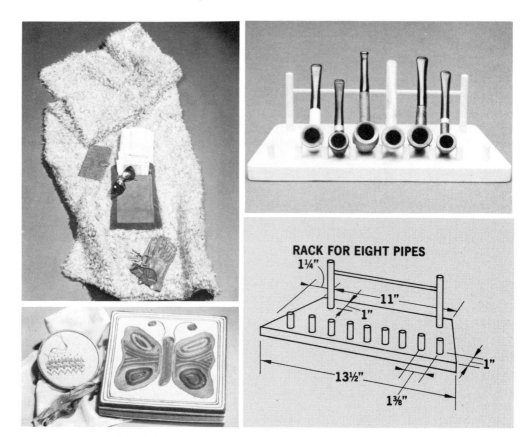

RACK FOR EIGHT PIPES

FAKE FUR LAP ROBE—Our robe has handy pockets for maps, guidebooks, pencils, etc. Cut two pieces of fur fabric, each 69"x31". For pocket, cut two pieces of suede 6"x8" and 8½"x11½". Edgestitch smaller pocket on top of larger one, then stitch ¾" from one long edge to make pencil slot in top pocket. Edgestitch pocket to right side of one fur piece. Right sides together, stitch fur pieces around edges, leaving 24" opening. Turn right side out. Whipstitch open edge.

"EMBROIDERED" EMBROIDERY BOX—Create a storage box for embroidery with embroidery floss. Cover a cardboard gift box with double-faced tape. Start your floss design at the center, looping the floss back and forth to cover the whole surface, including sides. Follow our design or create your own. Press floss firmly in place with fingertip.

RACK FOR EIGHT PIPES—Here's a gift for the pipe collector on your list. The only materials needed are a piece of clear pine lumber, wood dowels and plastic resin glue. Quick and easy.
MATERIALS: One 13½" length 1x6 clear pine; ⅜" doweling; ⅛" doweling; plastic resin glue; adhesive-backed felt.
DIRECTIONS: From ⅜" doweling, cut two 4" lengths and nine 1½" lengths. From ⅛" doweling, cut one 9½" length. Cut 1x6 pine as shown, sanding to round off corners and top. Refer to procedure in *Pipe Rack* on page 113, changing quantities and length of doweling only.

QUICHE PAN MIRROR FRAME—Three sizes of quiche pans soldered atop each other become a mirror frame. Cut edges at ½" intervals with metal shears. Bottom of largest quiche pan is soldered on back to hold mirror.

NEEDLEPOINT MONOGRAM PILLOWS—Give a personalized needlepoint pillow! With masking tape, bind the edges of a 6″ square of No. 10 Penelope canvas. With waterproof felt marker, draw a 4″ square in canvas center. Trace stencil initial in middle. Using your favorite stitch, work the initial and background with knitting worsted in contrasting colors. Block canvas then trim edges to ½″ of worked area. Machine-zigzag the canvas to one side of a removable pillow cover. Pin ribbon over canvas edges, mitering corners; slipstitch in place.

BRICK BOOKENDS AND DOORSTOP—Popsicle sticks, tongue depressors, sandpaper and magazine cutouts are glued on bricks to resemble windows and structural members of an apartment or town house. Sandpaper is glued to cedar shake for gambrel roof.

RIBBON-TRIMMED EASTER EGGS—Delight your family and friends with these elegant old-fashioned Easter eggs. To accomplish these timeless designs, paint emptied and dried eggshells a solid color, or rub with irridescent metallic wax for an antique patina. When completely dry, dress up in patchwork style with glued-on rows of lace, delicate floral embroidered ribbons, velvet or embroidery floss. Final results are pretty enough to enjoy year round—heaped in a glass bowl or individually displayed.

NAME-DROPPER PILLOW—This name-dropper pillow can be made by either adding labels to a pillow you already have or making new ones. Press labels carefully, turning under raw edges. Arrange and pin on the pillow surface until you are satisfied with the design, then whipstitch in place (or glue with fabric glue). Frame with a border of chain stitch.

51

POMANDER BAGS—To make from scraps of lining fabric and ribbon.
MATERIALS: Velvet and woven-satin ribbons; printed lining fabric, ⅓ yd.; lace edging and narrow velvet ribbon for ties, 1¼ yds. each.
DIRECTIONS: From lining cut two 9″ rounds for small bag, 12″ for large. Cover one with alternating ribbons, edgestitched. With edges even, baste lace to circle edges on right side. Pin lining over them. Stitch, leaving 4″ open. Turn right side out; stitch opening. To form casing, stitch ¾″ from edge all around; cut slash and insert ribbon. Make ice-pick holes in oranges or lemons. Insert cloves, covering fruit completely.

BOTTLECAP ADVENT CALENDAR—Caps to be turned in Advent are hung on felt tree glued to plywood.
MATERIALS needed are given in order used in Directions below.
DIRECTIONS: Use photo as a guide. *Pine board 12″x24″*—cut top and bottom edges in curved shape; sand edges; glue decorative molding to side edges; coat with gesso (a white liquid sealer); paint red. Attach sawtooth hanger to back.
Christmas tree: Cut from green and black felt and glue to board; paste large gold Christmas medallion at tree top, and smaller ones at random; screw 23 eyelets through felt into board, spacing them as in photo; screw 3 eyelets to board alone around tree top.
Angels: From felt, cut 2 angels; add magic marker strokes for features, hair and wings; glue to board at right and left of tree top.
Assorted sizes bottle caps and jar lids: Punch a small hole in the center of the lip; insert 1½″ copper wire and twist ends, leaving a ¼″ loop on top; spray with gold paint inside and out. When dry, glue gold foil strips around lips inside; glue felt circles with small Christmasy pictures pasted to center. On outside, paint in bright colors. Paste on gold foil medallions and black numbers, 1-24, in center of medallions. With red string, tie lids to eyelets (largest in center), with numbered side up; on each day of Advent, reverse one lid to show picture inside.

EIGHT-BOTTLE WINE RACK—You can make this eight-bottle wine rack of square pine stock and ⅜″ doweling for far less than the ones you buy. Extra sections can be added as your wine collection grows. To make this starter section, cut 10 feet of 1⅛″ square pine stock into twelve 10″ lengths. As a guide for dowel positions, make a heavy cardboard template, also 1⅛″x10″, and punch a pinhole 1″ from both ends in the exact center (⁹⁄₁₆″ from each side). Use the template to mark a pencil dot on each end of the 10″ pieces, as follows: Top and bottom pieces, three sides; all other pieces, four sides. Drill holes only halfway in at each dot with a ⅜″ electric drill (at slow speed), or ⅜″ auger brace and bit. Round off ends with medium, then fine, sandpaper. Cut 18 dowels, each 3⅝″ long and eight dowels, each 8⅜″ long, from four 3′ lengths of ⅜″ doweling. Smooth dowel ends with sandpaper. Slide two long dowels into three pieces of stock to make each layer. Put a drop of white glue into each hole in stock and insert 3⅝″ dowels to connect layers. When dry, finish rack with wax, stain, varnish or paint.

SEQUIN-COVERED GIFT BOXES—Here's a way to double a gift—make the box you give it in a treasure in itself. Permanently encrusted with twinkling sequins, the box may outlive the gift! Take any cardboard or wood box, draw a simple design on it (use a compass or ruler so it will look tidy), and then, using white glue and a toothpick, fill in the design with sequins, one color at a time. Start with the pattern you've drawn on the box lid. When you've completed decorating your box, let the glue set overnight and then brush on several coats of clear polyurethane, letting dry thoroughly between each coat.

EUROPEAN CHRISTMAS DECORATIONS—These ornaments have the look of costly handmade imports, but you can easily make them of today's available and inexpensive materials. Place a (FIG.1) delicate wooden star atop the tree—looks Polish, you might say, or perhaps Scandinavian. In truth, it's all wooden toothpicks and hors d'oeuvre forks cleverly glued together! You make the snowflakes on the tree, and the charming birds, the same way. As for those tiny bright-colored baskets, crochet them in single crochet stitch; spray starch them for extra body; fill them with colorful little candies and/or gum balls. Drawstring gift bags *(see the photo on page 56)* are made from scrap fabric.

Wooden Tree Ornaments—MATERIALS: Bamboo hors d'oeuvre forks; flat wooden toothpicks; round wooden toothpicks; ecru crochet cotton; lightweight cardboard; thick white glue; wax paper; masking tape; monofilament fishing line; pasta; pearl barley.

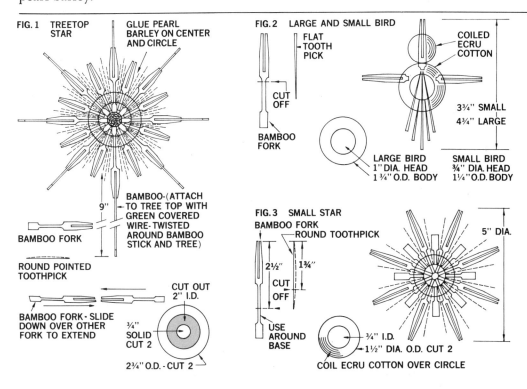

GENERAL DIRECTIONS:

1. Follow the construction diagrams in Figs. 1–6 to make ornaments. Cut two circles of lightweight cardboard for each ornament. Tape a sheet of wax paper on work surface. Spread glue on top of cardboard and place on wax paper.

2. Following diagrams, cut forks and toothpicks; glue on top of cardboard. When all picks are secured, spread glue on second circle and press on top of picks. Place a heavy object on top of ornament so that it will dry flat. Repeat.

3. When all ornaments are completed, spread glue on top of cardboard and decorate, as specified, with coiled crochet cotton or pasta or pearl barley.

4. Cut 6″ lengths of monofilament line for each ornament and tie into circle for hanger.

Optional: For added interest, decorate flat parts of bamboo forks with brown felt-tip pen lines.

Crocheted Christmas Baskets—Directions are given for a basket measuring 2″ across top.

MATERIALS: Coats & Clark's O.N.T. "Speed-Cro-Sheen" (100 yd. ball): One ball of desired color; steel crochet hook, Size 0 (zero), OR ANY SIZE HOOK WHICH WILL OBTAIN THE STITCH GAUGE BELOW.

GAUGE: 11 sc=2″.

Note: One ball will make three baskets.

DIRECTIONS: Starting at center of bottom section, ch 4. Join with sl st to form ring. *Rnd 1:* Ch 1, 6 sc in ring. Join with sl st to first sc. *Rnd 2:* Ch 1, 2 sc in same sc as joining, 2 sc in each sc around. Join with sl st to first sc—12 sc. *Rnd 3:* Ch 1, sc in same sc as joining, 2 sc in next sc, * sc in next sc, 2 sc in next sc; rpt from * around. Join to first sc—18 sc. *Rnd 4:* Ch 1, sc in same sc as joining, sc in next sc, 2 sc in next sc, * sc in each of next 2 sc, 2 sc in next sc; rpt from * around. Join as before—24 sc. *Rnd 5:* Ch 1, sc in same sc as joining, sc in each of next 2 sc, 2 sc in next sc, * sc in each of next 3 sc, 2 sc in next sc; rpt from * around. Join—6 incs

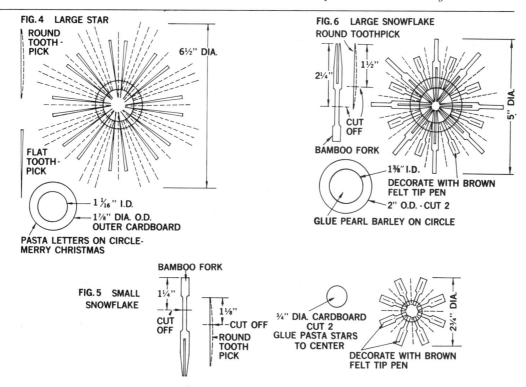

FIG.4 LARGE STAR
ROUND TOOTH-PICK
6½″ DIA.
FLAT TOOTH-PICK
1 ¹⁄₁₆″ I.D.
1⅞″ DIA. O.D.
OUTER CARDBOARD
PASTA LETTERS ON CIRCLE—MERRY CHRISTMAS

FIG.6 LARGE SNOWFLAKE
ROUND TOOTHPICK
1½″
2¼″
CUT OFF
BAMBOO FORK
5″ DIA.
1¾″ I.D.
DECORATE WITH BROWN FELT TIP PEN
2″ O.D. - CUT 2
GLUE PEARL BARLEY ON CIRCLE

FIG.5 SMALL SNOWFLAKE
BAMBOO FORK
1¼″
CUT OFF
1⅛″
CUT OFF
ROUND TOOTH PICK
¾″ DIA. CARDBOARD CUT 2
GLUE PASTA STARS TO CENTER
2¼″ DIA.
DECORATE WITH BROWN FELT TIP PEN

For knit and crochet abbreviations box, see Methods (Chapter 11)

made. *Rnd 6:* Ch 1, sc in same sc as joining, making 6 incs evenly spaced around, sc in each sc around. Join. *Rnd 7:* Rpt Rnd 6 (having one more sc before each inc than on previous rnd)—42 sc. *Rnd 8:* Ch 1, sc in same sc as joining, sc in each sc around. Join. *Rnds 9 through 15:* Rpt Rnd 8, 7 times—42 sc in each rnd. *Rnd 16:* Sl st in each sc around, sl st in first sl st. Do not break off.

Handle: Ch 25, sk next 20 sc, sl st in next sc; sl st in each ch st of ch-25, sl st in next sc on last rnd of basket. Break off and fasten.

Finishing: Spray each basket heavily with spray starch. Place on top of wax paper; shape as desired and allow to dry until stiffened.

Drawstring Gift Bags—MATERIALS: Solid and flower-printed cotton plain and/or quilted; bias tape or woven cord or velvet tube cord for pullstrings. The amounts depend on the size and quantity of bags to be made.

GENERAL DIRECTIONS:

1. Measure length and width of gift to be packaged and add sufficient to each figure to allow for the item's girth.

2. Cut measurements two times (one front and one back) from fabric (or pieced fabric, as shown in photo), adding 1″ seam allowance to length and width. *For lining,* cut same size pieces, adding 1½″ to length and 1″ to width for seam allowance.

3. With right sides together, stitch ½″ seams around sides and bottom of bag; repeat for lining; clip corners.

4. Turn bag right side out. Slip lining (as is) into bag, side seams and bottom corners matching; lining will extend 1″ from top of bag.

5. Turn lining top edge ¼″ under and press; now turn ¾″ over raw edge of bag top. Edgestitch all around to form hem and casing.

6. Clip a few stitches in one casing side seam and insert pullstring.

Optional Casing: For a bag with the casing below top edge, make two rows of stitching ½″ apart at desired distance from bag top. Clip seam; insert pullstring.

DESK ACCESSORIES—Colorful gift wrap turns ordinary file folders, clip boards and address books into welcome gifts. Staple ribbon ties to outside edges; use white glue to cover surfaces with paper. Cover with protective layer of clear self-adhesive plastic.

*Timeless classics and dozens
of accessories
to knit, crochet and sew*

This chapter is dedicated to the woman on the run—the woman who likes to do creative handiwork but doesn't have the time to take on big projects that take forever to complete. To be included here, the 30 items selected had to be quick to make as well as inexpensive. The choice ranges from dressy t-shirts (bought shirts you dress up with easy trims), to speedy crocheted sweaters and accessories, to dress-up aprons you can make in an evening, to whimsical jewelry. For the traveling woman there are nifty denim garment bag sets.

directions for items shown above appear on following page

57

CHAPTER 4

TRICOLOR CROCHETED CAP AND SCARF—We used an open and lacy crochet stitch so you could make up a cap and scarf set like ours in a hurry. The tricolor braid of yarn is made separately and stitched to the cap edge. Our scarf is 68″ long.

Directions are given for a woman's cap which fits all sizes.

MATERIALS: Bernat Krysta (2 oz. skeins): For cap or scarf: 2 skeins Color A, 1 skein each Colors B and C; Bernat-Aero crochet hook, Size J, OR ANY SIZE HOOK WHICH WILL OBTAIN THE STITCH GAUGE BELOW.

GAUGE: 4 clusters=3″; 2 rows/rnds=2″.

DIRECTIONS—**Cap:** With A, ch 7. Join with sl st to form ring. *Rnd 1:* Ch 4 to count as one tr, 17 tr in ring. Join with sl st to top of ch-4. *Rnd 2:* Sl st bet ch-4 and tr, *ch 4, dc in same place as sl st*—starting cluster made, ch 1, * *yarn over hook, draw up a loop bet next 2 tr, yarn over and draw through 2 loops on hook, yarn over, draw up a loop in same place, yarn over and draw through 2 loops, yarn over and draw through rem 3 loops*—cluster made, ch 1. Rpt from * around. Join last ch 1 to top of starting cluster—18 clusters. *Rnd 3:* In first sp make sl st and starting cluster, * ch 1, cluster in next ch-1 sp. Rpt from * around. Join. *Rnd 4:* In first sp make sl st and starting cluster, ch 1, * *in next ch-1 sp make (cluster, ch 1) twice* —inc made; (cluster in next ch-1 sp, ch 1) twice. Rpt from * around to last 2 sps, inc in next sp, ch 1, cluster in last sp, ch 1. Join—24 clusters. *Rnds 5 through 8:* Rpt Rnd 3 four times. Fasten off. *Braid Trim:* Cut sixteen 72″ strands each of A, B and C. Make a smooth braid and sew ends tog. Sew on top of lower edge.

Scarf: With A, ch 16 loosely. *Row 1:* Dc in 4th ch from hook, * ch 1, sk next ch, cluster (same as on Cap) in next ch. Rpt from * across—7 clusters. Ch 3, turn. *Row 2:* * Cluster in next ch-1 sp, ch 1. Rpt from * across ending with cluster in last sp, dc in top of ch-3—6 clusters. Ch 3, turn. *Row 3:* Dc in dc, * ch 1, cluster in next sp. Rpt from * across ending with ch 1, cluster in top of ch-3—7 clusters. Ch 3, turn. Rpt Rows 2 and 3 alternately until total length is 64″. Fasten off. **Fringe:** Cut seven 14″ strands of A. Fold strands in half, insert crochet hook through a ch-1 sp on narrow edge of scarf and draw folded loop through; pass free ends through loop and tighten. Make fringes of all 3 colors in sps along each narrow edge.

CROCHETED CLUSTER-TRIMMED BOLERO—This winter warmer is made in fisherman knit yarn in neutral eggshell tone.

          For knit and crochet abbreviations box, see Methods (Chapter 11)

Directions are given for size Small (8–10). Changes for sizes Medium (12–14) and Large (16–18) are in parentheses.

MATERIALS: Lion Brand Fisherman Knit (4 oz. skeins): 3(4, 4) skeins of #99 Eggshell; knitting needles, 1 pair No. 11, OR ANY SIZE NEEDLES WHICH WILL OBTAIN THE STITCH GAUGE BELOW; crochet hook, Size G.

GAUGE: 11 sts=4″. *Note:* Use 2 strands of yarn held together throughout.

MEASUREMENTS:			
SIZES:	SMALL	MEDIUM	LARGE
BUST:	32″	35″	38″
WIDTH ACROSS BACK AT UNDERARM:	16″	17½″	19″
WIDTH ACROSS EACH FRONT AT UNDERARM *(excluding border):*	8″	9½″	10″

Back: Starting at lower edge with 2 strands of yarn held together, cast on 44(48,52) sts. *Row 1 (wrong side):* P across. *Row 2:* * With yarn in back, sl 1 as if to p, yo, k 1, pass the slipped st over the yo and k st just made; rpt from * across. *Row 3:* P across. *Row 4:* K 1, with yarn in back sl 1, yo, k 1, pass slipped st over the yo and k st just made; rpt from * across, end with k 1. Rpt these 4 rows for pat. Work in pat until length is 7(7½,8)″ from beg; end with a wrong-side row.
Armhole Shaping: Keeping continuity of pat throughout, bind off 2(3,4) sts at beg of next 2 rows—40(42,44) sts. Work even until length is 7(7½,8)″ from first row of armhole shaping. Bind off all sts.
Left Front: Starting at lower edge with 2 strands held together, cast on 24(26,28) sts. Work same as for Back until same length as Back to underarm; end with a wrong-side row.
Armhole Shaping: Keeping continuity of pat throughout, bind off 2(3,4) sts at beg of next row. Work even over 22(23,24) sts until length is 5(5½,5½)″ from first row of armhole shaping; end at front edge.
Neck Shaping: Being careful to keep in pat, at front edge bind off 5(5,6) sts at beg of next row. Dec one st at neck edge every row 4 times. If necessary, work even over rem 13(14,14) sts until armhole is same length as on Back. Bind off all sts for shoulder.
Right Front: Work to correspond with Left Front, reversing shaping.
Finishing: Pin pieces to measurements on a padded surface; cover with a damp cloth and allow to dry; do not press. Sew shoulder and side seams.
Border: With right side facing, using 2 strands held together and crochet hook, attach yarn with sl st in center back of neck, * *yarn over hook, draw up a loop in next st on edge of bolero, pull up this loop to measure ¾″, (yarn over hook, draw up ¾″ loop in same st) 3 more times; yarn over hook, draw through 8 loops on hook, yarn over, draw through rem 2 loops on hook*—cluster made; * ch 1, sk next st (or row) along edge, make a cluster in next st; rpt from * around entire outer edge of bolero, end with ch 1. Join with sl st to top of first cluster. Break off and fasten. Turn border to right side of bolero and stitch loosely in place, easing in top edge of border to lay flat along corners. Starting at underarm, work border along each armhole edge in same way.

STRAPLESS RUFFLED TOP—Using easy single and double crochet stitches, you can make this slinky evening top in a couple of hours.

Directions are given for Small Size (6–8). Changes for Medium Size (10–12) and Large Size (14–16) are in parentheses.

MATERIALS: Coats & Clark's "Red Heart" Knitting Worsted, 4 Ply (4 oz. "Tangle-Proof" Pull-Out Skns): 10(12,13) ozs. No. 900 Melon; crochet hook, Size H OR

ANY SIZE HOOK WHICH WILL OBTAIN THE STITCH GAUGE BELOW; 1 yd. round elastic.
GAUGE: 7 sts=2″; 6 rows=2½″

FINISHED MEASUREMENTS:

SIZES:	SMALL (6–8)	MEDIUM (10–12)	LARGE (14–16)
TO FIT BUST SIZE (when stretched):	31½″	34″	38″
BACK OR FRONT WIDTH AT UNDERARM (without stretching):	15″	16½″	18¼″

Back: Start at lower edge, ch 53(58,65) loosely to measure 16(17¼,19¼)″. *Row 1 (right side):* Sc in 2nd ch from hook and in each ch across—52(57,64) sc. Ch 3; turn. *Row 2:* Sk first sc, dc in each rem sc—52(57,64) dc, counting turning ch-3 as 1 dc. Ch 1; turn. *Row 3:* Sc in each dc across, sc in top of turning chain. Ch 3; turn. Rpt Rows 2 and 3 alternately for pat. Work in pat until total length is about 20(20,21)″; end with an sc row. Break off and fasten.

Front: Work same as for Back.

Finishing: Block pieces to measurements. Sew side seams. *Top Edge:* Cut a piece of elastic to fit snugly around body at underarm, allowing ½″ for sewing. Overlap ends for ½″ and sew tog to form a circle. With wrong side facing, place circle of elastic along top edge of last row made; working over elastic, sc in each sc around. Join with sl st to first sc of this rnd. Ch 6; turn.

Ruffle: Make dtr in same sc used for joining, ch 1, * in next sc (dtr and ch 1) twice; rpt from * around. Join last ch-1 to 5th ch of ch-6 at beg of rnd. Break off and fasten.

T-SHIRTS WITH STYLE—We discovered that inexpensive T-shirts are great for "doing your own thing." You can create a new neckline and trim by appliqué-ing lace. Sew on rhinestones by the dozen. A zipper turns a pullover into a cardigan with ribbon trim.

Lace-Trimmed V-neck T-shirt—MATERIALS: T-shirt; floral-patterned cotton lace, 2½″-wide. Yardage depends upon sleeve width and desired width and depth of V neckline (we used about 1¾ yds.).

DIRECTIONS:

1. While wearing shirt, pin lace with one flower where you want the bottom of the V neckline to be located. Continue pinning around neck, around to the center front; overlap the ends ¼″. Mark the desired sleeve length. Remove shirt.

2. Starting at the underarm seam, pin lace around sleeve with lace straight edge at the marked sleeve length. Overlap lace ends ¼″.

3. Using a narrow zigzag, topstitch along the *top* edge of the lace on the sleeves and along the *bottom* edge of the lace around neck. Carefully cut away T-shirt fabric under the lace, on sleeves and neck, close to the stitching.

4. With tiny hand stitches, appliqué the overlapped lace ends; trim away the excess lace on the underside close to stitching.

Rhinestone-Trimmed T-shirt—MATERIALS: Round neck T-shirt with sleeves; rhinestones, about 4 gross; strong nylon thread; sharp, long needle; white pencil; stiff cardboard; ruler; yardstick.

DIRECTIONS:

1. Insert cardboard between shirt front and back to provide a firm, flat work surface for drawing and sewing.
2. On the front, draw the design as shown in photo, using white pencil, ruler and yardstick for the straight lines and a platter or any round object of suitable size for the arcs. Start with the vertical middle line to be sure design is even.
3. With double, knotted nylon thread, sew rhinestones to the marked lines, passing the needle through two of the stones' four holes. (Later, if you wish, sew through the other two holes for greater security.)
4. Also sew rhinestones in 12 groups of three around the neck and five groups of three on bottom front edge of sleeve. Sew additional rhinestones in a random pattern on both sides of the center design (*using photo as a guide*).

T-shirt Trimmed with Ribbon and Nailheads—MATERIALS: Round neck T-shirt with long sleeves; 16″ lightweight separating (jacket) zipper; 1″-wide grosgrain ribbon: 1 yd. pink, 2⅔ yds. yellow, ¾ yd. lavender; thread to match ribbons; gold-color nailheads, ¼″ in diameter, about 166 (available in sewing notions departments along with tool to attach them).

DIRECTIONS:

1. Fold shirt-front in half lengthwise. Baste along fold line.
2. Using the photo below as a color and placement guide, pin ribbons on shirt front with edges 1″ apart; cut one end of each on a slant, ⅜″ from center front line and turn other end under ¼″. Edgestitch ribbons with matching threads.
3. Cut shirt on basted center front line; bind edges with yellow ribbon. Sew in separating zipper. Bind neck edge with yellow ribbon.
4. Pin and edgestitch pink and yellow ribbons on sleeve bottom edge, spacing them ¼″ apart. Follow manufacturer's directions to attach nailheads to ribbon trim on sleeves and front, spacing them ½″ apart.

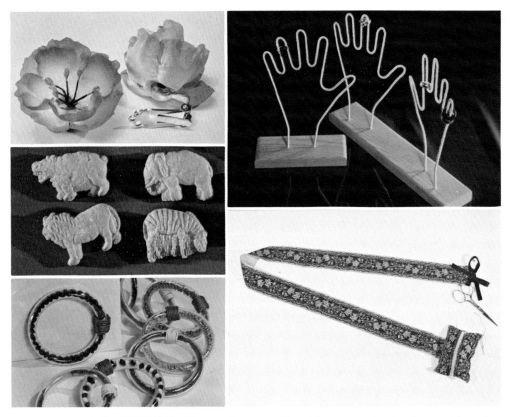

SILK POPPY EARRINGS—For an instant gift with a great look, drop white glue onto old or new earring backs; press firmly onto silk poppy bases.

ANIMAL CRACKER PINS—Paint animal crackers with three coats of varnish or clear nail polish; let them dry between coats. Use clear cement to attach pins.

PLASTIC TUBE BANGLES—Plastic tubing (3/8″ opening) is filled with beans, glued to short 3/8″ dowel plug, covered with twine.

HAND-SHAPED RING HOLDERS—With plier bend #12 white tape-covered floral wire to a hand shape traced on paper. Push wire ends into holes drilled 2″ apart in 6″ (12″ for double ring stand) length of 1″x3″ scrap lumber.

RIBBON SEW-HELP-ME—With this pretty helper around her neck, a seamstress can keep scissors and pins handy. Line fancy 1½″ ribbon with plain ribbon; edge-stitch. Add a covered pincushion. Attach the snipping scissors with velvet bow.

MUSLIN SACHETS—Sachets are sensational stocking stuffers. The shape is cut from muslin scraps, trimmed with sewing machine embroidery and filled.
MATERIALS (*for six 4″x5″ sachets*): 36″-wide unbleached muslin, 1/3 yd.; assorted color threads; 1 cup dried Rosemary; 1/3 cup dried thyme leaves; 3 cups dried mint leaves; 2 tsp. ground cloves.
DIRECTIONS: Cut muslin into 12 pieces 5″x6″. On six pieces, draw a freehand mushroom (or other design). Machine-embroider the design with satin and zigzag stitches of various lengths and colors. With right sides together, pin an embroidered piece to a plain piece; stitch around in 1/2″ seam, leaving 3″ open on one side. Turn right side out. Mix the spices thoroughly. Store in a covered con-

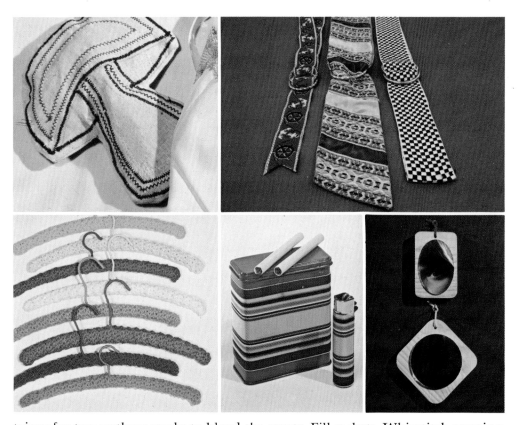

tainer for two or three weeks to blend the scents. Fill sachets. Whipstitch opening.

CROCHETED HANGER COVERS—Perennially popular and easy to make.
MATERIALS: Bucilla Machine washable Multi-Craft (2 oz. skeins): 1 skein (35 yds.
will make one hanger); crochet hook, Size K, OR ANY SIZE HOOK WHICH WILL
OBTAIN THE STITCH GAUGE BELOW; wooden clothing hanger; double sticking tape.
GAUGE: 8 sc = 3".
DIRECTIONS: At narrow end, ch 8 to measure 3½". *Row 1:* Sc in 2nd ch from hook,
sc in each ch across—7 sc. Ch 1, turn. *Row 2:* Working in the back loops only, sc
in each sc across—7 sc. Ch 1, turn. Rpt Row 2 until piece (when slightly stretched)
is same length as hanger. Fasten off. Pass hook through exact center of piece. Sew
narrow ends; then sew long edges tog. Wind hook with double sticking tape. Starting at end of hook, wind yarn evenly over taped hook; fasten end to crochet at
base of hook.

ADJUSTABLE RIBBON BELTS—Ribbon belts can be made in minutes. For
the nautical and checked belts buy ribbon to equal twice your waist measurement,
plus 16"; ¼ yard fusible webbing and, for the buckle, two metal rings with
diameters the width of the ribbon. Fold ribbon in half with wrong sides together
(rings at the fold); place webbing strips between. Fuse. Line stitched-together
bands of trim for the wider belt, adding ring at one end.

RIBBON TRIMMED CIGARETTE SET—Glue ribbon to a painted bandage
box and matching lighter.

PURSE-SIZE HANGING MIRRORS—Dime-store mirrors are glued to scraps
of lattice stripping. Lacing is knotted plastic cord.

GLAMOROUS APRONS—Definitely not for the kitchen.

GENERAL DIRECTIONS:

• Yardage requirements given are approximate and will vary according to your preference in skirt length.

• Cut pieces on fabric straight grain.

• Seam allowances are ½″ throughout, unless otherwise specified.

TIPS ON GATHERING: Set machine for longest stitch. Make a row of stitching ½″ from edge to be gathered and another row above the first. With right sides together, pin each end of edge to be gathered to the end of the section it is to join, also pinning together midway between the ends. Firmly holding the bobbin thread of each row of stitching, gather the fabric from one end to the pin at the middle until it fits the section. Secure thread ends. Repeat this procedure from the other end of the stitched rows. Distribute gathering evenly. Pin the two pieces together spacing pins about 1″ apart. Baste. With gathered side up, stitch *as directed in each instance*, ½″ from edge. Make a second row of stitching just above the first.

Blacksmith's Apron—MATERIALS (one size fits all): 1 yd. 36″ wide imitation suede cloth; ⅓ yd. 36″-wide lining fabric in matching color; 1 set of overall hooks; 2 giant grommets, ¾″ in diameter; brown wrapping paper.

DIRECTIONS: Please read GENERAL DIRECTIONS.

1. To enlarge bib and pocket patterns *(page 66)*, see directions in METHODS chapter.
2. Trace the bib pocket onto another piece of paper.
3. Cut out both enlarged patterns, *adding ½″ seam allowance to each on all edges.*
4. From suede cloth, cut the pieces shown in the cutting diagram, placing the bib and pocket patterns on areas A and B.
5. Before removing pattern from bib, mark the position of the buttons, *and* the corners of the pockets, with tailor's tacks.
6. From *lining fabric,* cut the pieces shown in lining cutting diagram, using the enlarged bib pattern to cut the facing on area G.

To make skirt

7. Turn under one long edge of hem facing ¼″; stitch.
8. With right sides together, and raw edges even, stitch facing to hem on bottom and side edges. Trim corners and seams.
9. Turn facing to wrong side. Fold under raw skirt side edges ½″; steam-press lightly (with iron at lowest steam setting). Baste the hemmed edge to skirt.
10. Turn skirt to right side; topstitch *evenly,* close to basting line. Remove basting.
11. Topstitch full length of skirt, ⅛″ from folded side edges; make a second row of stitching ⅜″ from the first.
12. Gather skirt top edge to a length of 18″ (*see* TIPS ON GATHERING above).

To make bib

13. With right sides together, stitch bib facing to bib on top and side edges. Trim corners and seams. Turn bib right side out.
14. Steam-press lightly.
15. Topstitch once, close to all edges.
16. Fold under ½″ on all edges of bib pocket (clipping curves); steam-press lightly. Topstitch a double row all around pocket (as for skirt side edges).
17. Pin pocket on bib, aligning corners with tailor's tacks. Topstitch directly on the outer, previously-stitched row, along top, bottom and side edges only (not curved edge).

To join bib and skirt

18. With right sides together, and raw edges even, center the gathered skirt on one long edge of the waistband; pin and stitch.

Denim
See
p. 130

19. Center bottom edge of the bib on the other edge of waistband; pin and stitch.

20. Steam-press seams toward waistband center, turning the remaining raw waistband edges under ½″; baste.

21. Turn under all edges of waistband facing ½″; baste. Pin and topstitch waistband to facing close to edges.

To make and attach ties

22. Fold each tie into thirds, lengthwise. Topstitch close to raw edge.

23. Set a large grommet in each end of waistband, ½″ from each end, following package directions.

24. Make a knot close to one end of each tie. Insert the other end into the grommet from the front to the rear and knot again behind grommet.

To add suspenders

25. Fold suspenders in half lengthwise, with right sides together. Stitch ½″ seam on long edge and on *one* short edge. (*Or,* to match the apron in our photograph on page 64, trim the one short edge into a point with its center exactly halfway between the seamline and the folded edge; stitch point in ½″ seam.) Trim seams. Turn right side out; steam-press lightly.

26. Slip the stitched end 1½″ through overall hook. Fold up and slipstitch.

27. Cut other end of each suspender on a slant; pin to waistband facing 2″ from each end—the slanted edges even with the lower edge of the facing. (Do *not* stitch at this point.)

28. Sew suspender buttons to bib in position marked.

29. Try on apron, crisscrossing suspenders in back. If necessary, unpin suspenders from waistband and move up or down to correct length; baste.

30. Turn apron to right side and topstitch the waistband on the previous stitching lines, across the width of each suspender. Remove basting.

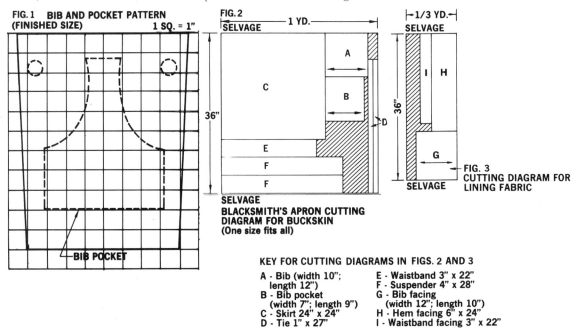

FIG. 1 BIB AND POCKET PATTERN (FINISHED SIZE)   1 SQ. = 1″

BIB POCKET

FIG. 2
SELVAGE   1 YD.
A
C
B
36″
D
E
F
F
SELVAGE
BLACKSMITH'S APRON CUTTING DIAGRAM FOR BUCKSKIN (One size fits all)

1/3 YD.
SELVAGE
I H
36″
G
FIG. 3
CUTTING DIAGRAM FOR LINING FABRIC
SELVAGE

KEY FOR CUTTING DIAGRAMS IN FIGS. 2 AND 3

A - Bib (width 10″; length 12″)
B - Bib pocket (width 7″; length 9″)
C - Skirt 24″ x 24″
D - Tie 1″ x 27″

E - Waistband 3″ x 22″
F - Suspender 4″ x 28″
G - Bib facing (width 12″; length 10″)
H - Hem facing 6″ x 24″
I - Waistband facing 3″ x 22″

Hoover Wrap Apron—MATERIALS for sizes 10 to 18: Please read GENERAL DIRECTIONS. About 2½ yds. 45″ wide polyester and cotton denim; 3¾ yds. 2½″ trim.

DIRECTIONS—*Cutting*

1. Cut waistband 4″ wide and 1½ times your waist measurement, plus 1″.

2. Cut three skirt sections, each half the width of your fabric and as long as you

want the skirt to be, plus ½".

3. Stitch apron side seams; press open.

4. Make ½" double-turned hem on raw edge of left-front apron section.

5. Turning raw edge under ½" so that it is caught in the stitching, topstitch trim on edge of right-front section, then all around bottom edge.

6. With right sides together, fold waistband in half lengthwise; seam each end.

7. Following TIPS ON GATHERING, pin and gather apron top edge to fit waistband; stitch.

8. Press under the seam allowance on the other long edge of the band; slipstitch to skirt along seamline.

9. Topstitch trim to waistband across right front, back, and only one inch beyond the left front seam (to avoid bulk at the waist).

10. Try on skirt, bringing right side over left to mark the position of snaps (or hooks and eyes). Sew on snaps or hooks.

Frontier Gingham Skirt—MATERIALS for all sizes: Please read GENERAL DIRECTIONS. About 2¾ yds. 45" wide polyester and cotton large-check gingham and about 1⅓ yds. small-check gingham; 2½ yds. ruffled eyelet with ribboned beading; skirt zipper.

DIRECTIONS—*Cutting*

1. From *large-check* gingham, *using full width of fabric,* cut skirt front and back as long as you want the finished skirt to be, plus 4" (or your choice) for hem.

2. For waistband, cut one strip 5" wide and as long as your waist measurement, plus 1".

3. From *small-check* gingham, cut apron 6" shorter and 15" narrower than skirt front.

4. The sash is made in three pieces: Cut *two* pieces 6"x42" (cutting one end of each piece on a slant) and *one* piece 6" wide. and long enough to fit across *only* the front of your waist, plus 1".

To Make Skirt

5. With top edges even, center apron on skirt front; pin and baste to skirt around all edges.

6. Pin eyelet trim to side and bottom edges of apron so that beading covers the raw, basted edges.

7. Topstitch beading strip close to both edges, through all thicknesses.

8. Topstitch the top edges of apron and skirt together. Remove basting.

9. Stitch skirt side seams ⅝" wide.

10. Insert zipper in left side seam, following directions on zipper package. Press seams open.

11. Fold the waistband in half lengthwise, with right sides together. Seam each end. Trim seams. Turn right side out.

   The sash is a separate piece (*sewn into the waistband seam only at the center front*) which covers the waistband when tied.

12. Stitch a ¼" double-turned hem on the long edges and the slanted ends of the longer sash pieces.

13. With right sides together, stitch the short straight ends to the middle sash piece. Press seams toward center.

14. Folding the middle sash piece in half lengthwise, topstitch the sash seams close to the seamlines.

15. Following TIPS ON GATHERING, with right sides together, pin and gather skirt to fit one long edge of waistband.

16. Now remove pin at center front and insert the raw edges of the sash.

17. Re-pin through all thicknesses and baste. Stitch.

18. Turn under seam allowance on other long waistband edge and slipstitch to skirt along seamline. Complete waistband with closure of your choice. Hem skirt.

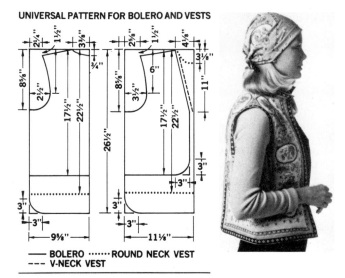

UNIVERSAL PATTERN FOR BOLERO AND VESTS

—— BOLERO ········ ROUND NECK VEST
--- V-NECK VEST

TRIANGULAR FRINGED SHAWL—The crocheted shawl you can make quickly. It takes only two skeins of acrylic yarn.

Directions are given for shawl to measure approximately 58″x31″.

MATERIALS: Coats & Clark's "Red Heart" Wintuk 4 ply (4 oz. skeins): 2½ skeins of No. 921 Vermillion; crochet hook, Size K, OR ANY SIZE HOOK WHICH WILL OBTAIN THE STITCH GAUGE BELOW.

GAUGE: 5 sc=2″.

DIRECTIONS:

Ch 141. *Row 1:* Sc in 2nd ch from hook, sc in each ch across—140 sc. Ch 2; turn. *Row 2:* Work in both loops of each sc, hdc in each sc across. Ch 3; turn. *Row 3:* Sk first st, sc in next st, * ch 3, sk next st, sc in next st; rpt from * across. Ch 1; turn—70 sps. *Row 4:* Sc in center of first ch-3 sp, * ch 3, sc in center of next ch-3 sp; rpt from * across. Ch 1; turn. There is 1 sp less than on previous row. *Rows 5 through 39:* Rpt Row 4. Ch 1; turn. *Row 40:* Sc in center of first ch-3 sp, * ch 3, sc in center of next ch-3 sp; rpt from * across to within last ch-3 sp; do not work in last ch-3 sp. Ch 1; turn. Rpt Row 40 until only one ch-3 sp rem. Fasten off.

Fringe: Wind yarn about 60 times around a 6½″ piece of cardboard; cut at one end to make 13″ strands. Continue to cut strands as needed. Hold 3 strands tog and fold in half to form a loop. Insert hook in a sp along a side edge and draw loop of strands through; draw ends of strands through loop on hook and pull tightly to form a knot. Tie 3 strands in each sp along the side and lower edges of the shawl. Trim the fringes evenly.

QUILTED FLOWERED SCARF VEST—To make the charming flowered vest, you need only two 24″ scarves with a very wide border. Machine-quilting around the edge gives a crisp finish.

MATERIALS (*for Small/Medium*): Two 24″ square scarves with wide borders or ¾ yd. 44″-wide fabric; 23″x44″ piece of polyester batting; ¾ yd. 44″-wide lining; 1 package regular bias tape; 3 yds. hem facing.

DIRECTIONS: Use pattern for round neck vest, using the 22½″ length and the dotted neckline.

Cutting (½″ *seam allowance*): Cut a pair of fronts (one left, one right) and one back from fabric, lining and batting. If you cut from scarves, use borders for hems and center fronts, keeping top border intact for standup collar and trim. You may piece at center back for better placement.

Sewing:

1. Place batting over wrong side of lining, then fabric right side up over batting. Baste across longest length and width. Quilt by machine, outlining motifs.

2. Seam sides and shoulders. Trim batting to stitching. Turn under each seam edge and slipstitch to lining. Face armholes with bias tape.

3. *Standup collar:* Cut two 9½″ strips from opposing corners of each top border. Depending on width of scarf border, cut the two collar strips 1″ to 1½″ wide, plus seams. Sew a center back seam at raw ends. Cut hem facing same size as collar. With right sides together, stitch facing to collar at ends and top edge. Trim, turn and press. Stitch outside layer to neckline, matching centers. Cut batting same finished size and slip into collar. Tuck neckline seam allowance under facing and slipstitch facing to neckseam.

4. With right sides together, stitch hem facing to bottom edges. Trim batting to stitching, turn facing to inside and slipstitch to lining. Face front edges in the same way. Quilt borders and collar for a crisp finish.

5. From each remaining top border, cut a narrow border about 15″ long plus seam allowance (we used the bold black portion of our border strip). Turn under seam allowance all around; pin over armholes from front to back. Edgestitch.

HER GOLF CLUB MITTS—Make these with washable rug yarn.
MATERIALS: Columbia-Minerva washable rug yarn (1¾ oz. pull skeins): 3 skeins Color A; 2 skeins Color B; Boye knitting needles No. 8 and No. 10½, OR ANY SIZE NEEDLES WHICH WILL OBTAIN THE STITCH GAUGE BELOW.
GAUGE: 7 sts = 2″; 5 rows = 1″.
DIRECTIONS: Start at wrist with A and No. 8 needles, cast on 27 sts. *Row 1:* K 1, * p 1, k 1. Rpt from * across. *Row 2 (right side):* P 1, * k 1, p 1. Rpt from * across. Rpt Rows 1 and 2 alternately 3 times; then rpt Row 1 once more. Change to No. 10½ needles and work in pat as follows: *Row 1 (right side):* K 3, * p 1, k 3. Rpt from * across. *Row 2:* K 1, p 1, * k 3, p 1. Rpt from * across ending with k 1. Rpt last 2 rows alternately for pat. **For No. 5 Mitt:** (Work 4 rows A, 2 rows B) 5 times. **For No. 3 Mitt:** Work 10 rows A, (2 rows B, 4 rows A) twice; 2 rows B, 6 rows A. **For No. 1 Mitt:** Work 16 rows A, 2 rows B, 12 rows A. **For All Mitts:** *Row 1:* With A, k across. *Row 2:* P 1, p 2 tog, * k 1, p 1, p 2 tog. Rpt from * across—20 sts. *Row 3:* K 2, * p 1, k 2. Rpt from * across. *Row 4:* P 2 tog, * k 1, p 2 tog. Rpt from * across—13 sts. *Row 5:* K 1, * p 1, k 1. Rpt from * across. *Row 6:* (P 2 tog) 6 times; p 1. Break off leaving an 18″ end. Thread a needle with this end; sl rem 7 sts onto it, draw tog and fasten: with same yarn, sew side seam.
Pompon *(make 3):* Wind B 100 times around a 4″ square cardboard. Sl strands off cardboard and tie securely at center. Cut loops at each end and trim. Fasten pompon to mitt tips.

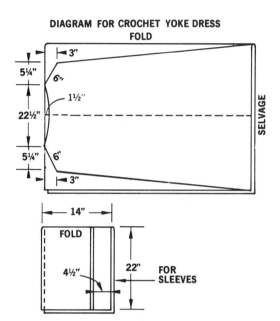

DIAGRAM FOR CROCHET YOKE DRESS

CROCHETED YOKE DRESS—The distinctive crocheted yoke and trim of this airy little dress can be attached to almost any fabric you like, plain or print. (We used a muslin-like cloth.)

MATERIALS: 2½ yds. of 45″ fabric; ½ yd. of elastic; 1 package of bias tape.

DIRECTIONS:

Dress: Cut 14″ from full width of fabric for sleeves.

1. Fold fabric in half crosswise, right sides together (*see Cutting Diagram*). Mark center with pins. Draw outline of dress dimensions on fabric as shown in diagram. Cut out.

2. Sew side seams together with ½″ seam allowance. Sew gathering rows ¼″ from top edge, using longest machine stitch. Pin Yoke (*directions follow*) to dress, covering the gathering stitching with the bottom edge of yoke. Gather dress in to fit yoke, matching centers. Baste in place. Topstitch with machine stitching along bottom edge of yoke.

Sleeves:

3. Fold the 14″ piece of fabric in half (*see diagram*). Slash along fold. Sew 14″ sleeve seam using ½″ seam allowance. Sew two rows of gathering stitches around top edge of sleeves ⅜″ and ¼″ from edge. Sew ½″ wide casing for elastic 4½″ from bottom edge. Press under ¼″ at sleeve hem.

4. Topstitch crocheted edging to sleeve edge. Pin sleeves to yoke, easing in fullness with gathering stitches, in same manner as for dress, and topstitch in place.

5. Cut elastic for each sleeve 2″ longer than wrist measurement. Pull through casing and stitch ends together securely. Hem to desired length and stitch crocheted edging to hem edge and sleeve.

Crocheted Yoke and Trim—Directions are given for Yoke to fit a Small Size garment. Changes for Yoke to fit Medium and Large Sizes are in parentheses.

MATERIALS: Size 10/2 Linen (8 oz. Tube): 1 tube for each size of Orange (or same amount of regular crochet cotton in any color); steel crochet hook, Boye No. 00

71

(double zero), OR ANY SIZE HOOK WHICH WILL OBTAIN THE STITCH GAUGE BELOW. *Note: To obtain linen yarn only write to: Frederick J. Fawcett Inc. Dept. FC, 129 South Street, Boston, Mass. 02111.*
GAUGE: 5 ch sts = 1″; first 3 rnds = 1″.

MEASUREMENTS:	SMALL	MEDIUM	LARGE
NECK EDGE (without drawstring):	26″	27½″	29″
WIDTH OF SLEEVE AT UPPER ARM:	15″	16½″	16½″
DEPTH AT CENTER BACK AND CENTER FRONT:	4″	4″	4″

Yoke: Starting at neck edge, ch 131(139, 147) to measure 26(27½,29)″. Being careful not to twist chain, join with sl st to first ch to form a circle. *Rnd 1:* Sc in same ch as joining, *ch 3, sc in same ch as last sc—***picot made;** * ch 3, sk next 3 ch, in next ch make sc, ch 3 for picot and sc; rpt from * around chain to within last 2 ch sts; do not join rnd—33(35,37) picots. *Rnd 2:* * Ch 3, sk next picot, in center ch of next ch-3 lp make sc, ch 3 and sc; rpt from * around, ending with ch 3, in center ch of first ch-3 lp of this rnd make sc, ch 3 and sc. *Rnds 3 and 4:* Rpt Rnd 2. *Rnd 5:* In each ch-3 lp (between picots) around make 7 dc. Join with sl st in top of first dc—32(34,36) shells. *Rnd 6:* Ch 1, in same dc as joining make sc, ch 3 and sc; ch 5, sk next 6 dc on same shell, in first dc of each 7-dc shell around make sc, ch 3, sc and ch 5. Join last ch-5 with sl st to first sc of this rnd. *Rnd 7:* Sl st in next ch, in same picot make sc, ch 3 and sc, * ch 5, sk next ch-5 lp, in next picot make sc, ch 3 and sc; rpt from * around, ending with ch 5. Join to first sc. *Rnds 8 and 9:* Rpt Rnd 7. *Rnd 10:* Sl st in next sc at base of same picot, sl st in next ch-5 lp, ch 4, 8 tr in same ch lp, make 9 tr in each ch-5 lp around. Join with sl st to top of ch-4—32(34,36) large shells. *Rnd 11:* Ch 1, in same ch as joining make sc, ch 3 and sc, * ch 3, sk next 3 tr, in next tr make sc, ch 3 and sc, ch 3, sk next 4 tr, in first tr of next 9-tr shell make sc, ch 3 and sc; rpt from * around, ending last rpt with ch 3. Join to first sc—64(68,72) picots.
Right Sleeve: *Row 1:* Sl st in first picot, sc same picot; (ch 3, in center ch of next ch-3 between picots make sc, ch 3 and sc) 20(22,22) times; ch 3, sc in next picot; do not work over rem sts. Ch 3, turn. *Row 2:* (In center ch of next ch-3 lp make sc, ch 3 and sc; ch 3) 20(22,22) times; sc in center ch of last ch-3. Ch 3, turn. Rpt last row 8(9,10) more times. Break off and fasten.
Left Sleeve: Sk next free 11(11,13) picots on last rnd of yoke for front edge; attach yarn to next picot (between shells below) and work same as for Right Sleeve.
Drawstring: Make a chain approximately 60(62,64)″ long. Break off and fasten.
Trim: Make a chain slightly longer than desired length, but having a number of sts divisible by 4, plus 2. In 2nd ch from hook make sc, ch 3 for picot and sc, * ch 3, sk next 3 ch, in next ch make sc, ch 3 and sc; rpt from * across chain. Break off and fasten. Use as trim for lower edge of garment and for lower edge of each sleeve.
Blocking: Pin yoke and sleeve sections to measurements on a padded surface; cover with a damp cloth and press with a warm iron. Remove when dry. To bring out the natural sheen of linen, press hard on the right side with iron alone. Starting at center front, draw chain through lps of rnd 1 at neck edge. Tie ends into a bow, pulling neck edge to desired fit.

GARTER STITCH SWEATER WITH CONTRASTING TRIM—For about $5 you can knit this nice little garter-stitch top of crochet cotton and edge it to match your favorite summer skirt.
Garter Stitch Sweater with Contrasting Trim—Directions are given for size Small (8–10). Changes for sizes Medium (12–14) and Large (16–18) are in parentheses.

MATERIALS: Size 10/2 Linen (8 oz. Tube): 1(2,2) tube White (A) and approximately 90(105,120) yards Orange (B) (or same amounts of regular crochet cotton); knitting needles, No. 8, OR ANY SIZE NEEDLES WHICH WILL OBTAIN THE STITCH GAUGE BELOW; steel crochet hook, Boye No. 00 (double zero).
Note: To obtain linen yarn only, write to: Frederick J. Fawcett Inc., Dept. FC, 129 South Street, Boston, Mass. 02111.
GAUGE: Before blocking—4 sts=1″; 8 rows=1″. After blocking—9 sts=2″; 6 rows =1″.
Note: Use 2 strands of same color held together throughout. Wind single tube into 2 equal parts.

MEASUREMENTS:

SIZES:	SMALL (8–10)	MEDIUM (12–14)	LARGE (16–18)
BUST:	33″	36″	40″
WIDTH ACROSS BACK OR FRONT AT UNDERARMS:	16½″	18″	20″
WIDTH ACROSS SLEEVE AT UPPER ARM:	12″	12¾″	13½″

Back: Starting at lower edge with 2 strands of A held together, cast on 68(80,89) sts. Work in garter st (k each row) until total length is 8(8½,9)″ without stretching; length will be stretched to 10(11,12)″ when blocking.
Armhole Shaping: Continuing in garter st, bind off 4(6,8) sts at beg of next 2 rows—60(68,73) sts. Place rem sts on a st holder.
Front: Work same as for Back. Place rem sts on a separate st holder.
Sleeves: Starting at sleeve edge with 2 strands of B held together, cast on 53(57,61) sts. *Rows 1 through 4:* K 4 rows. Cut B; attach double strand of A. *Row 5:* With A, k 2, with yarn in back sl 1 as if to p, * k 3, sl 1 as before; rpt from * across to within last 2 sts, k 2. *Row 6:* K 2, * with yarn in front sl 1 as if to p, k 3; rpt from * across, ending with sl 1, k 2. *Rows 7 and 8:* Rpt Rows 5 and 6. *Rows 9 through 14:* K 6 rows.
Underarm Shaping: Continuing in garter st, bind off 4(6,8) sts at beg of each of next 2 rows. Place rem 45 sts on a st holder.
Yoke: Slip sts from holders onto a needle in the following order: Back, one Sleeve, Front and other Sleeve—210(226,236) sts. *Row 1 (right side):* K across. *Row 2 (Dec Row):* K 0(6,6), * k 2 tog—dec made; K 8; rpt from * across—189(204,213) sts. *Rows 3 through 13:* K 11 rows. *Row 14 (Dec Row):* * K 2 tog, k 7; rpt from * across, ending last rpt with k 2 tog, k 7(4,4)—168(181,189) sts. *Rows 15 through 21:* K 7 rows. *Row 22:* K, decreasing 0(5,5) sts evenly spaced across—168(176,184) sts. K 0 (2,4) more rows. Cut A; attach double strand of B.
Neck Border: Row 1 (right side): With B k 1, * insert needle in st directly below next st in 4th row below and draw up a loop, pull up this loop to top edge of last row, k next st on lefthand needle, pass long loop over last st made, k 3; rpt from * across, ending last rpt with k 2. *Rows 2 and 3:* K 2 rows. *Row 4:* * K 2 tog, k 6; rpt from * across. Bind off tightly.
Crochet Loop Edging for Drawstring: With wrong side facing, using double strand of B and crochet hook, attach yarn to first st at neck edge, sc in same place, * ch 1, sk next st, sc in next st; rpt from * across neck edge, working last sc in last st. Cut yarn and fasten.
Finishing: Stretch and pin sweater (before sewing seam) to measurements on a padded surface, (stretching out garter st to measure 6 rows to 1″). Cover with a damp cloth and steam-press lightly. Remove when completely dry. Sew right back yoke seam, sew side and underarm seams.
Drawstring: With double strand of A, make a chain 52″ long. Cut yarn and fasten.

Starting at center front, draw chain through ch-1 sps along neck edging. Tie a knot at each end of chain. Tie ends into a bow at center front.

BASKETWEAVE KNITTED CARDIGAN–That beautiful basketweave knitted cardigan is made with linen yarn purchased by the tube at rock bottom price directly from the company. It looks great with a summer skirt, as here, or tossed over a bare dress.

Basketweave Knitted Cardigan–Directions are given for size Small (8–10). Changes for sizes Medium (12–14) and Large (16–18) are in parentheses.

MATERIALS: Linen Yarn, size 5/2 (8 oz. tubes): 3(4,4) tubes of White (or same amount of regular crochet cotton); knitting needles, No. 8, or ANY SIZE NEEDLES WHICH WILL OBTAIN THE STITCH GAUGE BELOW; steel crochet hook, Boye No. 00 (double zero).

Note: To obtain linen yarn only, write to: Frederick J. Fawcett Inc., Dept. FC, 129 South Street, Boston, Mass. 02111.

GAUGE: 9 sts = 2''; 6 rows = 1''.

MEASUREMENTS:

SIZES:	SMALL (8–10)	MEDIUM (12–14)	LARGE (16–18)
BUST:	33''	37''	41''
WIDTH ACROSS BACK AT UNDERARMS:	16''	18''	20''
WIDTH ACROSS EACH FRONT AT UNDERARMS:	8½''	9½''	10½''
WIDTH ACROSS SLEEVE AT UPPER ARM:	12''	14''	14''

Note: Body of cardigan is worked in one piece without side seams.

Body: Starting at entire lower edge, cast on 147(165,183) sts. *Row 1 (right side):* P 3, * k 3, p 3; rpt from * across. *Row 2:* K 3, * p 3, k 3; rpt from * across. Rpt. Rows 1–2 alternately until 20 rows in all have been completed. Now work in pattern as follows: *Row 1 (right side):* K 3, * p 6, k 3; rpt from * across. *Row 2:* P 3, * k 6, p 3; rpt from * across. *Rows 3 through 8:* Rpt last 2 rows (Rows 1–2) alternately 3 times. *Row 9:* P 3, * k 6, p 3; rpt from * across. *Row 10:* K 3, * p 6, k 3; rpt from *across. *Rows 11 and 12:* Rpt Rows 9 and 10. *Rows 13 through 56:* Rpt last 12 rows (Rows 1 through 12) for pattern 3 more times; then rpt Rows 1 through 8 once more.

To Divide For Back And Fronts: Row 57: Work in pattern across first 38(43,48) sts for Right Front. Place next 71(79,87) sts on a st holder for Back; place rem 38(43,48) sts on another st holder for Left Front. Turn. Work over sts on needle only.

Right Front–*Armhole and Neck Shaping: Row 58:* Bind off 4(6,7) sts at beg of row, keeping continuity of pattern, work across to end of row. *Row 59:* Keeping in pattern throughout, work across—34(37,41) sts. *Row 60:* Dec one st at beg of row (armhole edge); work in pattern across. *Row 61:* Work in pattern over first 3 sts, *with yarn in back sl 1 as if to p, work next st in pattern, psso*—dec made at neck edge after first 3 sts; complete row in pattern.

Note: Keep continuity of pattern throughout all shaping. Rpt last 2 rows (Rows 60 and 61) 2(2,3) more times—28(31,33) sts. Now, keeping armhole edge straight, continue to dec one st at neck edge after first 3 sts as before on every right-side row until 17(19,21) sts rem. If necessary, work even in pattern until length from first row of Right Front is 6½(7,7½)'', ending at armhole edge.

Shoulder Shaping: Next Row: Keeping in pattern, from armhole edge bind off 6(6,7) sts at beg of row. *Next Row:* Work even. Rpt last 2 rows. Bind off rem 5(7,7) sts.

     For knit and crochet abbreviations box, see Methods (Chapter 11)

Back—*Armhole Shaping:* Sl back sts from st holder onto a needle, with right side facing, attach yarn to right armhole edge. Keeping in pattern as established throughout back, work 1 row even. Bind off 4(6,6) sts at beg of each of next 2 rows. Dec one st at each end every other row 3(3,4) times in all—57(61,67) sts. Work even in pattern over these sts until length of armhole is same as on Right Front, ending with a right-side row.

Shoulder Shaping: Bind off 6(6,7) sts at beg of next 4 rows; bind off 5(7,7) sts at beg of following 2 rows. Bind off rem 23(23,25) sts for back of neck.

Left Front: Sl left front sts from holder onto a needle, attach yarn at armhole edge. Work to correspond with Right Front, reversing all shaping. To dec at neck edge: K 2 tog (or p 2 tog) according to pattern on every right-side row, before last 3 sts.

Sleeves: Starting at lower edge, cast on 37(43,43) sts. *Row 1 (right side):* P 2, (k 3, p 3) 5(6,6) times; k 3, p 2. *Row 2:* K 2, (p 3, k 3) 5(6,6) times; p 3, k 2. Rpt Rows 1–2 alternately until 21 rows in all have been completed, ending with Row 1. *Next Row (Inc Row):* Inc in first st (to inc k in front and back of same st), k 4, * p 3, inc as before in each of next 3 sts; rpt from * across to last 2 sts, p 1, p one st in row below, then p last st—54(63,63) sts. Now work in pattern as follows: *Row 1 (right side):* * K 3, p 6; rpt from * across. *Row 2:* * K 6, p 3; rtpt from * across. *Rows 3 through 6:* Rpt last 2 rows twice. *Row 7:* * P 3, k 6; rpt from * across. *Row 8:* * P 6, k 3; rpt from * across. *Rows 9 and 10:* Rpt Rows 7 and 8. *Rows 11 through 18:* Rpt Rows 1 and 2 alternately 4 times. Rpt last 12 rows (Rows 7 through 18) for sleeve pattern 5 more times (total length should be approximately 17″ from beg), ending with 18th row of sleeve pattern.

Sleeve Cap Shaping: Keeping continuity of pattern throughout, bind off 4(6,6) sts at beg of next 2 rows. Dec one st at each end every other row 3 times—40(45,45) sts. Keeping in pattern as established, work even for 10(12,14) rows. Dec one st at beg of each row until 30(32,32) sts rem. Working k 2 tog (or p 2 tog) according to pattern, bind off.

Belt: Cast on 6 sts. Work in garter st (k each row) for 54″ (or desired length). Bind off and fasten.

Note: Linen sweaters are machine or hand washable in hot or cold water. If desired, wash sections before finishing and place on a hanger to dry quickly.

Finishing: To block, pin each section to measurements on a padded surface; cover with a damp cloth and steam-press with a warm iron. Allow to dry completely. Fold fronts over back. Using a darning needle and same yarn, sew shoulder seams. Sew sleeve seams; fit sleeves into armholes and sew in place. With crochet hook, work 1 row of sl sts across back of neck.

Belt Loops: From right side, pick up and k 3 sts along last row of ribbing at side fold. Starting with a p row, work 8 rows in st st (p 1 row, k 1 row). Bind off. Sew bound-off edge to 8th row of pattern, directly above base of loop. Make belt loop at opposite side in same way. Slip belt through loops.

Button Loops: With pins, mark the position of 10 button loops evenly spaced along the right front edge, placing first pin at beg of neck shaping and last pin ½″ above lower edge. With wrong side facing and crochet hook, attach yarn in same st as first pin at neck, sl st in same st, * ch 5 for loop, sk 2 rows along front edge, sl st in each row to next pin; rpt from * across front edge, ending with ch 5, sk 2 rows, sl st in each rem row. Break off and fasten.

Button:(*Make 10*): With crochet hook, ch 4. Join with sl st to form ring. *Rnd 1:* 6 sc in ring. Do not join; mark beg of each rnd. *Rnd 2:* 2 sc in each sc around—12 sc. *Rnd 3:* Sc in each sc around. Stuff button with small piece of same yarn. *Rnd 4:* (Sk next sc, sl st in next sc) 6 times. Leaving a 14″ length for sewing, cut yarn and fasten. Using end of yarn, gather sts of last rnd tog; sew button on left front edge, opposite a button loop.

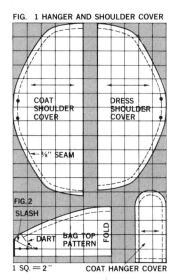

FIG. 1 HANGER AND SHOULDER COVER

COAT SHOULDER COVER

DRESS SHOULDER COVER

⅝" SEAM

FIG. 2
SLASH

DART   BAG TOP PATTERN   FOLD

1 SQ. = 2"   COAT HANGER COVER

CLOSET AND TRAVEL ACCESSORIES — Something that everyone wants but not everyone has—a great gift idea! The garment bags, shoulder covers and hangers shown here are made of denim-weight fabric, trimmed with felt and ribbon, hers at left, his at right.

GENERAL MATERIALS: Wrapping paper; dressmaker's carbon and tracing wheel; thread to match fabrics and ribbons. See YARDAGE CHART below.

YARDAGE CHART			
MAN'S	Bag	Shoulder cover	Hanger
44"-wide brown denim-weight fabric	2½ yds.	⅝ yd.	⅛ yd.
1½" grosgrain ribbon red and green, each	38½"	10"	4½"
batting			1¾ yds.
zipper	27"		
brown seam binding		1 pkg.	
brown ribbon			¾ yd.
WOMAN'S			
4"-wide orange denim-weight fabric	2¾ yds.	½ yd.	⅛ yd.
pink & green felt each	½ yd.	scraps	scraps
yellow felt	scraps	scraps	scraps
yellow seam binding		1 pkg.	
batting			1¾ yds.
zipper	30"		
yellow ribbon			¾ yd.

DIRECTIONS—*Enlarging patterns:* Following the directions in the METHODS chapter, enlarge the patterns needed for each item (FIGS. 1–3).

Cutting and Marking: Using enlarged patterns, cut two pieces for *shoulder cover* and four pieces for *hanger*. For each *garment bag*, cut two pieces of denim, ticking or other sturdy fabric, 28" wide, 38" long for women's and 39" long for men's. Fold each piece in half lengthwise, right sides together. Pin the enlarged bag—top pattern (Fig. 2) to the top of each folded piece in turn, with pattern top edge even with fabric top edge at the fold. Cut fabric, through both thicknesses, along the *top curved line* of the pattern. With dressmaker's carbon and tracing wheel, mark *the dart*. Measure off and mark a line across the bottom of the fabric pieces 2½" from the bottom edge. On man's bag, on one piece only, baste, or place pins along fold to mark center front line. In the same way, mark center front of one

76

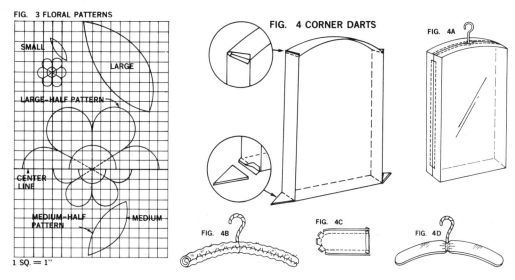

FIG. 3 FLORAL PATTERNS

SMALL

LARGE

LARGE—HALF PATTERN

CENTER LINE

MEDIUM—HALF PATTERN   MEDIUM

1 SQ. = 1"

FIG. 4 CORNER DARTS

FIG. 4A

FIG. 4B

FIG. 4C

FIG. 4D

piece of shoulder cover. Cut flower and leaves from felt using proper size pattern (Fig. 3) for each item.

Appliquéing Women's Accessories: On one piece of garment bag and dress shoulder guard, and two pieces of hanger cover, arrange flower petals, leaves and stems (on bag only) as shown in photo. Pin in place, then zigzag around each edge.

Trimming Men's Accessories: Edgestitch red and green grosgrain to front piece of garment bag and shoulder guard, with ribbon edge 7/8″ from marked center line. On two pieces of hanger cover, stitch the ribbons 1¼″ from the straight edge.

Sewing: *Note:* Seam allowance is 5/8″ throughout unless otherwise indicated. Stitch darts and seams with fabric right sides together.

Garment Bags:
1. Stitch darts in top corners of both pieces; reinforce with a second row of stitching over first. Trim darts; press open, as shown (Fig. 4).
2. At bottom corners of both pieces, fold fabric on marked line, right sides together. Stitch across; trim and press open, as shown (Fig. 4).
3. Pin the front and back pieces together along one long edge. Stitch a seam for a length of 2″ up from bottom and down from top, leaving rest of seam open for zipper. Following directions on package, insert zipper in opening; unzip zipper.
4. Pin front and back together along the remaining edges, matching the darts. Stitch, leaving a 3″ opening in top seam for hanger.
5. Turn bag right side out. Topstitch close to seam and opening edges between top darts, as shown (Fig. 4A). Press bag along crease lines, top and bottom. Cut a piece of heavy cardboard 4″x23″ and place in bottom of bag.

Shoulder Guards:
1. Stitch pieces together along curved edges, leaving a 3″ opening in center top for hanger. Clip seams; turn right side out.
2. Topstitch same as for garment bag. Bind straight edge with seam binding.

Hanger Cover:
1. Cut two pieces of batting, each 10½″ wide and 63″ long. Wind each piece around hanger on each side of hook, as shown (Fig. 4B). Catch-stitch long edges as shown. Sew short ends together at hook.
2. Press under 3/8″ on straight ends of cover sections. Stitch two sections together around other edges, taking 3/8″ seam, (Fig. 4C). Stitch other two sections together.
3. Slip one section over each end of hanger, with turned-under straight edges meeting in center. Sew these edges together, gathering to fit hanger (Fig. 4D). Wind ribbon twice around stitching; tie a bow.

EASY-TO-BUILD PLANT STANDS—Best way to get exactly the kind of indoor plant stand you want for your cherished greenery is to build it yourself. That way you can have the type and size that best suits your needs—and your plants. Here are eight free-standing stands you can build with common sizes of lumber and little effort and money: Starting at left, a cute cart (espe-

Whether you're a real plant nut with a jungle of greenery, or you haven't yet gone overboard into this popular hobby, you're bound to be pleased with our 34 green thumb gifts. For you who have entered Phase One (a hanging plant) we have directions for beautiful beaded

*Great gifts to make for
plant lovers, plus how-to
advice for successful growing*

$10

cially nice for a cactus garden); a tall stand for two showy plants; a butcher block platform on casters for a hefty monster (you won't have to lift it to rotate it in the light); a window box with a lower deck for a sizable collection; a stepladder that's fine for staging big and little plants; two pedestal stands for your particular favorites; and a tray table (good for your cuttings).

slings and knotted strings to glamorize your greenery in the air. For the dedicated hobbyist there is a selection of sturdy plywood and lumber planters for indoors and out. For tips on growing pot herbs, miniatures, and free plants (grown from cuttings), read on.

directions for items shown above start on following page

GENERAL DIRECTIONS: *To Waterproof Planters:* As shown on pages 78–79 our box-type planters are filled with pots set on saucers. However, should you wish to set the plants on pebbles without saucers, the boxes must be lined with plastic (heavy-weight garbage bags) or coated with asphalt paint.

Plant Cart (*cactus and succulents*)—MATERIALS: Two 1x6x33″ pine (A); two 1x6x16½″ pine (B); two 1x6x11″ pine (C—rounded at one end and drilled for axle, *as shown in* FIG. 1); 1x2x17½″ pine (D); two 1x2x16½″ pine (E); four 1x2x9¼″ pine (F); 21″ of 1¼″ dowel (G); two 1x3x21½″ pine (H—drilled for axle, *as shown in* FIG. 1); ½″x16½″x31½″ EXT plywood (J); two ½″x23″—diameter plywood wheels (K—drilled for axle); white glue; 4d, 6d finishing nails; wood putty; 1½″x1½″ butt hinge with screws; hook and eye; fourteen 1¼″ #6 flathead wood screws.

Tall Stand (*spathyphylum on top; maidenhair fern on bottom*)—MATERIALS: Four 1x2x43″ pine (A); four 1x3x8¾″ pine (B—notched, *as shown in* FIG. 2); white glue; 6d finishing nails; wood putty; paint.

Rolling Platform (*yucca*)—MATERIALS: 1½″x12″x12″ butcher block; four 1½″ spherical casters attached with ¾″ wood screws (*see* FIG. 3).

Window Box (*ruffle ferns on top; Rex begonias on bottom*)—MATERIALS: Two 1x6x28″ pine (A); two 1x6x7¼″ pine (B); 1x8x26½″ pine (C); 1x8x28″ pine (D—

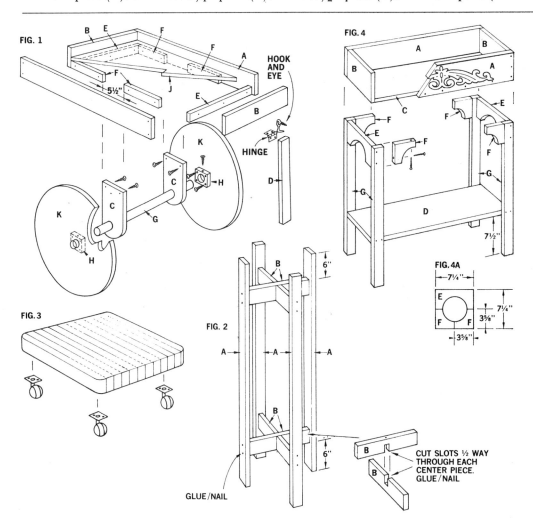

as shown in Fig. 4); two 1x8x7¼″ pine (E and F—cut *as shown in* Fig. 4A); four 1x2x26″ pine (G); appliqués; 4d, 6d finishing nails; white glue; wood putty.

Ladder (*bird's nest fern on top; all the rest are African violets*)—MATERIALS: Two 1x8x34″ pine (A—cut both ends on angle, *as shown in* Fig 5); two 1x8x14″ pine (B); two 1x6x25½″ pine (C); 1x10x16½″ pine (D); 15½″ of 1″ dowel (E); twelve 1½″ lengths of ⁵⁄₁₆″ dowel (F); 3d finishing nails; white glue.

Square Stand (*aralia*)—MATERIALS: Four 1x10x34½″ pine (A); two 1x10x8½″ pine (B—rip to 8½″ square); two 1x1x8½″ (C); two 1x1x7″ (D—*as shown in* Fig. 6); white glue; 3d, 6d finishing nails; wood putty.

Post Stand (*fuchsia*)—MATERIALS: 24″ turned post (A—available at building supply stores); 1″ pine, cut as follows: Two 6¾″ squares (B); two 3½″ squares (C); two 3″ lengths of ¾″ dowel (D—*as shown in* Fig. 7); white glue.

Tray Table (*all ferns: baby tears, maidenhair, ruffle, episcia; plus African violets*) —MATERIALS: Two 1x6x17¾″ pine (A—cut and drill, *as shown in* Fig. 8A); two 1x4x21¼″ pine (B); ¾″x16¼″x21¼″ plywood (C); four ¼″x¾″x4″ lattice strips (D); two 1x3x17¾″ pine (E); two 1x3x21¼″ pine (F); four 2x2x26″ pine (G); two 21¼″ lengths of 1″ dowel (H); two 16¼″ lengths of 1″ dowel (J—*as shown in* Fig. 8); eight ¼″ #10 flathead wood screws; 6d finishing nails; white glue; wood putty.

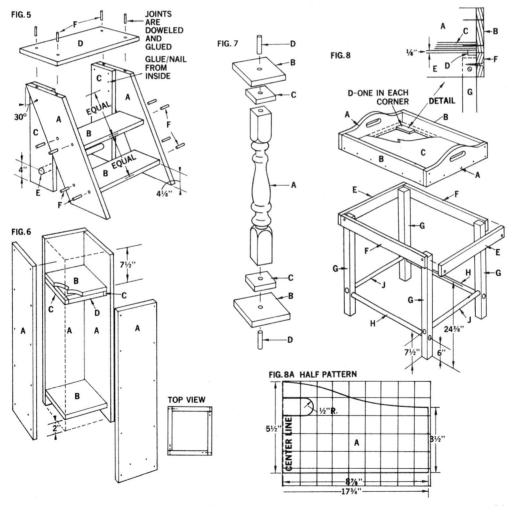

81

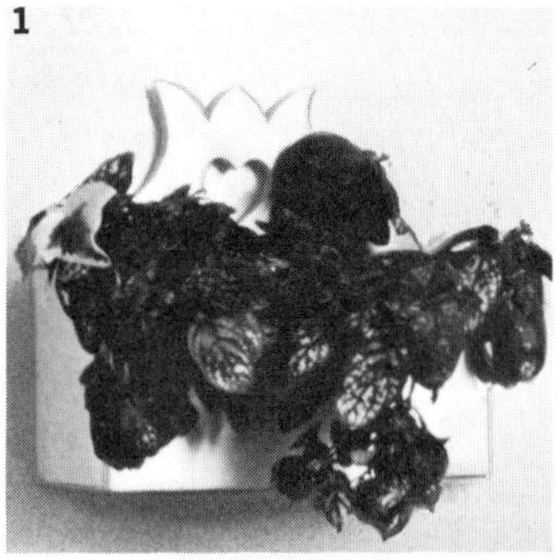

scroll saw.

FIG. 1
HALF
PATTERN –
UPPER
BACK
PIECE

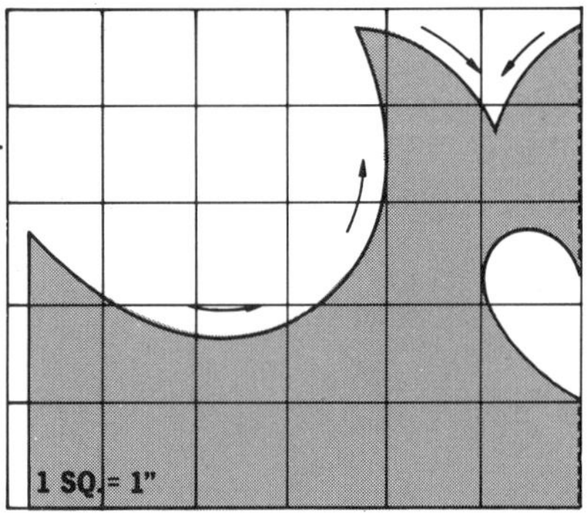

1 SQ. = 1"

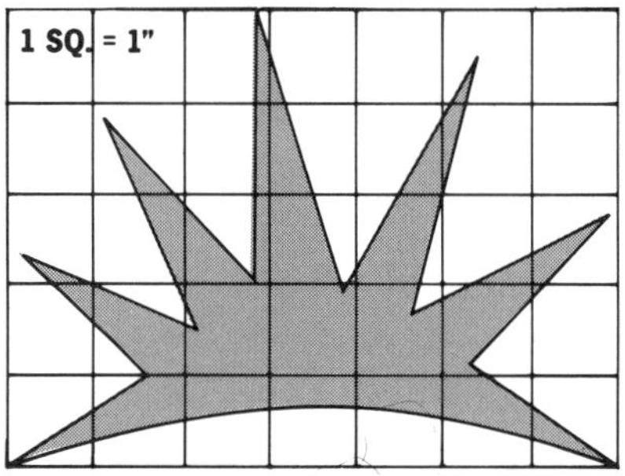

1 SQ. = 1"

FIG. 2
STENCIL
PATTERN
CACTUS
SHELF

PLANT SHELVES TO DECORATE A WALL—They're attractive, they're inexpensive, and you can make them in the time it takes to say *Cymbalaria muralis*. In a few hours, you can make a shelf for your prized Spiderwort, a plaque for little cacti, or any other of these wall-hung plant holders. (1) Pine box with a Swiss-style cutout on the back holds a plastic kitchen storage bin containing soil and a leafy plant. (2) This large 13½"x11½" cedar window box assembled with metal angle brackets was inspired by a Shaker wood box. (3) Wall plaque made from glued-together pine 1x4's has cutouts for eight small pots, a sunburst stencil decoration. (4) A stained 2x3 with notched dowels 9" apart can be made as long as you wish to hold a variety of hanging plants in any containers.

GENERAL INFORMATION AND MATERIALS:

● Shelves made of clear pine are intended for indoor use unless treated with a

82

wood preservative. Use carpenter's glue on pine pieces.

● Shelves made of cedar or redwood can be used indoors or out-of-doors. Use waterproof glue.

● MATERIALS needed for all items are: Crosscut saw; in some instances hand or electric drill with assorted bits; wood clamps; compass; nail set; wood filler, putty or wood plugs; medium, fine and extra-fine sandpaper; tack cloth; stain and/or finishing material, if necessary; paint brushes. See individual items for ADDITIONAL MATERIALS.

GENERAL DIRECTIONS:

1. Follow directions in METHODS chapter to enlarge patterns provided. Use carbon paper to trace patterns onto the wood; where half-patterns are given, turn pattern over to complete tracing. Saw on the tracing lines, cutting in the direction indicated by arrows on the patterns.

2. To mark corners for cutting, use compass opened to width indicated in DIRECTIONS. Set point at corner of wood and draw a quarter circle.

3. To insure accuracy and ease when cutting wood, clamp pieces down with scrap wood between clamp and piece to be cut.

4. Use a wet rag to wipe off excess glue before it dries.

5. *Preparing surface for finishing:* Countersink all nails with a nail set. Fill recess with a wood plug cut from a dowel of correct size and slightly rounded on top *or* with wood fill; let dry and sand.

● Before staining and applying preservative or varnish, sand the wood, first with medium sandpaper then with fine and extra fine. Wipe with tack cloth.

● Let each coat of stain, varnish or wood preservative dry thoroughly before proceeding to next step.

1. Pine Box—ADDITIONAL MATERIALS (*see* GENERAL MATERIALS): Clear pine 1x6, 4 ft.; saber saw; coping saw; Rubbermaid storage bin model No. 2324, to hold plants; wood preservative; 2 screws for hanging.

DIRECTIONS (*see* GENERAL DIRECTIONS): From pine, cut one lower backpiece 5⅜″ high and 11½″ wide at top tapering to 11″ at bottom; one frontpiece 3⅝″ high and 11″ wide at top tapering to 10½″ wide at bottom; two sidepieces 4″ wide x 5½″ high. Enlarge pattern for upper backpiece (*see* FIG. 1) and trace onto pine; cut out with saber saw in direction of arrows. At the center top point of heart, drill a hole large enough to insert the coping saw; cut out heart. On the lower backpiece, 1″ below top edge, drill a hole for hanger screw 1″ from each end.

Trace top edge of the side of the storage bin onto each pine sidepiece; cut on traced lines. Glue sides to back (using the bin as a brace) then glue frontpiece in place; clamp until dry.

Prepare surface and apply three or more coats of wood preservative on all surfaces. Insert bin.

2. Cedar Window Box—ADDITIONAL MATERIALS (*see* GENERAL MATERIALS): Rough sawn cedar, ⅝″x11½″, 6 ft.; 16 galvanized right angle brackets 4″x¾″; Flecto black rust-retardant spray paint; ¾″-long panhead topping screws; drill bit slightly smaller in diameter than screws; toggle bolt and washers for hanging.

DIRECTIONS (*see* GENERAL DIRECTIONS): Spray brackets and screws black. Cut three cedar pieces 13½″ long for front, back and bottom and two sidepieces 10½″ long.

Lay the corner and the center angle brackets on frontpiece as shown in photo on page 82; mark and drill holes for screws. Repeat on backpiece. Screw brackets to front and back. Set sidepieces in place between them; mark and drill holes for corner brackets; screw in place.

Screw a bracket at center bottom of each side panel. Place the assembly over the bottom piece and screw to the bottom from the inside.

In the center of one panel, 1″ from top edge, drill a hole of correct size for the toggle bolt. Screw box to wall.

3. Wall Plaque for Cactus—ADDITIONAL MATERIALS (*see* GENERAL MATERIALS): Sugar Pine 1/2"x31/2", 9 ft.; six wood screws; 16 roundhead nails; varnish; Venetian red acrylic paint; one 6"x9" stencil paper; one 13/4"x3" scrap leather for hanger; gray stain.

DIRECTIONS (*see* GENERAL DIRECTIONS): For back panel, cut from pine two pieces 191/4" long and two 163/4" long; cut two shelves 137/8" long. On each backpiece mark the corner cutting line with compass opened to 11/2"; cut off corners and save to use for shelf brackets.

Glue backpieces together as shown in photo on page 82; clamp until dry. Sand; rounding corners and edges. Stain gray.

On the shelf pieces, starting 1/2" from side edges and one long edge (the back) draw four evenly-spaced circles 21/2" in diameter. Cut out the circles, then cut the scalloped front edge 1/2" from the circles; stain gray.

Trace the stencil design (*see* FIG. 2) onto stencil paper; cut out. Tape stencil to back panel, as shown in photo. Paint design red.

Glue and nail brackets to the back, the upper one 91/2" from the bottom, the lower one 21/2" from the bottom. Glue shelves on brackets; nail in place through the back.

Cut a 3/4" diameter hole in leather scrap; round off one end (the top). Nail hanger to center back top edges. Apply varnish to entire shelf.

4. Wall Peg Plant Hanger—ADDITIONAL MATERIALS (*see* GENERAL MATERIALS): Clear pine 2x3, one 2 ft. wall strip; 3/4" doweling, 21/2 ft.; 11/16", 1/4" and 1/2" drill bits; two 1/2" wood plugs; 1/2" chisel; two 3" toggle bolts for hanging; gray Varathane #109; red wood stain.

DIRECTIONS (*see* GENERAL DIRECTIONS): Sand the pine wall strip well, rounding off the corners. Starting at one end, measure off and mark dowel hole locations at 3", 12" and 21". Drill holes at marks, using the 11/16" bit. On the same side, evenly centered between the dowel holes, drill two holes for the mounting bolts, using a 1/4" bit and a 1/2" countersink bit. Stain strip and wood plugs red.

Cut three 9" lengths of doweling. Place each dowel, in turn, in a vise; 11/4" from one end, make two saw cut 1/4" deep and 1/2" apart. Chisel out the wood between the cuts to make a notch. Sand the other dowel-ends to fit the holes drilled in the wall strip. Paint dowels gray; when dry, hammer dowels in place. Attach back strip to wall with toggle bolts; countersink. Hammer wood plugs into recesses.

MINIATURE HOUSEPLANTS—If you'd like to grow lots of houseplants and have very little space, or if you simply are fascinated by wee things, you can indulge your most extravagant gardening fantasies with these miniatures. Elfin roses that will grow in teacups, gloxinias so small they can be potted in thimbles—this is the Lilliputian world of miniature houseplants, and growing them is the most creative and the least difficult of all indoor gardening games.

Miniature plants are of various kinds. Look for them in local greenhouses and florist shops. Some are flowering species: In addition to roses and gloxinias, you can have tiny African violets, begonias, geraniums, even daffodils, tulips and hyacinths. There are miniature evergreens, tiny cacti and succulents that fit into pots no bigger than a candlestick holder, and small ferns that will flourish in a champagne glass.

To fill out a collection of true miniatures, you can use small species and seedlings of slow-growing, standard-size plants. Because small containers inhibit the root growth that governs plant development, a plant grown from a citrus seed, for instance, can live in a nutshell for two or three years before it needs a larger pot.

Exotic as the miniature plants appear to be, they are among the easiest of all houseplants to find room for. In a small, dark apartment, half a dozen miniature

MINIATURE HOUSEPLANTS TO GIVE—Miniature sedum spills out of salt cellar (1) in front of "Pixie Blue" African violet (2). Dwarf fern (3) grows in wine glass; shot glass houses tiny ivy "Glacier" (4). African violet "Coco" blooms in goblet (5); miniature gloxinias use thimbles as pots (6). In glass, mini-violet "Tiny Ellie" (7); Miniature crassula in candlestick (8); Cactus grows in inkwell (9); in front, more gloxinias in thimbles. Crystal vase and crystal salt cellar hold dwarf fern (10) and mini-cactus (11). In cup hybrid tea rose "Windy City" (12) seems huge behind tiny cacti in ashtray (13).

geraniums will bloom in that one sunny corner of the windowsill. Under lights, stacked in glass-domed compartmented candy jars, you can grow literally dozens of everblooming Sinningias. A whole landscape of dwarf foliage plants fits into a small glass fishbowl, each plant a diminutive history of unfurling leaves, swelling buds, maturing branches.

Any container big enough to hold the root ball of a miniature is a suitable pot. If it has no drainage hole, add only as much water as is needed to moisten the soil. Water the tiniest of minis with an eyedropper.

The rules for handling standard-size plants apply to minis of the same species, with a few differences. Minis need fine potting soil with a high content of humus. Add a handful of ground peat moss to every 2 quarts of regular potting mixture for miniatures not described here. Don't layer container bottoms with sand for drainage: The soil allotments are so small, the plants absorb moisture quickly. The rule for watering all houseplants is: The smaller the container, the more often it must be checked for moisture. This is particularly pertinent to minis. A doll's teacupful of soil can be moist at breakfast, dry at dinner.

To keep the miniatures flourishing and flowering once bloom starts, keep fading blossoms picked, and repot often—every three or four months. Add fertilizer two or three times a year to keep nutrients balanced.

Here's how professionals handle the individual types of miniatures most commonly grown as houseplants:

Miniature African Violets

Varieties: Favorites include "Pixie Blue" and other Pixies, Tiny Ellie, Pink Trail and Violet Trail, the white-flowered Silver Bell, and others in the Bell series.

Small-leaved types are particularly appealing, though hard to find. Look for Edith's Toy and Allen's Toy.

Light: South windows in winter; east or west windows in summer. But they'll bloom almost anywhere, and bloom especially well under fluorescent lights.

Soil: African violet commercial mixtures are fine, or make grower Michael Kartuz's mix; 6 quarts ground sphagnum peat moss, 4 quarts vermiculite, 4 quarts perlite, 2 tablespoons ground limestone, all moistened before planting with 1 quart lukewarm water.

Watering: Keep soil moist, but not soggy. Plants thrive on a bed of wet pebbles.

Containers: Plastic 1½- to 2½-inch pots are fine, or household finds of similar sizes.

Fertilizing: Feed plants three out of four waterings with a commercial African-violet fertilizer.

Temperatures: Between 70° and 80° Fahrenheit during the day, with a low of 52° at night is ideal.

Small Begonias

Varieties: There are three categories of begonias grown indoors—the small ever-blooming wax begonias; the taller rhizomatous types; and the rexes, angelwing begonias with colorful leaves. Small wax begonias include Andy, Pied Piper and Pistachio. Rhizomatous begonias with dainty blossoms on long, arching stems include Beatrice Haddrell, Bowerae, Bow-Arriola, Bow-Joe, a favorite, China Doll and Chantilly Lace. Small rexes fairly easy to find include Baby Rainbow, Lorraine Closson and others in the Closson series—Red Berry, Bantam Gem, Wood Nymph, Dew Drop and Robin.

Cultural instructions: Similar to the preceding African violets, with one main difference—fertilize only every third or fourth watering, and keep the rexes just out of direct sunlight.

Tiny Gloxinias (Sinningias)

Varieties: These, among the most adorable of small houseplants, bloom all the time under the right conditions. *Sinningia pusilla,* which has lavender flowers, is the smallest of all the minis and really will grow in a thimble. White Sprite is a sort of *Sinningia pusilla.* Bright Eyes is a little larger, and has white-eyed purple flowers; Cindy, Cindy-Ella, Coral Baby, a pink, Freckles, Hircon, Minarette, Norma Jean and Patty Ann are variations. Among the easiest to find are Poupee, Snowflake and Tinker Bells.

Light: Early-morning sun is fine, but they'll bloom in a north window with no sun, too, or under fluorescent lights.

Watering: Grow the Sinningias under glass. They require moist greenhouse conditions to maintain their blooms. Terrariums and bottle gardens make good homes. Water them just as you would African violets.

Containers: Use 1-inch plastic or glass containers for beginning Sinningias, or appropriate household items. Move plants to larger pots if they become crowded.

Fertilizing: Fertilize as African violets.

Temperatures: Ideal is 65° to 75°.

Small Ferns

Varieties: Baby ferns of many species can be grown as miniatures. Some pretty ferns that stay small are *Adiantum bellow, A. capillus-veneris* and *A. hispidulum,* all tiny maidenhairs; *Polystichum tsussimense,* a dwarf that's wonderful in terrariums; and *Pteris ensiformis evergemiensis,* a mini with silver and green fronds.

Cultural instructions: Handle small ferns as African violets, but avoid direct sunlight in summer.

Miniature Roses

Varieties: There are enchanting hybrid tea, floribunda and moss roses in pinks, reds, yellows, whites and variegated shades. Many are scented. Some climb and some are offered for hanging basket culture. Recommended for pot culture are Janice, a medium pink; White Madonna; Fire Princess, an orangy-red; Willie Mae, a red; and Max Caldwell, another red. Windy City is a deep pink double, and Gold Coin is a lovely yellow double. A favorite is Janna, a white frilled with deep pink. Frosty is a fragrant white.

Light: Roses need sun, but they can also be grown under fluorescent lights. Use two or three daylight tube fixtures held 4 to 6 inches above plant tops and leave them on 12 to 16 hours daily. Keep roses in a southwest window in fall and winter, in an east or west window in late spring and summer. Or summer outdoors.

Containers and potting: Plant in plastic pots ½ inch below the original soil levels. Use a mixture of 1 part sterilized soil (commercial soils are usually sterilized), 1 part ground peat, 1 part perlite or sand. Mix in it, at the amount recommended by the manufacturer, fish fertilizer, bat guano or blood meal. If you are using garden soil that is alkaline in the potting mix, fertilize with acid azalea or camellia fertilizer. Place newly potted roses in a sunny, cool spot at 50° to 55° for two to four weeks. When you notice that growth has begun, move them indoors.

Watering: Keep roses damp but not soggy. Allow the soil to dry out every three to four weeks, then water thoroughly. Every three to five weeks, water heavily twice within a period of 10 hours, then let the plants dry thoroughly before returning to their regular watering schedule.

Fertilizing: Feed with a commercial rose fertilizer or 10-10-5 at half-strength every two to three weeks.

Temperatures: Ideal conditions are 50° to 60° at night, 70° or higher during the day. An open window will lower nighttime tempertures.

Pruning: After a flowering period, pinch branch ends off to keep plants bushy.

Spraying: Control aphids and red spider with Malathion and Captan. For black spot and mildew, use Phaltan and Manzate. Aramite controls red spider mites.

Miniature Geraniums

Varieties: There are at least 75 minis, with names like Fairy Tales, Minx, Tiny Tim. I've had good luck with Firefly, Claudius, Tweedlededee and Sneezy.

Light: A south window is ideal in winter; in summer, east or west facing windows.

Soil: Mix regular potting soil half and half with sand.

Watering: Be sure to keep mini geraniums damp.

Containers: Clay or plastic pots 2½ inches in size will house miniature geraniums for quite a long time, but eventually you will have to shift them into a 3-inch pot.

Fertilizing: Feed with regular houseplant formula every three to four weeks; slow the program if leaves grow instead of flowers.

Temperatures: Ideal during the day is 65° to 75°; at night, 55°.

Succulents and Cacti

Varieties: Cacti and succulents suited to miniature collections are too many to name. A few favorites are *Monanthes polyphylla*, a tiny hen-and-chickens type plant only ½ inch tall. *M. muralis* is like a diminutive bonsai, 3 inches tall. *Sedum dasyphyllum* is a sprawler and *Crassula schmidtii* looks like a snake plant.

Light: Semi or full sun.

Soil: Potting soil mixed half and half with coarse sand.

Watering: Keep plants moist during summer; in other seasons, let them dry out before watering.

Containers: Sizes ½ to 1 inch fit the minis, and the containers can be quite shallow because their root systems are on the surface.

Fertilizing: Fertilize every three to four waterings in summer.

Temperatures: Hot will do; so will cool. The cacti and succulents are wonderful apartment plants because they can stand overheating and unusually dry atmospheric conditions.

INEXPENSIVE PLANTS THAT GROW EXPENSIVE Here's how to have large, thriving, expensive houseplants to give as gifts—without spending a large amount of money! The trick is to substitute your own time and efforts for those of professional growers and to follow what many ingenious householders have done for a long time with their outdoor plants: Raise big, beautiful plants from little baby ones.

Of course, mature plants like those you've admired at garden centers won't grow overnight. If it were that easy, the growers' price tags would have much lower figures; they're worth what is asked. But with a modicum of patience (which every gardener acquires sooner or later), the ability to follow directions and a willingness to put in some interesting hours, you'll soon have plants that command admiration. You will have acquired the "green thumb" gardeners boast of, for these plants will be uniquely your own.

There are two ways to go about it. The easier method is to start with baby plants, the sort that come already rooted in two- to three-inch pots. You will find an astonishing array of these young plants at garden centers, nurseries or florists as well as supermarkets and department and dime stores. Since most plants sold this way come with name labels stuck in the pots, you can be confident you're buying the baby versions of the large expensive plants you eventually want in your indoor garden. Mail-order seedsmen's catalogs also offer a good selection of plants in small sizes; so if you live in an area remote from nurseries, you can still become a houseplant green-thumber via mail order.

Oleander, dwarf palms, bougainvillaea and any number of other large plants that grow outdoors in the warmer regions of the country are available as baby plants by mail and can be gown indoors in the northern, colder states. For warm-climate gardeners, larger versions of these same plants can still be bought at reasonable prices from nurseries or garden centers. Once they've grown even larger, you can transfer them to big pots or tubs to keep indoors or move out onto the terrace.

The second way to produce large plants from little ones is not as direct, but it is more fun. You make cuttings from a big plant of the sort you like, root them and then give them the same care you would give baby plants. Cuttings are pieces, six to eight inches long, removed from the tips of shoots or branches of mature plants. Some plants will even root from just the leaves (with stems intact). Cuttings should be taken from plants only during their more vigorous growing period— before December 1 and after February 15.

How to Root Your Cuttings

Water rooting: Leaves alone as well as leaf-and-stem cuttings may be rooted in water. African violets, gloxinia, peperomia, and pickaback plant leaves (complete with stems) are good subjects. The African violets, gloxinia and peperomia will form roots and plantlets at the stem base, so it's best to suspend the leaf blade above the water line. Pickaback forms roots at the base of the leaf blade and should be positioned so the blade barely touches the water. When plantlets are an inch high, transplant them into pots of soil.

Sprigs of ivy, wandering Jew, philodendron, Chinese evergreen, oleander and pandanus can also be successfully rooted in water.

Some leaf-and-stem cuttings such as begonia and geraniums may be rooted in water, but their soft stems are apt to rot. A moist medium rooting (*see below*) is better. The other plants mentioned above may also be rooted in a moist medium.

Moist medium rooting: The classic medium is a 50-50 mixture of sand (you can use boxed bird sand) and peat moss; but vermiculite or vermiculite and perlite

can also be used successfully for most plants. (Cactus is the exception; this should be rooted in all sand.) For a few cuttings, use a flowerpot covered with a glass jar or cheese dome; or enclose it in a plastic bag sealed with paperclips. For several cuttings, use a covered transparent plastic box (such as a shoe or bread box). All of these covered containers will help maintain the right level of humidity during rooting. Note: When using a flowerpot, lightly stuff drain holes of the pot with a piece of nylon stocking to permit drainage and prevent soil from washing out.

When rooting cuttings in a covered transparent box, be sure to keep the medium moist—never wet, because there is no drainage in the box. Press any excess water out of the medium before putting a two-inch layer in the box. Pack it down lightly.

Cuttings should be no more than six inches long. Remove all leaves from the lower stem, leaving only three or four at the top; also take off any flowers or seed pods. Cut the stem just below a leaf joint using a razor blade or sharp knife. With a pencil, make a hole in the rooting medium, insert the cutting at least 1½ inches and press the medium firmly around it. The cutting should stand erect, with the stem in full contact with the medium. When all cuttings are placed, put the cover on the box or pot. When water drops appear on the cover you'll know proper humidity is being maintained. If little or no moisture appears, the medium may be too dry. Add a small amount of water, but avoid making it too wet. Otherwise, do not remove the cover.

In a cold room it's a good idea to place the box on a shelf above a radiator for extra warmth. Place two layers of corrugated boxboard between the box and radiator for insulation against too much heat.

Potting the Plants

After two weeks, test for rooting: Gently tug a cutting out of the medium. If it comes out easily, it is not sufficiently rooted. Replace it and firm the medium again. If it carries a root ball of up to an inch, the cutting is ready to be potted. Plant it in a three-inch pot filled with a 50-50 mixture of potting soil and vermiculite, keeping the roots about halfway down in the pot. Firm the soil well around roots and stem, water well and let the pot drain. Keep the soil moist but not wet thereafter and do not feed it plant food for the first month.

Baby plants purchased already rooted should be transferred immediately into five-inch pots (larger if plants are big) to allow growth. Stuff a piece of nylon stocking in the drain hole to prevent the soil's washing out and fill with soil to allow the top of the plant root ball to come about ½ inch below the pot rim. Fill around with a good potting soil; water, drain, keep moist and, the first month, do not feed.

Continuing care: Plants need light as well as water and food. Follow the plant's needs for light (sun to partial shade) and feed often but lightly. Too much feeding causes a buildup of fertilizer salts in the soil and hurts rather than helps plants. Use a standard houseplant food diluted according to manufacturer's label instructions. Water according to the plant's natural needs. Cacti and succulents need very little water compared to the rain forest tropical plants. But water is needed for all, so soil nutrients can be taken up in solution and used by the plant mechanisms.

Repot to a larger-size container, using the same soil mixture, as often as the roots begin to crowd their home.

As you can see, rooting and potting your own plants is really very easy. What's more, it's a satisfying project because you end up with big, beautiful plants to share with friends—for a very small investment in time and money.

1. **Plywood slot-together box, 16″x16″x20″, for topiary evergreens: 4 hours, $10.**
2. **Plywood tray, 24″x12″x6″, for herb garden: 4 hours, $10.**
3. **Redwood window box, 36″x7½″x7½″, for perennials: Build in 3 hours for $8.**

OUTDOOR PLANTERS—The prices you pay for beautiful outdoor containers for flowers, plants and shrubs are almost prohibitive—yet inexpensive planters are the most effective way to decorate your "outdoor room." The planters themselves, and the plants they contain, provide color, add drama where spots are bare and enhance any outdoor setting in lovely, interesting groupings. Our planters are easy to make in a short time and are remarkably low in cost. They're designed to house just about every growing thing and require no special gardening skills. We used two readily available, low-cost materials: plywood and garden grade redwood.
GENERAL DIRECTIONS: Low-cost materials are used for all the planters. Lumber is "construction-grade." Redwood can be "garden-grade" unless otherwise indicated. Plywood should be "Ext." for exterior use (APA grade-trademarked). For many of the planters, you can probably find the plywood you need in your lumber dealer's odd-size or leftover pile.

All planters should have ⅝″ drain holes drilled in the bottoms. All are raised on base supports to allow for drainage.

Because of its extreme resistance to decay, redwood requires no finish—it will weather over the years to a mellow silvery gray. For longer life, lumber and plywood should be painted or finished with a preservative; the finish for each planter is given in the individual MATERIALS list. Lumber and plywood planters must also be protected on the inside. Brush on asphalt roofing paint after assembly.

1. Plywood Slot-together Box for Topiary Evergreens (*boxwood*):
MATERIALS: Ext. or MDO plywood, ⅝″x4′x4′; 2x2x3′ lumber; 6d galvanized finishing nails; waterproof glue; asphalt paint; exterior white paint.
CUTTING DIRECTIONS: Four 17″x19½″ plywood sides (cut decorative tops and notch *as shown in* FIG. 1); 12⅜″x12⅜″ plywood bottom; four 2x2x9″ base supports.

2. Plywood Tray for Herb Garden (*chives and thyme*):
MATERIALS: Ext. plywood, ⅝″x24″x48″; ¼″x¾″x4′ lattice; 3d galvanized finishing nails; waterproof glue; asphalt paint; dark green paint; clear polyurethane finish.
CUTTING DIRECTIONS: Plywood: two 6″x24″ sides, two 7½″x12″ ends, 12″x22¾″ bottom, two 6⅞″x12⅜″ dividers; three 13¼″ lattice base strips (*see* FIG. 2).

3. Redwood Window Box for Perennials (*chrysanthemums*):
MATERIALS: Construction Heart redwood: 1x8x8′, 1x8x3′, ½″x¾″x2′; 6d galvanized finishing nails.

90

CUTTING DIRECTIONS: Two 1x8x10″ ends, curved as shown; two 1x8x34½″ sides; 1x8x34½″ bottom ripped to 6″ width; three ½″x¾″x7½″ bottom support strips (see FIG. 3; if box is to be mounted on a window ledge, use thicker strips and cut to fit slope of ledge).

FIG. 1 —
PLYWOOD
SLOT-TOGETHER
BOX — for topiary
evergreens

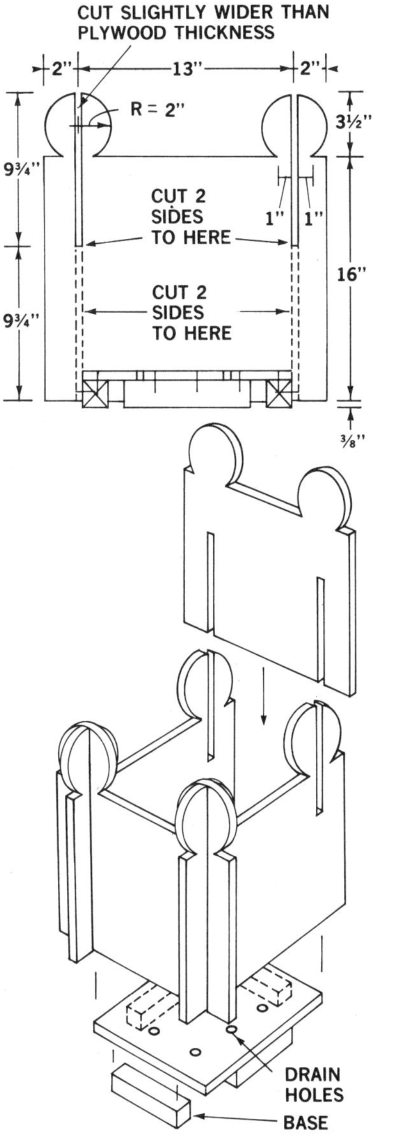

CUT SLIGHTLY WIDER THAN
PLYWOOD THICKNESS

2″   13″   2″
R = 2″
3½″
9¾″
CUT 2
SIDES
TO HERE
1″ 1″
16″
9¾″
CUT 2
SIDES
TO HERE
⅜″

DRAIN
HOLES
BASE

FIG. 2 — PLYWOOD TRAY —
for herb garden

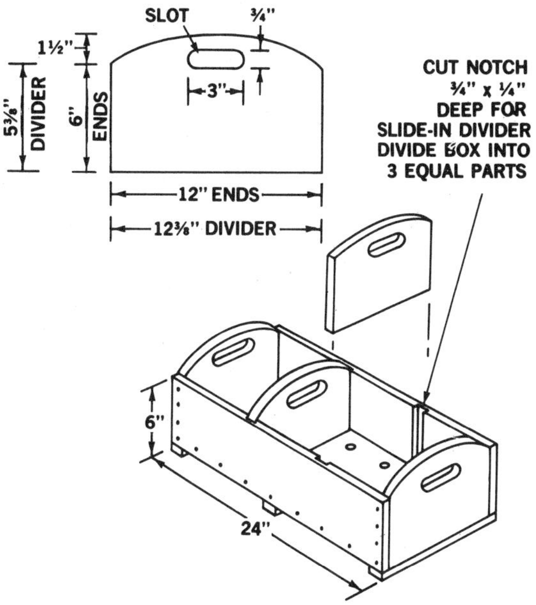

SLOT   ¾″
1½″
5⅜″ DIVIDER
6″ ENDS
3″

CUT NOTCH
¾″ x ¼″
DEEP FOR
SLIDE-IN DIVIDER
DIVIDE BOX INTO
3 EQUAL PARTS

12″ ENDS
12⅜″ DIVIDER

6″
24″

FIG. 3 — REDWOOD
WINDOW
BOX —
for perennials

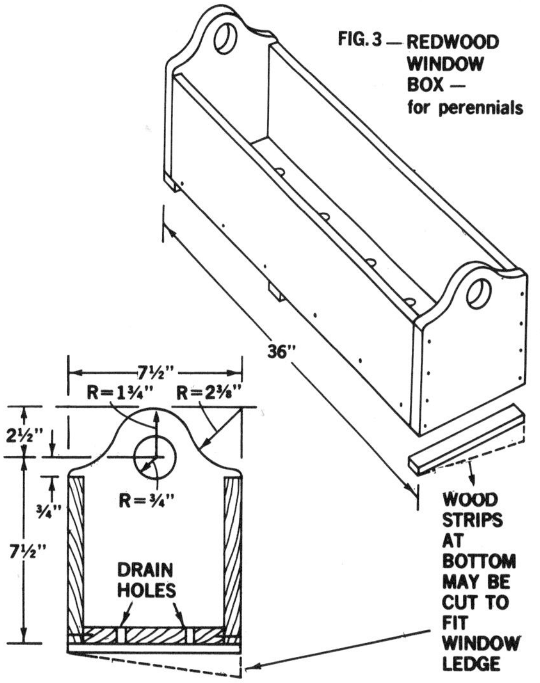

36″

7½″
R=1¾″   R=2⅜″
2½″
R=¾″
¾″
7½″
DRAIN
HOLES

WOOD
STRIPS
AT
BOTTOM
MAY BE
CUT TO
FIT
WINDOW
LEDGE

GIVE FLOWERPOT HERBS TO GOURMETS—Best way to have fresh herbs continually at hand to work their magic in your cooking is to grow your own—year round. Many herbs thrive about as well indoors in pots as outdoors in your garden. All they really need is adequate light, a warm but not too hot atmosphere, proper soil, sufficient moisture and humidity, and an occasional application of plant food—and that's about all there is to it (*see* Chart). If you don't have a sunny window, it is possible to supply "daylight" with fluorescent bulbs placed about a foot above the top of the plants. You can lengthen the growing day this way, too. Some plants need more water than others, so you must adjust watering to the plant's needs (*see* Chart). A shallow baking tin filled with gravel for the pots to sit on and drain into will help to supply humidity. Feeding is best accomplished with a soluble-in-water houseplant fertilizer. The 20-20-20 formula (read the label) is best, but a 10-15-10 kind will do pretty well. Feed *once* a month.

If your apartment has a balcony or terrace, you can put the pots out there for the summer if you like. If you live in a house, give the plants an outdoor vacation over the summer in their pots in the garden or on the terrace. But you *can* keep them indoors all year long.

The following pot herbs can be grown quite easily from seeds, except for tarragon—it must be bought as a plant.

Basil. An annual plant, raised each year from seed. For growing indoors, discard old plants and start two or more new crops a year from seed. Either the green- or purple-leafed kind may be used, fresh or dry, to flavor a wide variety of dishes.

Mint. A perennial, it has vigorous roots that produce new growth year after year. Spearmint is the kind most grown indoors; its fresh or dried young tips and leaves are matchless in flavor and tang.

Oregano. A perennial, usually grown as an annual in pot culture. Cut short sprigs, pick off the oval gray-green leaves; discard stems before using fresh or drying.

Rosemary. A decorative and woody perennial with pungent needle-like grayish leaves. It likes a somewhat sandy soil and frequent waterings. Keep it low and bushy by cutting back shoots. Use leaves only, fresh or dried, and discard stems.

Sage. A shrubby perennial with fascinating pebbly silver-green leaves that are used fresh, or dried and then pulverized.

Sweet Marjoram. An erect bushy perennial plant that is grown as an annual. Use leaves and tender young stems, fresh or dried. Trim back shoots often to keep it producing. Keep the soil barely moist.

Tarragon. A small, vigorous, spreading perennial that must be purchased as a plant, for it doesn't produce seeds. (Seeds offered for sale are from a weak-sister relative, not the true French tarragon.) Each spring and fall, un-pot, divide the roots, discard old roots or plant them in the garden, retaining a young root with two shoots on it for pot culture. Force new growth by frequently cutting off tops, using fresh new leaves or drying them.

Thyme. A charming perennial with woody stems studded with tiny leaves. Cut it back to two inches each spring, then cut new growth twice a season. Cut a sprig or two and use only the leaves, fresh or dried.

Planting and Caring for Herbs. *Planting seeds:* Any shallow containers will do to start your seeds in: flat cans, cottage cheese or pint-size milk containers, shallow clay or plastic pots—about three inches deep. Provide drainage holes, cover them with broken pieces of pot or gravel, then fill containers to within ½ inch of top with a good grade of commercial potting soil. (Or mix equal parts of garden soil, peat moss, sand.) Water well and let drain; refill soil to proper level.

Sow only 12 to 16 seeds per pot, spacing them at least ½ inch apart. Sift soil over them—barely covering small seeds, covering big ones about ¼ inch. Cover pots with plastic wrap held tightly by a rubber band. Keep pots warm; not below 50° at night nor above 70° daytimes.

Seeds sprout, according to kind of plant, in six days to four weeks (*see* Chart). When sprouts are up a half inch, remove plastic cover and place pots in full sun. Keep soil always slightly moist, watering gently once a day to once a week, depending on temperature and humidity.

Transplanting: When pots have two pairs of leaves (10 days to 2 weeks), put in permanent pots. (*See Chart for pot sizes.*) The day before transplanting, prepare pots as above with same kind of soil to ½ inch from top. Water and let drain. Lift out seedlings with a good block of soil around roots, using a table fork thrust in deeply. Avoid injuring roots. Plunge a table knife into the permanent pot soil and press it from side to side. Insert the seedling root and soil into this slit, placing plant at the level it had been growing. Press soil gently to close slit. Put large seedlings into individual pots, small seedlings four or five together per pot.

herb	planting depth	pot size (diam.)	soil	water	sun/ shade	germina- tion
Basil	⅛″–¼″	5″–6″	average	moderately	S–PSH	6–7 days
Mint*	¼″	6″–8″	rich, moist	often	S–SH	3 weeks
Oregano*	⅛″	5″–6″	rich, moist	moderately	S–PSH	to 3 weeks
Rosemary*	¼″	6″–8″	light, sandy	often	S	3–4 weeks
Sage*	¼″	6″	light	moderately	S	2–3 weeks
Sweet Marjoram#	⅛″	5″–6″	average	moderately	S–PSH	to 2 weeks
Tarragon*	(plants)	10″	average	moderately	S	

* Availble as plants as well as seeds
\# Soak 24 hours in tepid water before planting, to speed germination.

S = Sun   SH = Shade   PSH = Part Shade

Plant care: In two weeks, thin out and discard the poorest plants, saving the strongest. Turn pots each week to ensure balanced growth on all sides. Keep watered according to weather and the plant's needs (*see* Chart); feed once a month; keep trimmed back for use and to force new, fresh growth.

Leaves of most herbs can be picked for use in cooking after four to six weeks. Woody perennials take longer.

Drying and Freezing Herbs—*Drying:* Cut sprigs in the morning. Tie several sprigs in a bunch, hang up to dry in a cool shady spot. To store, strip off dried leaves. Or, strip leaves immediately and let dry flat on paper towels in a cool spot. Store in tightly stoppered colored bottles to keep color.

Freezing: Hold a few sprigs with tongs, plunge into boiling water for one minute, then into ice water for two minutes. Drain, place in plastic bags, seal and freeze immediately. Or, wash herbs, chop up leaves (all one kind or mixtures), measure into small amounts and freeze in individual bags. Defrost at room temperature; use immediately. Never refreeze.

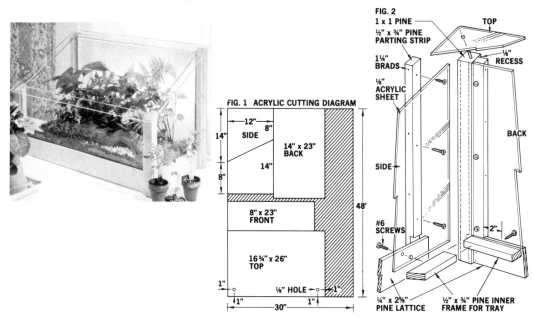

FIG. 1 ACRYLIC CUTTING DIAGRAM

A TOM THUMB-SIZE GREENHOUSE—If your gardening fantasy is to have your own greenhouse, but you don't have the space or money for one, our miniature greenhouse will fulfill your dream. It's 16¼″ high, 24″ wide and 13½″ deep, and, like a full-sized greenhouse, creates a warm, humid environment for a variety of plants. You can use it as a terrarium, or cultivate potted plants in it—tropical or flowering varieties such as African violets, or seedlings for your indoor or outdoor garden. To make sure the greenhouse will get enough light, place it on a deep windowsill, on a table or shelf in front of a window, or under a fluorescent plant light. Fill the plastic plant tray in the bottom of the greenhouse with gravel for potted plants or seedlings, or with soil for terrarium plants.

MATERIALS: ⅛″x30″x48″ sheet acrylic; 11″x22″x2½″ plastic plant tray or old roasting pan; scrap pine and lumber or ½″x¾″x16′ pine parting strip; 1x1x5′ pine lumber; ¼″x2⅝″x6′ pine lattice; ¾″ and 1¼″ brads; 6¾″ panhead self-tapping screws; 4d finishing nails; white glue; pentachlorophenol wood preservative. (The cost of sheet acrylic brings this greenhouse about $7 over our $10 limit.)

DIRECTIONS: Cut sheet acrylic (see FIG. 1). Drill ⅛″ holes as indicated. Cut lumber as follows: 1x1, two 12″ and two 18″ lengths; pine lattice, two 12″ and two 23″ lengths; ½″x¾″ parting strip, two 23″ and two 10½″ lengths for inner frame, four 12″ and four 18″ lengths for corner posts. Cut a 1¼″x2⅝″ notch in one end of each of the 12″ and 18″ lengths of parting strip. Assemble a pair of 18″ rear and 12″ front corner supports by attaching 2 parting strips with glue and 1¼″ brads to adjacent sides of the 1x1's. Mark each corner post 2⅛″ up from bottom and position acrylic side piece on this line. Mark off the angle of the acrylic on posts; cut and sand. With ¾″ brads and glue, attach rear corner posts to ends of one 23″ length of lattice. Attach front posts to other. Attach front to back with 12″ lengths of lattice. Place frame over plant tray; adjust square. Remove tray. Coat frame and remaining parting strips with wood preservative, following manufacturer's directions. With ¾″ screws attach acrylic back and front to respective corner posts through pre-drilled ³⁄₃₂″ holes; then attach sides. Attach parting strips for inner frame with screws through ³⁄₃₂″ holes pre-drilled through the lattice and acrylic—¼″ below the upper edge of the lattice, 2″ from each corner and in the center of the front and back (see FIG. 2). Nail 4d finishing nails into tops of rear supports to hold acrylic top.

94

PRETTY FLOWERPOT COVERS—If your humble terra-cotta flowerpots have taken on a rather seedy look, you can easily remedy that by slipcovering them—or even covering new ones—to go with favorite curtains, tablecloths or furniture slip-covers. Here are covers you can make of fabric scraps and yarn.

1. Chintz Cover (*for pot 5½″ in diameter and 5¼″ high*)—DIRECTIONS: Cut a paper pattern 5½″ high and 5¼″ wide at top, tapering to 3¾″ at bottom. Use pattern as is to trace and cut four cardboard side pieces; add ½″ on pattern edges to cut four pieces of chintz or similar fabric. Now trim ⅛″ from the pattern edges and cut four felt pieces.

Center the cardboards on wrong side of fabric pieces; glue in place. Fold excess fabric around cardboard edges; glue in place. Cut 16 five-inch lengths of ⅜″ wide grosgrain ribbon. Glue a ribbon to each cardboard side edge 1″ from top and 1¼″ from bottom. Glue felt to cardboard backs to conceal ribbon-ends. Tie ribbon bows. Slip pot into cover.

2. "Upholstered" Pot—DIRECTIONS: Cut paper pattern to fit the rim and one to fit the pot. Adding ½″ to all pattern edges, cut the rim pattern on the straight grain of the fabric and the pot pattern on the bias. Turn under and glue ½″ on top and bottom edges of both pieces. Gluing one end in place, wrap each strip tightly around pot; fold other end under ½″ and glue. Lap folded end over beginning end; glue.

Grasscloth Tie-on Cover (*for pot 4½″ in diameter and 4″ high*)—DIRECTIONS: Press a 1″-wide strip of masking tape along each edge of wrong side of a 6″x16″ piece of grasscloth. Centered on the right side, draw a 4¼″x14¾″ rectangle; cut on drawn line through tape. Add pieces of tape on the corners to keep edges firm. Round off corners, cutting them identically. Bind edges (over whatever tape remains) with bias fabric strips cut 1⅞″ wide. *For ties,* cut two 1¾″x12″ fabric strips. Fold each in half lengthwise with right sides together; cut one end diagonally. Stitch ¼″ seam on long edge and diagonal end. Turn right side out; press. Center the straight end of each tie 2″ from front edge of cover; stitch in place. Glue crescent-shape suede shield over each tie end. Wrap cover around pot and saucer; tie bow.

3. Multicolored Crocheted Pot Cover—Use leftover 2-ply knitting worsted in a variety of colors (we used ten colors) and stitches, figuring on a gauge of 9 stitches to measure 2″ with a size E crochet hook, OR ANY SIZE HOOK WHICH WILL OBTAIN THAT GAUGE.

DIRECTIONS: Make a row of chain stitches equal to the circumference at the bottom of the flower pot. Add as many rows of single, double and triple crochet as necessary for the height of your pot, changing colors and stitches with every row and increasing 8 to 10 to 12 stitches per row to accommodate the increase in the pot size from bottom to top. In the last row, make a picot every 8 to 10 stitches for a pretty top edge. Sew band short edges together and slip over pot.

HOUSEPLANTS TO GROW FOR CHRISTMAS GIVING—If you start them in October all the pretty plants here will grow in time for you to give as Christmas gifts. Seeds will sprout, bulbs will bloom, and cuttings will root in weeks. Cool house temperatures, weekly misting, proper watering and feeding will do it. The wreath requires a coat-hanger frame (easy to make). Be sure to enclose care instructions with your gift plants.

Bulb Plants: Unpotted bulbs for forcing into winter bloom are for sale (Oct.) in garden stores. Amaryllis is the easiest to handle and quickest to bloom—3 to 4 weeks. Paperwhites bloom in 6 to 7 weeks; hyacinths in 8 to 10 weeks.

Amaryllis—Plant one bulb per pot in all-purpose potting soil with the top third above soil level. Set in bright light with 1 to 2 hours direct sun daily, keeping soil evenly moist. Best blooms are at indoor temperatures of 62° to 75°. Feed blooming plant food weekly after blooming until August. Sometime in August, place plant in the dark for 8 weeks and let soil become almost dry (water a little if soil becomes completely dry). Then clear dead leaves, repot in fresh soil, return to light, resume weekly watering and feeding.

Paperwhites—Plant 4 to 6 bulbs 1 to 2 inches apart in all-purpose soil in an 8-inch bulb pan (broad as it is deep), with tips just above soil level. Keep evenly moist. Or place bulbs in a 4-inch-deep bowl containing pebbles and water, with bulb bases ½ inch under water. Keep water level with and touching bulb bases, and change weekly. Set to root in the dark at 55° to 65° for 3 to 4 weeks. When top growth is good, move to sunny east or west window, or a bright north window. Indoor temperatures of 60° to 70° give best blooms. Continue caring for plants after they bloom; plant outdoors in early spring.

Hyacinths—Plant as paperwhites, but 2 or 3 to a pot. Rooting is best at 40° to 50°. Hyacinths bloom best indoors at 50° to 60°, but will bloom at 70° if there's lots of moist, fresh air available.

Ivy Wreath: Seed catalogs and some florists and garden stores sell long-branched, small-leaved ivies especially for training as topiaries. The wreath in the picture is made from a potted "Merion Beauty" ivy with branches 36 inches long. To form, twist two coat hangers together into a long wire and mold into a double circle 14 inches across; cross the two ends and push them firmly into the soil (use all-purpose soil). Tie the branches to the form and cut away twigs and large leaves to make a symmetrical arrangement. As new branches grow 2 to 3 inches long, tie to

96

wreath and pinch off tips. Some leaves will die the first few days—remove them. Place the wreath in moderate light for 3 days, then in a bright north window or 2 to 3 feet back from an east or west window. Mist after tying and every few days for 3 weeks, then weekly. Indoor temperatures of 60° to 70° and lots of fresh air promote good growth. Add a bow at Christmas time and your living wreath is ready to give.

Begonia: Wax begonia seeds are sold in seed stores and by mail order and grow year round. Plant 8 to 10 seeds in a 5-inch pot in slightly moist African-violet soil. Cover with $\frac{1}{4}$ inch vermiculite. Water lightly, cover with plastic wrap and place in moderate light to germinate. Keep soil moist, not soaked. Water enough so excess drains into saucer; empty saucer after an hour. When seedings are growing vigorously, remove plastic and place pot in a sunny east or west window. Remove weakest seedlings as pot gets crowded. Feed blooming plant food after plants are 3 inches high. Indoor temperatures of 60° to 70° are best. Keep tips pinched for compact growth.

Herbs: Herb seeds are sold in seed stores and by mail order and grow year round; plant as begonias. Or cut 4-inch tips from a mature herb plant and root in water in a sunny window. Plant cuttings in all-purpose potting soil in 2- or 3-inch pots and place in the sunniest spot you have, in a tray containing pebbles and water. (Water level should be just below—not touching—pot bottoms.) Keep soil evenly moist (test smaller pots twice daily for moisture).

Pineapple sage is for scenting, plain *sage* for seasoning. Both sages grow easily from seed or tip cuttings.

Chive plants grow from seed. Or, divide the roots of a mature plant into clumps and plant in 3-inch pots. Snip off half the growth after planting. If plants look sickly, treat to a two-week rest in your refrigerator. Keep chive tips at 3- to 4-inch length till 10 days before you give away the plant, then let grow.

Rosemary grows from seeds or tip cuttings and does best in plastic pots.

Rose geranium grows easily from seed—but slowly. So instead, plant tip cuttings in all-purpose soil with one-fourth part sand. If weather is overcast, place under fluorescent lights or plants will yellow and grow spindly.

Terrariums: Use a champagne glass or any wide-rimmed stemmed glass to hold lacy cedar-like ground pine and red-berried bittersweet. (Use a small inverted fish-bowl as a cover.) A mushroom-shaped glass (sold specifically for terrariums at florists and garden stores for about $5) can use these two, plus another wildling, Princess pine. Line your terrarium bottom with $\frac{1}{4}$ to $\frac{1}{2}$ inch of pebbles and top with a sprinkling of small charcoal chips and 1 to 2 inches of terrarium soil. Dig the plants from the forest floor with as much root and soil as possible. Place gently in terrarium soil in an attractive arrangement and firm another $\frac{1}{2}$ inch of soil around roots. Water just enough to settle soil. Top with moss, cover glass—keep covered—and water only when lid shows no condensed moisture. Set in light of a bright north window or several feet back from east or west windows. As plantlets grow and crowd the terrarium, remove them to larger containers and replace with new forest findings. Don't feed.

Pepper Plant: Pepper plants can be grown from store-bought seed but also from hot red-pepper seeds from your spice shelf. (But they must be whole, not ground—and fresh.) Plant as begonias. Soil for peppers must be kept evenly moist, or leaves fall. To promote rapid growth, mist daily after plants begin to grow. Warm air helps peppers, but it must be freshened frequently. Feed blooming plant food weekly. Tiny white flowers will wither, and from them pods will develop—at first white, then yellow, then red. Keep withering peppers picked so fruiting continues. Place plants outdoors during summer; before frost, cut back by half and bring indoors. In spring, start new plants from picked seeds.

(1) **A simple sling of white jute in basic macramé knots, trimmed with blue beads.**
(2) **A regular florist's hanging pot decked out in red beads you string on the wires. Add swags of more beads on the side. (3) Fishnet sling of red jute, quickly created with simple knots. Add dangling clear yellow beads. (4) Another fishnet sling—this one of yellow jute strung with rainbow-colored beads (extra pretty around a clear bowl of cut flowers). (5) The same design as 3 and 4, a brown jute sling shining with tortoise-shell-colored beads.**

SPARKLING BEADED PLANT HANGERS—When the sun catches the clear beads of these pretty plant hangers, they glisten like jewels. You won't believe how easy they are to make.

1. White Sling—MATERIALS: White jute, 24 strands, 2 yds. long; plastic beads: $5/16''$ in diameter, 120 green and 120 blue; $3/4''$ in diameter, 12 faceted blue.

DIRECTIONS: Align strands; tie overhand knot at one end, leaving 5" long tassel. Thread each tassel strand with three small beads, alternating blue-green-blue and green-blue-green. Secure beads with overhand knot $1\frac{1}{2}''$ from tassel end.

Section 1: Holding two strands together in each hand, tie a double knot 1" above tassel; repeat five times. Repeat 1" above the first six knots, using one cord from one knot and one cord from the adjacent knot.

Section 2: Straighten out each group of four strands and tie $1\frac{1}{2}''$ of square knots (see FIGS. 1A to 1F).

Section 3: String a pair of small beads (1 blue, 1 green) on each *outer* strand, then make an overhand knot (anchor strands hang free until Section 2 is repeated). With a double knot, tie two adjacent outer strands $2\frac{1}{4}''$ from beads. Make an overhand knot $1\frac{3}{4}''$ further along these *outer* strands and string another pair of beads.

Sections 4 and 5: Repeat Sections 2 and 3.
Section 6: Repeat Section 2.

98

Top Beads: On each outer cord, string one small blue and green bead, then an overhand knot to keep beads in place. Make another overhand knot 1½″ above previous one. String four more beads, alternating colors and secure with overhand knot.

Adding Big Bead Drops: Thread needle with long double strand of white sewing thread. At all the intersections of the outer strands in Sections 3 and 5, push the needle through the double knot leaving a 3″ tail. Thread a large blue bead and one small green and bring needle back through blue; make a double knot, drawing thread up tight. Tie; cut off excess thread.

Finishing: Smooth out strands and tie an overhand knot at proper place for desired height of planter. Trim off excess 1½″ above knot.

2. Bead-Strung Hanger—MATERIALS: Purchased basket with wire hanger; plastic beads—¾″ in diameter, 33 each in pink, red and mauve.

DIRECTIONS: Alternating colors, thread 18 beads onto the planter's three suspension wires. From remaining beads make three swags of 15 beads each on doubled thread; tie to the wires.

Slings 3, 4 and 5—*see Universal Diagram in* FIG. 2.

3. Red Sling—MATERIALS: Red jute, 14 strands, 2 yds. long; plastic beads—⁵⁄₁₆″ in diameter, 28 yellow; ¾″ in diameter, 28 faceted yellow (directions follow).

4. Rainbow Sling—MATERIALS: Yellow jute, 14 strands, 2 yds. long; plastic beads—⁵⁄₁₆″ in diameter, 98 each of red, yellow, green, blue and purple (directions follow).

5. Brown Sling—MATERIALS: Brown jute, 14 strands, 2 yds. long; plastic beads—⁵⁄₁₆″ in diameter, 406 brown.

GENERAL DIRECTIONS (for No. 4 and No. 5):

1. Align strands; tie overhand knot leaving a 5″ tassel.

2. Thread five beads on each tassel strand, securing at top and bottom with overhand knots.

3. Holding one strand in each hand, tie together in a double knot 3″ above the tassel; repeat 6 times for remaining strands.

4. Beginning with the first pair of knotted strands, thread six beads on the strand at right. Moving to the right to the second pair of knotted strands, thread six beads on the left-hand strand. Tie beaded strands together with double knot. Repeat for remaining strands.

5. *For Brown Sling*—repeat step 4 for three more rows. *For Rainbow Sling*—repeat step 4 for five more rows.

6. *Finishing:* See Finishing, White Sling, No. 1.

Red Sling (No. 3)—Follow GENERAL DIRECTIONS step 1, then step 3, tying double knots only 1½″ above tassel. Follow step 4, omitting beads and tying double knots 2″ apart. Repeat step 4 two more times. Attach yellow beads (*see Adding Big Bead Drops* in Sling No. 1). Finish as in White Sling No. 1.

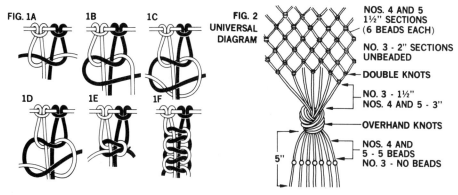

FIG. 1A 1B 1C

FIG. 2 UNIVERSAL DIAGRAM

NOS. 4 AND 5 1½″ SECTIONS (6 BEADS EACH)

NO. 3 - 2″ SECTIONS UNBEADED

1D 1E 1F

DOUBLE KNOTS

NO. 3 - 1½″ NOS. 4 AND 5 - 3″

OVERHAND KNOTS

NOS. 4 AND 5 - 5 BEADS NO. 3 - NO BEADS

5″

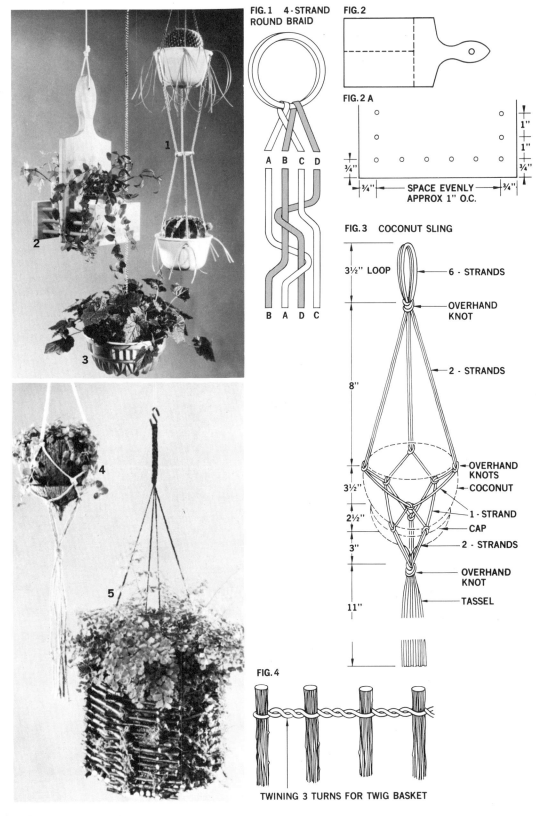

FIG. 1 4-STRAND ROUND BRAID

A B C D

B A D C

FIG. 2

FIG. 2 A

1"

1"

¾"

¾" SPACE EVENLY APPROX 1" O.C. ¾"

FIG. 3 COCONUT SLING

3½" LOOP ← 6 - STRANDS

OVERHAND KNOT

2 - STRANDS

8"

OVERHAND KNOTS

COCONUT

3½" 1 - STRAND

2½" CAP

2 - STRANDS

3" OVERHAND KNOT

TASSEL

11"

FIG. 4

TWINING 3 TURNS FOR TWIG BASKET

5 HANGING PLANTERS TO MAKE—Beautiful ways to hang your greenery in the air.

1. White Plastic Bowl Planters for Cactus—MATERIALS: Two large nondairy whipped topping containers; one spool natural color plastic lacing; two white plastic buckle rings without posts, 1¾″ in diameter.

DIRECTIONS: Punch or drill three holes in the rim of the bottom container and six holes in the top container, spacing evenly. To make nine 4-strand round braids, cut 18 strips of plastic lacing, each 42″ long. Following the diagram in FIG. 1, use two plastic strips for each braid to tie three 8″-long braids on the top ring, and six 8″-long braids on the bottom ring. Using the bottom ring, tie every other braid into every other hole in the top container securing each with square knot. Now knot the braids from the top ring into the remaining holes of the top container. Tie the remaining braids from the bottom ring to the bottom container. Cut all cord ends evenly.

2. Cutting Board Herb Planter—MATERIALS: Two cutting boards, 7″ wide x 15″ long or 2′ of 1x8 pine (you can save money by tracing one of your own cutting boards on pine and cutting out); 7′ of ⅜″ doweling; white glue; wood preservative; 2′ of ⅛″ nylon rope; sandpaper.

DIRECTIONS: Cut two 3½″x7″ end panels from one board (*see* FIG. 2), and sand edges smooth (or cut pieces from 1x8 pine). Mark the other cutting board (or board shape cut from pine) and drill ⅜″ holes (*see* FIG. 2A).

Now drill ⅜″ holes in the end panels, ½″ deep, *or less,* if board is less than ¾″ thick. To be sure holes will line up, place one piece against corresponding side of large board, mark location of holes by tracing. Cut ten 7¼″ lengths of ⅜″ doweling, slide into main board, placing a small amount of glue at center. Place a small amount of glue in holes of end panels; press onto dowels. Apply several coats of wood preservative, as directed. Draw cord through hole in board handle and tie loop for hanging from a ceiling hook.

3. Fancy Tube Mold Planter—MATERIALS: Fancy aluminum tube mold; tree tar; one nut; one eyebolt and two washers; non-rusting chain, 1 yd. (or a dog leash chain); small key ring.

DIRECTIONS: Paint the inside of the mold with tree tar. Place the washer on the tube; slip the bolt into it and secure from the bottom with another washer and a nut. Attach chain to eyebolt with a small key ring.

4. Coconut Planter—MATERIALS: One coconut; 1 qt. wood preservative; 1 ball 2-ply polished India twine; household bleach; handsaw.

DIRECTIONS: With the coconut held securely in a vise, or V-block—or by someone else wearing utility gloves—carefully cut off the end opposite the eyes with the handsaw. This little cap becomes the hanger "saucer." Drain off coconut milk and dig out the flesh. Soak the coconut in wood preservative, following directions on can. Meanwhile, bleach three 80″ strands of the jute to lighten it. After the cap was soaked in wood preservative, we stood it in ½″ bleach to lighten edges.

To Make Sling: Fold strands of twine in half to make six 40″ lengths. Make an overhand knot 3½″ from the fold to form a loop. To keep the strands taut as you work, hang the loop from a coat hook or around the neck of a hanger hooked over the top of a door. Using a pair of strands held together, make three overhand knots 8″ from the first knot (*see* FIG. 3). Now take one strand from one pair and one strand from the adjacent pair and make three more overhand knots 3½″ from the previous ones; repeat knotting, leaving 2½″. Now gather the strands and make one final overhand knot at bottom, 3″ from the last knots, leaving about a 10″–12″ tassel with ends trimmed even.

5. Twig Basket Planter—MATERIALS: For our 7″-high octagon we used 96 twigs about ¼″ in diameter for the side panels, each cut 5½″ long, and fifteen 12″-long slightly thicker twigs (about ⅜″ in diameter) for the bottom; waxed brown thread, one large spool.

Note: Our twigs were cut from trimmed cherry tree branches. (If you use fallen twigs, make sure they are not dried out.) It is important to select fairly straight pieces without too many cross branches.

DIRECTIONS: Divide the 5½″ twigs into 8 piles, 12 twigs each. The panels are made separately, then interlocked to form the octagon. To make one panel, cut two 50″ lengths of thread. Fold in half, around a twig, ¾″ from the twig end (*see* FIG. 4) Crisscross the threads to twine three times, then add another twig; repeat until all 12 twigs are used and knot threads at the end; cut off excess. Now use the other piece of thread to assemble the opposite end. Repeat for remaining seven piles of twigs. The twining between the twigs allows just nough room to insert the twigs from the next panel when it comes time to interlock the octagon.

Interlocking the Panels: Cut a yard of thread off the spool and knot it around one twig where you tied off the twisted threads. Interlock another panel into the first so that the twig threads are as close as possible to each other. Slip the other end of the knotted thread into a tapestry needle and weave it back and forth around the twig threads to hold the panels together; knot at the end. Add remaining panels the same way, being sure to raise or lower the height by one twig every other panel to keep the basket height even all around.

Basket Bottom: Turn the basket over and slip seven 12″ twigs in place at the center part of the basket under the first row of twigs. Knot each twig end in place, over the cross twig that covers it. Now slip four twigs in place on each side of the first ones. Mark these twigs with a pen so you can cut off the excess.

For Braided Hangers: Cut twelve 1-yd. lengths of thread, and use three for each braid. Align three threads and fold in half around one top twig of the basket. Using two threads held together as one, make a pigtail braid about 15″ long and secure temporarily with a paper clip. Make another braid on the opposite panel, then on the middle panels between the first two, giving you braids at North, South, East and West. Bring all the braid-end threads together. Divide into three groups and make another pigtail braid 8″ long. Fold this braid in half to form a loop and secure it by binding with the end threads. Pull excess through binding.

JOINING SQUARE CORNERS

WOODEN FLOWERPOT COVERS—The natural look of wood grain, highlighted by color, plus a protective wax coating, make our vase and flowerpot covers both beautiful and practical.

MATERIALS: *For tall sleeve:* ½x10 clear pine, 2′; 1¼″ brads; Minwax—Americolor #102, Lexington Green; 32-oz. juice bottle "vase." *For short sleeve:* 1x8 clear pine, 2′; 4d or 1½″ finishing nails; Minwax—Americolor #103 Liberty Blue; small olive oil bottle to hold flowers.

DIRECTIONS—*Cutting:* For *tall sleeve,* cut four 4″x11″ pieces of ½″ thick pine. *For short sleeve,* cut four 6″ lengths of 1x8. For *both sleeves,* fasten as shown. Finish with two coats of stain and wax, following package directions. (Nails may be countersunk and filled before finishing.)

102

Prices slashed on clothes and accessories any man would enjoy receiving

It's virtually impossible these days to find really nice gifts for men that cost less than $10. That's why we are so proud of the 24 selections in this chapter. Those who can knit will be pleased with the variety of hats, scarves and sweaters. We even give directions for crocheted loafers! For those who would rather sew, there are ideas galore—a shave sarong from a towel, a drip-dry robe from an on-sale sheet, a hang-up toilet kit for his business trips. Even a child can make Dad the stenciled work gloves and handy chamois travel bags.

directions for item shown above appear on following page

103

MAN'S OR BOY'S KNITTED CAP–Stockinette and cable-knit stitches make this man's or boy's cap extra warm. One size fits all. Directions are given for a man's ski cap which fits big boys, too.

MATERIALS: Bernat Krysta (2 oz. skeins): 2 skeins; Bernat-Aero knitting needles, No. 13, OR ANY SIZE NEEDLES WHICH WILL OBTAIN THE STITCH GAUGE BELOW.

GAUGE: 5 sts = 2"; 7 rows = 2".

DIRECTIONS–**Cuff:** Cast on 67 sts. *Row 1* (right side): * P 1, (k 1, p 1) twice; k 6. Rpt from * across ending with p 1. *Rows 2 and 4:* K 1 * p 6, k 1, (p 1, k 1) twice. Rpt from * across. *Row 3:* * P 1, (k 1, p 1) twice; *sl next 2 sts onto a toothpick and hold in front of work, k next 2 sts, k 2 sts from toothpick*–**front cable made;** k 2. Rpt from * across ending with p 1. *Row 5:* * P 1, (k 1, p 1) twice; k 2, *sl next 2 sts on toothpick and hold in back of work, k next 2 sts, k 2 sts from toothpick*– **back cable made.** Rpt from * across ending with p 1. *Row 6:* Rpt Row 2. Rpt Rows 3 through 6 for pat. Work in pat until total length is 6" ending with Row 5. This completes cuff; reverse pat as follows:

Cap: *Row 1:* With wrong side of Cuff facing, p 1, * k 6, p 1, (k 1, p 1) twice. Rpt from * across. *Rows 2 and 4 (wrong side):* * K 1, (p 1, k 1) twice; p 6. Rpt from * across ending k 1. *Row 3:* P 1, * front cable over 4 sts, k 2, p 1, (k 1, p 1) twice. Rpt from * across. *Row 5:* P 1, * k 2, back cable over 4 sts, p 1, (k 1, p 1) twice. Rpt from * across. *Row 6:* Rpt Row 2. Rpt Rows 3 through 6 of Cap until total length is 12" ending with Row 6. *Top Shaping: Row 1:* P 1, * work in pat over 6 sts, (k 2 tog) twice; p 1. Rpt from * across–55 sts. *Row 2:* K 1, * p 8, k 1. Rpt from * across. *Row 3:* K 2 tog, k 1, * back cable over 4 sts, k 2 tog, p 1, k 2 tog. Rpt from * across ending k 2 tog, p 1–43 sts. *Row 4:* K 1, * p 6, k 1. Rpt from * across. *Row 5:* K 2 tog across ending k 1. Break yarn leaving a 16" length. Thread a needle with this length, draw through rem sts, pull up tightly and fasten securely; with same yarn, sew back seam.

SARONG–Turn your talents to menswear. You can make a shave sarong from a towel in no time.

Cut 19½" off each end of a bath-size towel. With right sides together and raw edges at waistline, stitch pieces together at selvages to form center back seam. Turn up 2" hem at bottom and iron in place with fusible webbing. Stitch hook portion of Velcro® waist closure to left edge on right side, 1" down from top and 5¾" from edge. Turn under 1" at top; zigzag over raw edge to form casing, stopping 1½" from right side edge. Pull elastic through casing, adjusting to fit man's waist size; stitch ends. Stitch remaining casing. Turn in side edges 1½" to form facings and fuse with webbing. Sew Velcro loops to inside top right edge. From remaining towel, cut 8¼" square pocket. Turn pocket top ⅝" to right side and stitch ⅝" wide seams; turn. Tuck raw edges under and edgestitch to the sarong.

MAN'S DRESSY DENIM SHIRT–Dress up a favorite shirt. Cut patterns for patchwork gingham yoke, cuffs. Add ¼" on all edges. Turn edges under; topstitch. Reinforce the cuff buttonholes.

WORK GLOVES–Cotton gloves are personalized for Mom or Dad with dime-store stencils and permanent felt-tip markers.

CHAMOIS TRAVEL BAGS–Sew dime-store chamois into tote bags; add stenciled markings and leather laces.

STENCILED SHOE BAGS–Easy-to-sew red flannel shoe bags (trace shoe for pattern) keep clothes clean when traveling.

MAN'S STRETCH BELT–Buy a leather buckle kit (fitted with a brass harness buckle) and stitch a strip of stretch belting to the ends–and you've got a super belt! Or you can add belting to the salvaged buckle portion of a worn-out belt.

104

MAN'S GARTER STITCH PULLOVER—A sweater he can wear with everything. It's speedy-to-make with the easy garter stitch. Directions are given for size Small (36–38). Changes for sizes Medium (40–42) and Large (44–46) are in parentheses. The Small size (36–38) can also be used for older teenagers or for husky youngsters. Because young men seem to hate wearing anything tight, we made this sweater in the garter stitch which has lots of "give." The wide-open neckline is comfortable to wear over a dress shirt with regular collar, and looks terrific with a turtleneck jersey.

MATERIALS: Lion Brand Yarn, Knitting Worsted, 4-ply (4 oz. 100% wool skeins): 6(7,8) skeins of Natural Heather; knitting needles, 1 pair No. 11, OR ANY SIZE NEEDLES WHICH WILL OBTAIN THE STITCH GAUGE BELOW; 2 large st holders.

GAUGE: 3 sts = 1"; 9 rows (4½ ridges slightly stretched) = 2".

Note: Work with 2 strands of yarn held together throughout. Entire sweater is worked in garter st (k each row).

MEASUREMENTS:

SIZES:	SMALL (36–38)	MEDIUM (40–42)	LARGE (44–46)
CHEST:	38"	42"	46"
WIDTH ACROSS BACK OR FRONT AT UNDERARMS:	19"	21"	23"
WIDTH ACROSS SLEEVE AT UPPER ARM:	18"	20"	21"

DIRECTIONS: Starting at a sleeve edge with 2 strands of yarn held together, cast on 32(34,36) sts. Work in garter st (k each row) for 28 rows (14 ridges). *Row 29:* K 1, inc in next st, k across to last 2 sts, inc in next st, k 1—inc made at each end. *Rows 30 through 36:* K 7 rows. Rpt last 8 rows (Rows 29 through 36) until there are 48(50,52) sts, end with an inc row. Now inc one st at each end every other row until there are 56(60,64) sts. Work 4 rows even. *Next 2 Rows:* Continuing in garter st, at beg of each of next 2 rows cast on 38(40,42) sts for Back and Front—132(140,148) sts. Work even in garter st over these sts for 28(32,36) rows or 14(16,18) ridges.

Neck Shaping: *Row 1:* K 63(67,70) place these sts just worked on st holder for Back; bind off next 6(6,8) sts for side of neck; k rem sts. For Front, working in garter st over 63(67,70) sts on needle only, dec one st at next edge on next row, then every other row 3 times in all—60(64,67) sts. Work even for 16(16,18) more rows. Inc one st at neck edge on next row, then every other row 3 times in all—63(67,70) sts, end at neck edge; place these sts on another st holder. For Back, slip sts from first holder onto a needle; attach yarn at neck edge. Working in garter st, dec one st at neck edge on next row. Work even over 62(66,69) sts for 24(24,26) rows; inc one st at neck edge on next row, end at neck edge; cast on 6(6,8) sts for side of neck; slip Front sts onto free needle and k across these sts—132(140,148) sts. Work even over all sts for 28(32,36) rows on 14(16,18) ridges. Bind off 38(40,42) sts at beg of each of next 2 rows—56(60,64) sts rem. For Sleeve, continuing in garter st throughout, work 4 rows even. Dec one st at each end of next row, then every other row until there are 48(50,52) sts. Now, dec one st at each end every 8th row until 32(34,36) sts rem. Work even over rem sts for 28 rows (14 ridges). Be sure to have same number of rows as on first sleeve. Bind off.

Finishing: Pin sweater to measurements on a padded surface; cover with a damp cloth and allow to dry; do not press. Fold piece in half, matching ends of row. Sew side and sleeve seams. Turn up cuffs at lower edges of sleeves.

MAN'S AND BOY'S KNITTED COSSACK HAT AND GLOVES—These sets for father and son, are knitted from warm, tweedy-look yarn.

Man's Knitted Cossack Hat and Gloves: Directions for Gloves are given for Small Size. Changes for Medium and Large Sizes are in parentheses. Hat will fit all Sizes.

MATERIALS: Coats & Clark's Red Heart "Wintuk" Sport Yarn, 2-ply, 2 oz. "Tangle-proof" skeins, No. 327 Camel and No. 858 Navy: 2 ozs. of each color for Hat; 2(3,4) ozs. of each color for Gloves; knitting needles, 1 pair No. 6; double pointed needles, 1 set No. 3 OR ANY SIZE NEEDLES WHICH WILL OBTAIN THE STITCH GAUGE BELOW; crochet hook, Size G; stitch markers.

GAUGE: On No. 6 needles: 5 sts = 1"; 7 rows = 1".
　　　　 On No. 3 needles: 11 sts = 2"; 8 rows = 1".

GLOVES—FINISHED MEASUREMENTS			
SIZES:	SMALL	MEDIUM	LARGE
MEASUREMENTS AROUND PALM:	8"	9"	10"

Note: Work with one strand of each color held together throughout for each article.

Man's Hat: Starting at outer edge of ribbed band with one strand each of Camel and Navy held tog and No. 6 needles, cast on 112 sts. *Row 1:* P 2, * k 5, p 3. Rpt from * across, ending with p 1 instead of p 3. *Row 2:* K 1, * p 5, k 3. Rpt from * across, ending with k 2 instead of k 3. Rpt first and 2nd rows alternately until 16 rows of ribbing in all have been completed. Now work as follows: *Rows 1 through 18:* Work in st st (k 1 row, p 1 row). *Row 19 (right side):* K 2, * p 5, k 3. Rpt from * across, ending with k 1 instead of k 3. *Row 20:* P 1, * k 5, p 3. Rpt from * across, ending with p 2 instead of p 3. *Row 21:* K 2, * p 2, *working loosely, k in front, back and front of next st (3 loops made in one st); turn, p 3; turn, k 3 tog—* **bobble st made;** p 2, k 3. Rpt from * across, ending last repeat with k 1 instead of k 3. *Rows 22 and 23:* Rpt Rows 20 and 19. Last 5 rows form Bobble Band. *Row 24:* P across —112 sts. *Top Shaping: Row 1 (right side):* K 2 tog—**dec made;** k 52, sl 1, k 1, psso— **another dec made;** place a marker on needle; k 2 tog, k 52, sl 1, k 1, psso—4 sts decreased. *Row 2:* Sl marker, p across. *Row 3 through Row 6:* Sl marker, work in st st, ending with a p row. *Row 7:* K 2 tog, k across to within 2 sts before marker, sl 1, k 1, psso, sl marker, k 2 tog, k across to within last 2 sts, sl 1, k 1, psso. Rpt last 6 rows (Rows 2 through 7) 4 more times—88 sts. If necessary, work even in st st until length is 4¼″ from last row of Bobble Band, ending with a p row. Bind off. Using a darning needle and same yarn, sew ends of rows together for back seam; sew top seam from back seam to center front. Turn over ribbing band to right side at lower edge.

Man's Gloves: *Right Glove:* Starting at lower edge of cuff with one strand each of Camel and Navy held tog and using 2 dp needles tog, cast on 45(51,57) sts. Remove one needle; divide sts evenly among 3 needles, having 15(17,19) sts on each needle. Being careful not to twist sts, join. Mark end of each rnd. Work in rnds of k 2, p 1 ribbing for 2½(2¾,3)″, dec 0(1,2) sts on last rnd—45(50,55) sts. *Bobble Band: Rnd 1:* * K 2, p 3. Rpt from * around. *Rnd 2:* Rpt last rnd. *Rnd 3:* * K 2, p 1 working loosely, *K in front, back and front of next st (3 loops made in one st); turn, p 3; turn, k 3 tog—***bobble st made;** p 1. Rpt from * around. *Rnds 4 and 5:* Rpt first rnd. *Thumb Gore: Rnd 1:* K 1, place a marker on needle. *p and k in next st—***inc made;** k and p in next st, place a marker on needle; k to end of rnd. *Rnds 2 and 3:* Sl markers, k around. *Rnd 4:* K 1, sl marker, inc in next st as before, k across to within one st before next marker, inc in next st, sl marker, k to end of rnd. Rpt last 3 rnds (Rnds 2, 3 and 4) until there are 14(14,16) sts between markers. Work 2 rnds even. *Next rnd:* K 1, removing markers, sl next 14(14,16) sts onto a double strand of yarn; cast on 2 sts for inner side of thumb, k to end of rnd—45(50,55) sts. Work even in st st (k each rnd) for 1½″ from thumb opening or until glove, when tried on, reaches base of fingers. *Little Finger:* K 18(19,20) for palm, sl these sts just made onto a double strand of yarn; k next 10(12,13) sts for Little Finger, sl rem sts onto a separate double strand of yarn for back of hand. Divide sts for Little Finger on 3 needles, cast on 2 sts for inner side of finger. Join—12(14,15) sts. Work in rnds of st st for 2(2¼,2½)″ or ¼″ shorter than desired length. *Tip Shaping: Rnd 1:* * K 1, k 2 tog. Rpt from * around, ending with k 0(2,0). *Rnd 2:* K around. *Rnd 3:* * K 2 tog. Rpt from * around. Break off, leaving a 6″ length of yarn. Thread a darning needle with this end, draw through rem sts, pull up tightly and fasten off securely on wrong side. *Ring Finger:* From palm of hand, sl last 5(5,6) sts from double strand onto a needle, attach yarn and with another needle, pick up and k 2 sts along base of last finger made, from back of hand, k 5(6,7) sts from back strand of yarn, cast on 2 sts—14(15,17) sts. Divide sts on 3 needles and work in rnds of st st for 2½(2¾,3)″ or ¼″ shorter than desired length. *Tip Shaping: Rnd 1:* * K 1, k 2 tog. Rpt from * around, ending with k 2(0,2). *Rnd 2:* K around. *Rnd 3:* * K 2 tog. Rpt from * around. Break off, leaving a 6″ length of yarn. Finish same as for last finger made. *Middle Finger:* From palm of hand, sl 5(6,6) sts from strand onto a needle, attach yarn and pick up and k 2 sts along base of last finger made, from back of hand, k 6(6,7) sts from strand of yarn, cast on 2 sts—15(16,17) sts. Divide sts on 3 needles and work in rnds of st st for 3(3¼,3½)″ or ¼″ less than desired length. *Tip Shaping: Rnd 1:* * K 1, k 2 tog. Rpt from * around, ending with k 0(1,0). Break off, leaving a 6″ length of yarn. Finish same as before. *Index Finger:* Sl rem palm sts onto a needle; attach yarn, pick up and k 2 sts along base of last finger made, k rem sts on back strand—16(17,18) sts. Divide sts on 3 needles and work in st st until length of finger is same as ring finger before tip shaping. *Tip Shaping: Rnd 1:* * K 1, k 2 tog. Rpt from * around, ending with k 1(2,0). *Rnd 2:* K around. *Rnd 3:* K 2 tog around, ending with k 1(0,0). Break off, leaving a 6″ length and finish as before. *Thumb:* Sl sts of thumb gore onto 2 needles, with 3rd needle, pick up and k 2(3.2) sts along the cast-on sts on thumb opening—16(17,18) sts. Divide sts on 3 needles and k around. Work in st st, dec one st at center of picked-up sts on inner side of thumb on next rnd; then work even over 15(16,17) sts for 2(2¼,2½)″. Shape Tip same as for Middle Finger.

Left Glove: Work same as for Right Glove until the Bobble Band has been completed. *Thumb Gore: Rnd 1:* K around to within last 3 sts, place a marker on needle, inc in each of next 2 sts, place a marker on needle, k 1. Position of thumb gore is now established. Work to correspond with Right Glove up to base of fingers. *Little Finger:* K 17(19,22) sts, sl these sts just made onto a double strand of yarn for back of hand; k 10(12,13) sts for Little Finger, sl rem sts on a separate double strand for palm of hand; cast on 2 sts for inner side of finger. Divide sts on 3 needles and complete finger same as for Right Glove. Work other fingers to correspond with Right Glove.

Boy's Knitted Cossack Hat and Gloves: Directions for Gloves given for Small Size. Changes for Medium and Large Sizes are in parentheses. Hat will fit all Sizes.

MATERIALS: Coats & Clark's Red Heart "Wintuk" Clansman Sport Yarn, 2-ply, 1¾ ozs. "Tangleproof" skeins; 3½ ozs. for Hat; 3½(4¼, 5) ozs. for Gloves; knitting needles, 1 pair No. 6 and double-pointed needles, 1 set each No. 2 and No. 6 OR ANY SIZE NEEDLES WHICH WILL OBTAIN THE STITCH GAUGE BELOW; crochet hook, Size G; stitch markers.

GAUGE: On No. 6 needles: 5 sts = 1″; 7 rows = 1″.
On No. 2 needles: 6 sts = 1″; 17 rows = 2″.

GLOVES—FINISHED MEASUREMENTS			
SIZE:	SMALL	MEDIUM	LARGE
MEASUREMENTS AROUND PALM:	5¾″	6½″	7½″

Note: Work with 2 strands of yarn held together throughout for each article.

Boy's Hat: Starting at outer edge of ribbed band with 2 strands of yarn held together and long No. 6 needles, cast on 97 sts. *Row 1:* P 2, * k 5, p 3. Rpt from * across, ending last rpt with p 2 instead of p 3. *Row 2:* K 2, * p 5, k 3. Rpt from * across, ending last rpt with k 2 instead of k 3. Rpt first and 2nd rows alternately 5 more times, ending with 2nd row. Now work in st st (k1 row, p1 row) until total length is 4″, ending with a p row. *Bobble Band: Row 1:* K 2, * p 5, k 3. Rpt from * across, ending last rpt with k 2 instead of k 3. *Row 2:* P 2, * k 5, p 3. Rpt from * across, ending with p 2 instead of p 3. *Row 3:* K 2, * p 2, *working loosely, k in front, back and front of next* st (3 loops made in one st); turn, p 3; turn, k 3 tog—**bobble st made;** p 2, k 3. Rpt from * across, ending last rpt with k 2 instead of k 3. *Rows 4 and 5:* Rpt Rows 2 and 1 of Bobble Band. Last 5 rows form Bobble Band. Now, starting with a p row, work 5 rows in st st, thus ending with a p row and dec one st on last row. *Top Shaping: Row 1:* K 1, k 2 tog—**dec made;** k 42 sl 1, k 1, psso—**another dec made;** k 1, place a marker on needle; k 1, k 2 tog, k 42, sl 1, k1, psso, k 1 —4 sts dec. Always slip marker. *Rows 2,3 and 4:* P 1 row, k 1 row, p 1 row. *Row 5:* K 1, k 2 tog, k across to within last 3 sts before marker, sl 1, k 1, psso, k 1, sl marker, k 1, k 2 tog, k to within last 3 sts, sl 1, k 1 psso, k 1. Rpt last 4 rows (Rows 2 through 5) 3 more times—76 sts. Work even in st st until length is 4¼″ from last row of Bobble Band, ending with a p row. Bind off. Using a darning needle and same yarn, sew ends of rows tog for back seam; sew top seam from seam to center front. Turn over ribbing band to right side at lower edge. Push in corners at top edge.

Boy's Gloves: *Right Glove:* Starting at lower edge of cuff with 2 strands of yarn held tog and using 2 No. 2 dp needles tog, cast on 36(42,45) sts; remove 1 needle; divide sts evenly on 3 No. 2 needles, having 12(14,15) sts on each needle. Being careful not to twist sts, join. Mark end of each rnd. Work in rnds of k 2, p 1 ribbing for 2(2¼,2½)″, dec 1(2,0) st on last rnd—35(40,45) sts. *Bobble Band: Rnd 1:* * K 2, p 3. Rpt from * around. *Rnd 2:* Rpt last rnd. *Rnd 3:* * K 2, p 1, make bobble st in next st same as for Hat, p 1. Rpt from * around. *Rnds 4 and 5:* Rpt Rnd One. *Thumb Gore: Rnd 1:* K 1, place a marker on needle; *p and k in next st*—**inc made**; *k and p in next st*—**another inc made**; place a marker on needle; k to end of rnd. *Rnds 2 and 3:* Slipping markers, k around. *Rnd 4:* K 1, sl marker, inc in next st as before, k to within last st before next marker, inc in next st, sl marker, k to end of rnd. Rpt last 3 rnds (rnds 2, 3 and 4) until there are 12(12,14) sts between markers. Work 2 rnds even. *Next rnd:* K 1, removing markers, sl next 12(12,14) sts onto a double strand of yarn; cast on 2 sts for inner side of thumb, k to end of rnd—35(40,45) sts. Work even in rnds of st st (k each rnd) for 1¼(1½,1½)″ from thumb opening or until glove, when tried on, reaches base of fingers. *Little Finger:* K 13(15,17), sl these sts just worked onto a double strand of yarn for palm of hand; k next 8(9,10) sts for Little Finger; sl rem 14(16,18) sts onto a separate double strand for back of hand. Divide sts for Little Finger on 3 needles, cast on 2 sts for inner side of finger. Join—10(11,12) sts. Work in rnds of st st for 1½(1⅝,1¾)″ or ¼″ shorter than desired length. *Tip Shaping: Rnd 1:* * K 1, k 2 tog. Rpt from * around, ending with k 1(2,0). *Rnd 2:* K around. *Rnd 3:* * K 2 tog. Rpt from * around, ending with k 1(0,0). Break off, leaving a 6″ length of yarn. Thread a darning needle with this end, draw through sts and pull up tightly; fasten off. *Ring Finger:* From palm of hand, sl last 4(5,5) sts from strand of yarn onto a needle; attach double strand of yarn and with another needle, pick up and k 2 sts along base of last finger; from back strand, k 4(5,6) sts, cast on 2 sts—12(14,15) sts. Divide sts on 3 needles and work in rnds of st st for 1¾(2,2¼)″ or ¼″ shorter than desired length. *Tip Shaping: Rnd 1:* * K 1, k 2 tog. Rpt from * around, ending with k 0(2,0). *Rnd 2:* K around. *Rnd 3:* K 2 tog. Rpt from * around. Finish same as for Little Finger. *Middle Finger:* From palm of hand, sl 4(5,6) sts from strand onto a needle; attach double strand of yarn and pick up and k 2 sts along base of last finger; from the back of hand, k 4(5,5) sts from strand of yarn, cast on 2 sts—12(14,15) sts. Divide sts on 3 needles and working finger ½″ longer, work same as for Ring Finger. *Index Finger:* Sl rem palm sts onto a needle; attach double strand, pick up and k 2(3,2) sts along base of last finger, k rem sts on back strand—13(14,15) sts. Divide sts on 3 needles. Work in st st until length of finger is same as ring finger. *Tip Shaping: Rnd 1:* * K 1, k 2 tog. Rpt from * around, ending with k 1(2,0). *Rnd 2:* K around. *Rnd 3:* * K 2 tog. Rpt from * around, ending with k 1(0,0). Finish same as for other fingers. *Thumb:* Sl sts of thumb gore onto 2 needles, with another needle, pick up and k 2(3,2) sts along the cast-on sts on thumb opening—14(15,16) sts. Divide sts on 3 needles and, dec one st at inner side of thumb on first rnd, work until ¼″ shorter than desired length. Shape Tip and finish same as for Index Finger.

Left Glove: Work same as for Right Glove until Bobble Band has been completed. *Thumb Gore: Rnd 1:* K around to within last 3 sts, place a marker on needle, inc in each of next 2 sts, place a marker on needle; k 1. Position of thumb gore is now established. Work to correspond with Right Glove up to base of fingers. *Little Finger:* K 14(16,18) sts, sl these sts just worked onto a double strand of yarn for back of hand; k 8(9,10) sts for Little Finger; sl rem sts onto a separate double strand of yarn for palm of hand; cast on 2 sts. Divide sts on 3 needles and complete finger same as for Right Hand.

Work other fingers to correspond with Right Glove.

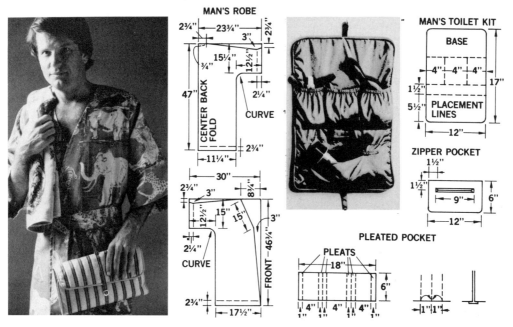

MAN'S DRIP-DRY ROBE AND HANG-UP TOILET KIT—This terrific drip-dry robe is made from a twin-size sheet. The hang-up toilet kit is perfect for travel.
Man's Drip-Dry Robe—MATERIALS: One single flat sheet.
DIRECTIONS: Make paper pattern for front and back, following diagram. For back neck facing and front facing, trace the edges of the pattern for outside lines, then draw inside lines 3″ away. Cut pocket, 9¼″x11⅝″.
Sewing:
1. Open both hems. Cut 6″ off length, for belt.
2. Fold sheet lengthwise. Cut back and back neck facing (both on fold), front and front facing. Pocket is cut from single fabric. (Be sure to cut all pieces in same direction if using a sheet like ours.)
3. Sew shoulder and underarm seams. Clip curves, press seams open.
4. Seam facings at shoulders. Press under ¼″ at inside edge and edgestitch.
5. With right sides together, sew facing to robe. Trim seams; clip curves. Turn and press.
6. Stitch 2″ hems at sleeve and bottom edges. Topstitch ⅜″ from faced edges.
7. Make 2″ hem in top of pocket, turn under edges and topstitch to robe at comfortable position.
8. Fold belt in half lengthwise. Stitch long edges. Turn and press. Slipstitch ends.
Man's Hang-up Toilet Kit—MATERIALS: ⅜ yd. water-repellant fabric for inside base; ½ yd. lengthwise striped fabric for outside base; 12″x34″ piece of batting; one package ½″ bias tape; 9″ zipper; 12″ elastic, ⅜″ wide; ½″ buckle.
DIRECTIONS: Make paper patterns for base and two pockets, following diagram. Cut base from outside and inside fabric and from a double layer of batting; cut two pockets in inside fabric; cut two strips of outside fabric 7½″x1½″ and 5″x 1½″ for straps.
Sewing:
1. Turn under edges and ends of straps ¼″. Fold in half lengthwise right sides out. Edgestitch.
2. Quilt outside base to batting on stripes.
3. Stitch long strip to outside, centered, 5″ from bottom edge. Sew buckle to one end of short strap. Stitch other end, centered, 2½″ from top.
4. *Zipper pocket:* Draw 9″ center line as shown in diagram. Slash, clipping to

corners ½″ from each end. Fold under edges ¼″; place over zipper and edge-stitch. Turn under pocket top ½″. Pin pocket to inside base, with bottom and side edges matching. Edgestitch.

5. *Elastic pocket:* Turn under top ¼″ and again ½″ to form casing. Stitch. Turn under bottom ½″. Make pleats at bottom edges to form three 4″ pockets (*see* diagram). Leave ¼″ free at side edges by making pleat only ¾″. Position on inside base 1½″ above lower pocket. Edgestitch across bottom, securing pleats. Pull 12″ of elastic through casing. Edgestitch sides in place, catching elastic but leaving pleat free. Distribute gathers evenly and topstitch between pleats from top to bottom to form pockets.

6. Stitch inside base to quilted base, right sides out. Bind stitched edges with tape.

PIPE RACK AND HUMIDOR SET—The pipe rack is designed to hold his very special pipe. It's easy to make from scrap pine lumber and dowels. The humidor is half-round strips of molding applied to coffee can with water-thinned white glue.

Pipe Rack—MATERIALS: One 12″ length 1x6 clear pine; ⅜″ doweling; ⅛″ doweling; plastic resin glue; rubber bands; adhesive-backed felt.

DIRECTIONS: Drill six ⅜″ holes (*see* diagram). Sand pine to round off corners and top. From ⅜″ doweling, cut two 4″ lengths and three 1½″ lengths. From ⅛″ doweling, cut one 3¾″ length. Sand dowels (*see* Note). Drill a ⅛″ hole 1″ from one end of each 4″ dowel, *only half way into dowel, not through*. Mix glue as directed on can. Glue the ⅛″ dowel into the holes in the 4″ dowels to connect them. While still wet, glue to the pipe rack. Glue remaining 1½″ dowels to the base, (*see* Note) where indicated. Remove excess glue. Finish underside with felt.

Note: To Sand and Glue Dowels—Sand ends of dowels smooth by rotating over sandpaper on a flat surface. *To glue,* start dowel into the hole. Turn object over and add a few drops of glue in hole. Spread glue around with a match or tooth-pick. Turn object back over and press dowels down until flush with back or bottom. If tight, dowels may be hammered down with a mallet or a block of wood—*never with a conventional iron hammer.*

Humidor—MATERIALS: 1 tall 1-pound coffee can with plastic top (plus 1 extra plastic top); 1 heavy brown paper bag; white glue; 8′ of ¾″ half-round molding; small piece of sponge.

DIRECTIONS: Cut molding into seventeen 5″ lengths; cut a piece of brown paper 4½″x17″. Brush both sides with a mixture of 2 parts glue to 1 part water (mix on wax paper). Wrap tightly around can, centering between can top and bottom. Sand ends smooth. Place four rubber bands around can. Place one plastic top on can bottom. Glue flat side of molding pieces in place by sliding each under the rubber bands. When dry, remove bands. Place dampened sponge in humidor, when you fill with tobacco. Cover with plastic top. Place humidor where indicated.

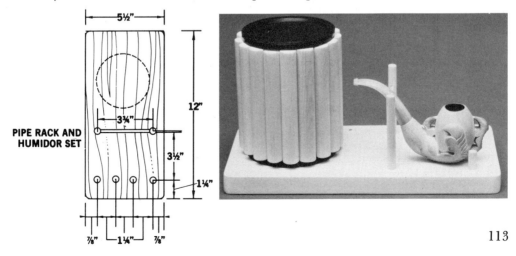

PIPE RACK AND HUMIDOR SET

COLLEGIATE STRIPED HAT/SCARF SETS—Your guys will love winter warmers made in their school colors.

Vertical Stripe Scarf and Hat: Scarf measures 8½"x68", plus fringe. Directions are given for hat to fit all sizes.

MATERIALS: Bucilla Knitting Worsted, 4-ply (4 oz. balls): 2 balls Blue (A), 1 ball Red (B); knitting needles, 1 pair No. 9, OR ANY SIZE NEEDLES WHICH WILL OBTAIN THE STITCH GAUGE BELOW.

GAUGE: 4 sts = 1"; 8 rows (4 ridges) = 1".

Scarf: Starting at one long edge with A, cast on 270 sts. Work in garter st (k each row) for 22 rows (11 ridges). Mark first row for right side. Break off A; attach B.

With B, continue in garter st for 22 more rows (11 more ridges). Break off B; attach A. With A, work 22 additional rows (11 more ridges) in garter st. Bind off loosely.

Fringe: Wind A 5 times around a 7″ square of cardboard; cut at one edge, making 14″ strands. Hold strands together and fold in half to form a loop. With right side of scarf facing, working along ends of rows, insert a large size hook from back to front in end of first row, draw loop of strands through st on hook, draw loose ends through loop, pull tightly to form a knot. Tie 3 more A groups of 5 strands each evenly spaced along A stripe. Tie 4 B groups of 5 strands each evenly spaced along B stripe and 4 A groups along next A stripe. Tie fringe across opposite end in same way. Trim evenly.

Hat: Starting at center back with A, cast on 45 sts. *Rows 1 through 6:* Work 6 rows in garter st (k each row). *Row 7 (Short row):* K 37. Turn. *Row 8:* K across all sts. *Rows 9 through 16:* Rpt Rows 1 through 8. Break off A; attach B. *Rows 17 through 32:* With B, work same as for Rows 1 through 16. Break off B; attach A. Rpt Rows 1 through 32 four more times—there are 5 stripes A and 5 B in all. Bind off. Sew bound-off edge to cast-on edge for back seam, forming a tubular piece. Using a darning needle, gather narrow end of tube closely together and fasten securely. Fold 2½″ cuff to right side at lower edge.

Pompon: Cut 2 cardboard circles, each 3″ in diameter. Cut a hole 1½″ in diameter in center of each circle. Cut 4 strands of A each 8 yards long. Place cardboard circles tog and holding the 4 strands tog, wind yarn around double circle, drawing yarn through center opening and over edge until center hole is filled. Cut yarn around outer edge, between circles. Double ½ yard of A, slip between cardboard circles and tie securely around strands of pompon. Remove cardboard and trim evenly. Tack to center top of hat.

Horizontal Stripe Scarf and Hat: Scarf measures 8½″x66″, plus fringe. Directions are given for hat to fit all sizes.

MATERIALS: Lion Brand Knitting Worsted, 4-ply (4 oz. balls); 2 balls each of Green (A) and White (B); knitting needles, 1 pair No. 8, OR ANY SIZE NEEDLES WHICH WILL OBTAIN THE STITCH GAUGE BELOW.

GAUGE: *Ribbing*—6 sts = 1″; 6 rows = 1″.

Scarf: Starting at one narrow edge with A, cast on 53 sts. *Row 1 (right side):* K 1, * p 1, k 1; rpt from * across. *Row 2:* P 1, * k 1, p 1; rpt from * across. Rpt Rows 1 and 2 alternately for pat. *Rows 3 through 12:* Rpt Rows 1 and 2 alternately 5 times. Break off A; attach B. Working as Rows 1 and 2 throughout, * make 12 rows B and 12 rows A; rpt from * until total length is approximately 66″ ending with 12 rows A. Bind off in ribbing.

Fringe: Wind B several times around an 8″ square of cardboard; cut at one edge, making 16″ strands. Continue to cut strands as needed. Hold 5 strands together and fold in half to form a loop; with right side facing, insert a crochet hook from back to front in first st on one end of scarf, loop crochet hook from back to front in first st on one end of scarf, draw loop through, draw loose ends through loop on hook; pull tightly to form a knot. Tie a 5-strand group in same way in every 4th st across end of scarf. Tie fringe across opposite end in same way. Trim evenly.

Hat: Starting at outer edge of cuff with A, cast on 95 sts. Work same as for Scarf until total length is about 12″, ending with 10 rows B. *Dec Row:* With B, k 1, * k 2 tog; rpt from * across. Leaving a 12″ length, break off yarn. Thread a darning needle with this end and draw through rem sts. Pull Thread tightly tog and fasten securely on wrong side.

Pompon: Cut 4 strands each of A and B, each 4 yds. long. Using A first, then B strands, work same as for Pompon for Vertical Stripe Hat. Tack pompon to center top of hat. Fold 2½″ cuff to right side at lower edge.

BUCKLED CROCHETED LOAFERS—Pick up some striped canvas belting, a brass buckle kit and you can make this Belt—instantly. And, how about crocheted loafers with classic buckle trim! Directions are given for size Small (9½–10). Changes for sizes Medium (10½–11) and Large (11½–12) are in parentheses.

MATERIALS: Phentex Twist Yarn: 1(2,2) skeins Brown or desired color; crochet hook, Size I OR ANY SIZE HOOK WHICH WILL OBTAIN THE STITCH GAUGE BELOW; 2 narrow buckles (or desired ornaments), about 2¾″ long.

GAUGE: 7 sc = 2″; 4 sc rnds = 1″.

Note: Work with 2 strands of yarn held together throughout. Wrong side of sts is right side of slipper; this will give you a knobby texture.

Slipper (*make 2*)—**Sole:** Starting at center with 2 strands of yarn held together, ch 21(24,28). *Rnd 1:* 3 sc in 2nd ch from hook, sc in each of next 8 ch, hdc in each of next 3 ch, dc in each of next 7(10,14) ch, hdc in each of next 3 ch, sc in each of next 8 ch—44(50,58) sts. Do not join rnds, mark beg of each rnd. *Rnd 2:* 2 sc in each of next 3 sc, sc in each st to within 5-dc group at toe; 2 sc in each of next 2 dc, 3 sc in next dc, 2 sc in each of next 2 dc, sc in each rem st to end of rnd—53(59,67) sts. *Rnd 3:* (Sc in next sc, 2 sc in next sc) 3 times; sc in each sc around—56(62,70) sts. *Rnd 4:* (Sc in each of next 2 sc, 2 sc in next sc) 3 times; sc in each of next 20(23,27) sc, (2 sc in next sc, sc in next sc) twice; 3 sc in next st, (sc in next sc, 2 sc in next sc) twice; sc in each of next 18(21,25) sc—65(71,79) sts. *Rnd 5:* 2 sc in next sc, (sc in each of next 3 sc, 2 sc in next sc) 3 times; sc in each next 10 sc, hdc in each of next 3 sts, dc in each of next 6(9,13) sc, (dc in each of next 2 sts, 2 dc in next st) 5 times; dc in each of next 6(9,13) sts, hdc in each of next 3 sts, sc in each rem st—74(80,88) sts. *Rnd 6 (Sole Ridge):* Working in front loop only of each st, sc in each st around. Do not break off. Back loops of sts form a ridge on right side of slipper.

Upper Of Slipper—*Rnd 7:* Working through both loops of each st, sc in each st around. *Rnds 8 and 9:* Rpt last rnd twice. At end of last rnd sl st in next 2 sc. Break off and fasten. Now work short rows for back shaping as follows: With a small safety pin, mark center dc of 5-dc group at toe on Rnd 1. Mark sc directly in line with marked dc on last rnd for center of toe. Do not turn. *Row 1:* Sk 10 sc after center of toe st on last rnd, attach double strand to the 11th st, sc in same st, working toward back of slipper, sc in each sc to within last 10 sts before marked center front st, sl st in next sc; do not work over rem sts. Break off and fasten. *Row 2:* Do not turn; sk first 4 sc at beg of last row made, attach yarn to next (5th) sc, sc in same sc, sc in each sc to within last 4 sc of last row, sl st in next st, break off and fasten. Rpt last row 4(4,5) more times. Do not break off at end of last row. *Last Rnd:* Do not turn; sl st in each st around entire top edge of upper. Join with sl st to first st. Break off and fasten.

Tongue: Starting at side edge with 2 strands of yarn held together, ch 13(15,17). *Row 1:* 2 sc in 2nd ch from hook, sc in each ch to last ch, 2 sc in last ch—14(16,18)

For knit and crochet abbreviations box, see Methods (Chapter 11)

sc. Ch 1, turn. *Row 2:* 2 sc in first sc, sc in each sc to last sc, 2 sc in last sc—inc made at each rnd. Ch 1, turn. *Rows 3 and 4:* Rpt Row 2 twice—20(22,24) sc. Ch 1, turn. *Row 5:* Sc in each sc across. Ch 1, turn. *Rows 6 and 7:* Rpt last row twice. Ch 1, turn. *Row 8: Draw up a loop in each of first 2 sc, yarn over book, draw through all 3 loops on hook*—**dec made;** sc in each sc to last 2 sc, dec over last 2 sc. Ch 1, turn. Rpt last row 2 more times. Turn. *Next Row:* Sk first sc, sl st in each sc to last 2 sc, sk next sc, sl st in last sc. Break off and fasten. With knobby side of sts on the outside, place tongue in place, having center of one shaped end at center st of toe edge of upper; pin tongue evenly to top edge of upper, adjusting to most comfortable position when tried on. Using a large eyed darning needle and double yarn, from right side, overcast outer edge of tongue to top edge of slipper, forming a ridge on upper edge. Sew buckle across top of slipper.

MAN'S TURTLENECK DICKEY—Ribbing of alternate k sts and p sts. Directions are for one size to fit all, for either a man or woman.
MATERIALS: Bucilla Multi-Craft Yarn (2 oz.ball) or Bear Brand Twin-Pak Knitting Worsted (4 oz.ball) or Bear Brand Twin-Pak Machine-Washable Win-Knit (4 oz. ball): 7 oz. of White; knitting needles, 1 pair No. 9, OR ANY SIZE NEEDLES WHICH WILL OBTAIN THE STITCH GAUGE BELOW; 3 stitch holders; tapestry needle.
GAUGE: 9 sts *(when stretched)* = 2″; 5 rows = 1″.
Note: When using Knitting Worsted, use 2 strands held tog throughout.
Back: Starting at lower edge, cast on 57 sts. *Row 1:* P 1, * k 1, p 1. Rpt from * to end of row. *Row 2 (right side):* K 1, * p 1, k 1. Rpt from * to end of row. Mark the right side of work. These 2 rows establish ribbing. Rpt Rows 1 and 2 alternately until length is 6″ from beg ending with Row 2 (when measuring length be sure to stretch width to 12½″).
Shoulders: Purling the p sts and knitting the k sts, bind off the first 17 sts for shoulder, continue in ribbing as established until there are 23 sts on right-hand needle; slip these 23 sts just worked onto a stitch holder for back of neck; bind off rem 17 sts.
Front: Work same as Back until length is 9″ from beg ending with Row 2.
Neck Shaping: Row 1: Work in ribbing across the first 21 sts, slip these 21 sts just worked onto a stitch holder for right side; work across next 15 sts, slip these 15 sts just worked onto another stitch holder for front of neck; work across rem 21 sts for left side.
Left Side: Row 1: Work in ribbing to within 2 sts before front-of-neck stitch holder, decrease by k 2 tog. *Row 2:* Work in ribbing as established across. Rpt Rows 1 and 2 alternately 3 times more—17 sts rem. Work 5 rows in ribbing. Starting at neck edge, bind off same as back shoulders.
Right Side: Starting at side edge, slip sts from right side holder onto knitting needle having point at neck edge. Attach yarn at neck edge. *Row 1:* Decrease as follows: Sl 1, k 1, psso, complete row in ribbing. *Row 2:* Work in ribbing as established across. Rpt Rows 1 and 2 alternately 3 times more—17 sts rem. Work 5 rows in ribbing. Starting at side edge, bind off same as back shoulders. Sew right shoulder seam.
Turtleneck Collar: With right side facing, starting at left shoulder, pick up and knit 13 sts along left front neck edge—this is right-hand needle; slip the 15 sts on front stitch holder onto left-hand needle, then work in ribbing as established across these 15 sts; with right-hand needle pick up and k 13 sts along right front neck edge to shoulder seam; slip the 23 sts on back stitch holder onto left-hand needle, then work in ribbing as established across these 23 sts—64 sts in all. Work in k 1, p 1 until collar measures 5″ from back of neck. Bind off loosely in ribbing.
Finishing: Sew left shoulder seam. Sew collar seam having seam on wrong side when collar is turned to right side, as shown. Pin back and front sections to measure 12½″ wide. Steam lightly through damp cloth.

⊠ LIGHT GREY   ◤ BLACK
⊡ LIGHT NATURAL   ☐ EGGSHELL

FAIR ISLE PULLOVER AND CAP (for experienced knitters). Directions are given for size Small (38–40). Change for sizes Medium (42–44) and Large (46–48) are in parentheses. Cap fits all sizes.

MATERIALS: Coats & Clark's Red Heart Fabulend, (4-ply, 4 oz. skeins): 2(3,3) skeins of No. 111 Eggshell and 1 skein each of No. 12 Black, No. 406 Lt. Grey and No. 407 Lt. Natural for each size; knitting needles, 1 pair each of No. 8 and No. 10, OR ANY SIZE NEEDLES WHICH WILL OBTAIN THE STITCH GAUGE BELOW.
Gauge: 4 sts = 1″; 5 rows = 1″.

MEASUREMENTS

SIZES:	SMALL (38–40)	MEDIUM (42–44)	LARGE (46–48)
CHEST:	41″	45″	49″
WIDTH ACROSS BACK OR FRONT AT UNDERARM:	20½″	22½″	24½″
LENGTH FROM SHOULDER TO LOWER EDGE:	24″	25″	26″
LENGTH OF SIDE SEAM (*excluding armhole band*):	15″	15½″	16″

Note: When changing colors always twist the color not in use around the other to prevent making holes. Carry the color not in use loosely on wrong side of work. Pattern is worked in stockinette st (k 1 row, p 1 row). Chart shows one half of pattern. To follow Chart for each row, start at line at right side edge indicating size being made; follow each row across to left side edge, knitting all sts including center stitch; to complete row, do not work center stitch again, but follow same row back from left side to starting line.

Pullover—Back: Starting at lower edge with No. 8 needles and Eggshell, cast on 75(83,91) sts. *Row 1 (wrong side):* P 1, * k 1, p 1. Rpt from * across. *Row 2:* K 1, * p 1, k 1. Rpt from * across. Rpt Rows 1 and 2 alternately until ribbing measures 3″ ending with Row 1 and inc 8 sts evenly spaced across last row—83(91,99) sts. Change to No. 10 needles and work in pattern as follows: *Row 1:* K across. *Row 2:* P across. *Row 3–4:* Rpt Rows 1 and 2. Attach Black. *Row 5:* * With Eggshell k 1, with Black k 1. Rpt from * across, end with Eggshell k 1. *Row 6:* * With Black p 1, with Eggshell p 1. Rpt from * across, end with Black p 1. Starting with Row 7 on Chart, work until Row 40 on Chart is completed. Rpt last 34 rows (Rows 7 through 40) for pat. Work in pat until total length is 15(15½,16)″, end with a p row.

Armhole Shaping: Continuing in pat throughout, bind off 5(6,7) sts at beg of next 2 rows. Dec one st at each end every other row 6(7,8) times in all—61(65,69) sts. Work even in pattern until length from first row of armhole shaping is 9(9½, 10)″, end with a p row. *Next Row:* With one color, bind off first 16(17,18) sts for right shoulder, work across next 29(31,33) sts, place these sts on a stitch holder for neckband, bind off rem 16(17,18) sts.

Front: Work as for Back until length from first row of armhole shaping is 5½(6, 6½)″, end with a p row.

Neck Shaping: *Row 1:* Work in pat across first 24(25,26) sts, place rem 37(40,43) sts on a stitch holder. *Row 2:* Working over sts on needle only, bind off first 2 sts, complete row. *Row 3:* Work in pat across. *Row 4:* Rpt Row 2. Continue in pat, dec one st at neck edge every other row until 16(17,18) sts remain. Work even in pat until length of armhole is same as Back, end with same Row of pat as on Back. With same color yarn, bind off remaining sts. Leaving center 13(15,17) sts on stitch holder, slip rem sts onto a No. 10 needle, attach corresponding color yarn at neck edge and work to correspond with the opposite side, reversing the shaping. Pin pieces to measurements on a padded surface; cover with a damp cloth and allow to dry; **do not press.** Sew left shoulder seam.

Neckband: With right side facing, using Eggshell and No. 8 needles, k across sts on back stitch holder, pick up and k 15(17,17) sts along left side edge of neck, k across sts on front stitch holder, pick up and k 14(16,16) sts along right side edge of neck—73(79,83) sts. Work ribbing same as on Back for 5 rows. Bind off loosely in ribbing. Sew right shoulder seam, including neckband.

Armhole Bands: With right side facing, using No. 8 needles and Eggshell, pick up and k 89(93,97) sts along entire armhole edge. Work ribbing same as on Back for 5 rows. Bind off loosely in ribbing. Sew side seams, including armhole bands.

Cap: Starting at cuff with Eggshell and No. 8 needles, cast on 83 sts. Work 2 rows in ribbing same as on Back. Change to No. 10 needles; work in st st for 4 rows. Starting with Row 11 on Chart, following line at right side edge indicating Small Size, work in pat until Row 20 on Chart has been completed. *Next Row:* Change to No. 8 needles starting with Row 1 of ribbing as for Back, work in ribbing for 2½″, end with a wrong side row. *Next Row:* Change to No. 10 needles, k across dec 10 sts evenly spaced—73 sts. *Next Row:* P across. *Next 6 rows:* Working over 73 sts, work the same color design as Rows 21–26 on Chart. *Following Row:* With Eggshell, dec 8 sts evenly spaced, k across—65 sts. Work 3 rows even. Now work in pattern as follows: *Row 1:* * With Grey k 1, with Natural k 7. Rpt from * across, end with Grey k 1. *Row 2:* With Natural p 1, * Grey p 1, with Natural p 5, with Grey p 1, with Natural p 1. Rpt from * across. *Row 3:* With Natural k 2, * with Grey k 1, with Natural k 3. Rpt from * across, end with Natural k 2. *Row 4:* With Natural p 3, * with Grey p 1, with Natural p 1, with Grey p 1, with Natural p 5. Rpt from * across, end with Natural p 3. *Row 5:* With Natural k 4, * with Grey k 1. with Natural k 7. Rpt from * across, end with Natural k 4.

Top Shaping—*Row 1:* * K 4, k 2 tog. Rpt from * across to last 5 sts, k 5—55 sts. *Row 2:* P across. *Row 3:* * K 3, k 2 tog. Rpt from * across. *Row 4:* P across. Continue dec in this manner, having one st less between decreases every other row until 22 sts remain. *Next Row:* * K 2 tog. Rpt from * across. Break off, leaving a 12″ length of yarn. Thread a needle with this length and draw through rem sts, pull tightly and then continue sewing back seam up to center of ribbing, then sew remainder of seam from the reverse side. Steam lightly. Turn up cuff.

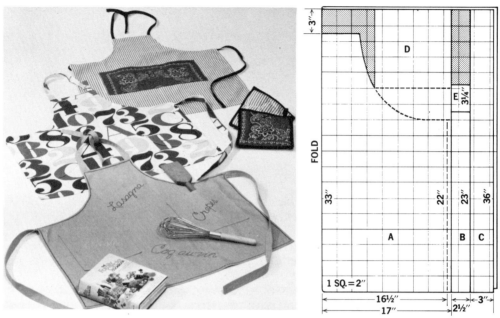

TRIO OF APRONS FOR MEN (PLUS POTHOLDERS)—Make aprons for the men in your life. Each is cut from a yard of fabric and the pattern is the same for all. For the ticking coverup we subdivided one red bandana handkerchief into pockets and companion potholders.

MATERIALS: 1 yd. each 45″-wide denim, 45″-wide printed cotton duck, and 33″-wide ticking; 1 set brass D-rings for print apron; 1 red bandana kerchief (21″x 22″); 5½ yds. polyester woven foldover braid and 20″x40″ thin polyester quilt batting for the ticking apron with potholders.

DIRECTIONS: Following the directions in the METHODS chapter, enlarge and cut out the apron pattern.

Cutting: Fold fabric lengthwise and cut out pattern (A) as shown—using 16½″ line for ticking and 17″ line for other fabrics: Cut straps B and C for denim and print aprons. Cut loop for D-rings (E) for print apron only. Cut 10″x10″ pockets (D) for denim apron. For print apron, cut pockets D, following *curved* broken line for pocket bottom.

Denim Apron:
1. Turn all raw edges of apron to inside ⅝″, turning raw edge under again ¼″. Zigzag close to inner edge.
2. Turn all pocket edges under ⅝″, turning top raw edge under again ¼″. Press. Topstitch top edge of pocket.
3. *For embroidered apron:* Choose names of favorite dishes and write them out in appropriate size and script on tissue paper. Pin paper on apron and pockets. Machine or hand embroider through paper to fabric. Tear away paper.
4. Topstitch pockets to apron.
5. For neck and waist ties, fold each strip lengthwise, right sides together. Stitch one end and side in ¼″ seams. Turn. Press. Stitch ⅛″ from raw edge at open end; overcast. Edgestitch all finished edges.
6. On inside, place neck strap ends at upper front edges. Stitch securely in place.
7. On inside, place waist ties at upper side corners of apron. Stitch.
8. Topstitch pockets in place 8″ from bottom and 2½″ from side edges.
9. Using bright thread zigzag stitch around apron, ⅜″ from finished edge.
Printed Apron: Sew edges, pockets and waist ties and *only* one neck tie as for

DENIM APRON. Stitch neck tie inside upper right corner of bib. Make loop for D-ring (E) as for other straps. Pull through D-ring and fold in half. Stitch both edges to upper left corner of apron bib.

Ticking Apron:

1. Finish raw edges of apron as for denim apron.

2. Cut bandana in half to make rectangle. Fold raw edge under ¼"; press. Use this as bottom edge of pocket. Center on apron 11" up from bottom edge. Edge-stitch in place at sides and bottom. Stitch once down the center to form two pockets.

3. Cut two strips of foldover braid 18" long for neckties and two more 36" long for waist ties. Finish raw edges and edgestitch foldover braid to close. Place and stitch ties as for denim apron.

Potholders:

1. Cut remaining half of bandana in half to form two squares. Using batting double, layer it between ticking and bandana fabric. Pin or baste securely in place. Using zigzag stitch, quilt together, outlining bandana design.

2. Cut two 5" lengths of braid; edgestitch open edge closed and fold in half to make loop. Sew to one edge of bandana side of potholders 1½" from a corner.

3. Use remaining braid to bind raw edges of both potholders, mitering corners.

MAN'S BELTED PULLOVER—Handsome knitted pullover sweater can be worn with or without a belt. Directions are given for Small Size (36,38). Changes for Medium (40,42) and Large (44,46) are in parentheses.

MATERIALS: Columbia-Minerva Nantuk 4-ply Knitting Worsted: 22(26,30) oz. of any color; knitting needles, 1 pair each of No. 5 and No. 8, OR ANY SIZE NEEDLES WHICH WILL OBTAIN THE STITCH GAUGE BELOW; crochet hook, Size G; 2 markers; 3 stitch holders; 1 belt slide; 4 buttons, ¾" in diameter.

GAUGE: 9 sts (st st) = 2"; 6 rows = 1".

Back: Starting at lower edge with No. 8 needles, cast on 90(98,108) sts. Work 4 rows of k 1, p 1 ribbing increasing one st on last row—91(99,109) sts. *Row 1 (right side):* K 27(29,32), place a marker on needle, p1, * k 3, p 1. Rpt from * 8(9,10) times; place a marker on needle, k 27(29,32). *Row 2:* P 27(29,32), slip marker, k 2, * p 1, k 3. Rpt from * 7(8,9) times; p 1, k 2, slip marker, p 27(29,32). Rpt Rows 1 and 2 alternately for pat. Work in pat until total length is 20" ending with a wrong-side row. **Armhole Shaping:** Keeping continuity of pat bet markers throughout, bind off 4(4,5) sts at beg of next 2 rows. Bind off 2(3,3) sts at beg of following 2 rows—79(85,93) sts. Dec one st at both ends of every other row 5(6,7) times—69(73,79) sts rem. Work even until length is 8½ (9½,10)″ from first row of armhole shaping ending with a wrong-side row. **Shoulder and Neck Shaping:** *Row 1:* Keeping the center sts in pat, work across 24(26,27) sts; place these last sts worked on a stitch holder for shoulder; work across next 21(21,25) sts and place these last sts worked on another stitch holder for back of neck; work across rem 24(26,27) sts. *Row 2:* At armhole edge, bind off 7(8,8) sts, complete row. *Row 3:* At neck edge, bind off 2 sts, complete row. Rpt Rows 2 and 3; then bind off rem 6(6,7) sts. Work other shoulder to correspond. **Front:** Work same as Back until length is 7½(8½,9)″ from first row of armhole shaping ending with a wrong-side row. **Neck Shaping:** *Row 1:* Same as Row 1 of Shoulder and Neck Shaping of Back. *Row 2:* Work in pat across. *Row 3:* At neck edge, bind off 2 sts, complete row. Rpt Rows 2 and 3—20(22,23) sts rem. Work even until length from first row of armhole shaping is 8½(9½,10)″ ending at armhole edge. **Shoulder Shaping:** *Row 1:* At armhole edge, bind off 7(8,8) sts, complete row. *Row 2:* Work in pat across. Rpt Rows 1 and 2. Bind off rem 6(6,7) sts. Work other side to correspond. **Sleeves:** Starting at lower edge with No. 5 needles, cast on 68 (72,76) sts. Change to No. 8 needles and work in st st for 19(19½,20)″. **Top Shaping:** Bind off 4(4,5) sts at beg of next 2 rows. Bind off 2(3,3) sts at beg of following 2 rows. Dec one st at both ends of every other row until 26 sts rem. Bind off 3 sts at beg of next 4 rows. Bind off rem 14 sts. **Cuff** *(make 2)*: With No. 5 needles, cast on 43 sts. *Row 1:* K 6 for band, * p 1, k 1. Rpt from * across ending with k 2 (instead of k 1). *Row 2:* * K 1, p 1. Rpt from * across to within last 7 sts, k 1, p 5, k 1. *Rows 3 and 4:* Rpt Rows 1 and 2. *Row 5:* K 2, bind off next 2 sts for buttonhole, k 2 complete row in ribbing as established. *Row 6:* Work as for Row 2 only casting on 2 sts over the 2 sts bound-off for buttonhole. Rpt Rows 1 and 2 alternately 4 times. Rpt Rows 5 and 6; then work 2 rows even. Bind off knitting the k sts and purling the p sts. Sew on buttons ½″ in from edge opposite the buttonholes. Button the cuff. Sew sleeve seam. Gather lower edge of sleeve to fit cuff. Then, having overlap of cuff opposite sleeve seam, sew lower edge of sleeve to edge of cuff. Finish other sleeve being sure the overlap of cuff is in opposite position. Sew side and right shoulder seams. **Neckband:** With right side facing and No. 5 needles, pick up and k 10 sts along front neck edge to holder, k across sts on holder, pick up and k 17 sts along neck edge to next holder, k across sts on holder, pick up and k 7 sts along rem front neck edge—76(76,84) sts. Work 4 rows of k 1, p 1 ribbing. Bind off in ribbing. Sew left shoulder seam incl neckband. Sew sleeves in. **Belt:** With No. 5 needles, cast on 11 sts. *Row 1:* K 1, (p 1, k 1) 5 times. *Row 2:* K 2, (p 1, k 1) 4 times; k 1. Rpt Rows 1 and 2 until total length is 43″ or desired length. Bind off in ribbing. Fasten belt slide to one end. **Belt Loop** *(make 2)*: With crochet hook make a tight chain 5″ long. Sew loops in place to side seam. Make another chain 5″ long. Join ends and pass belt through.

FINISHED MEASUREMENTS

SIZES:	SMALL (36–38)	MEDIUM (40–42)	LARGE (44–46)
CHEST:	38″	42″	46″
WIDTH ACROSS BACK OR FRONT AT UNDERARM:	19″	21″	23″
LENGTH OF SIDE SEAM:	20″	20″	20″
LENGTH FROM SHOULDER TO LOWER EDGE:	28½″	29½″	30″
SLEEVE SEAM *(including 3″cuff)*:	22″	22½″	23″
SLEEVE WIDTH AT UPPER ARM:	15″	16″	17″

Useful gifts for the home, with the accent on good design and economy

You've heard of the Peter Principle? Of Parkinson's Law? Well make way for the Family Circle Premise: i.e., that the quality of your daily life improves in direct proportion to the beauty of the objects you most frequently use. Why shouldn't a trivet be beautiful (see above, made from a scrap of plywood)? It's easy to do and costs nothing but time. It serves its purpose admirably and pleases the eye. Our premise prevails throughout. All 50 housewares shown are made from scrap, found at home or (for pennies) at a lumberyard.

directions for item shown above appear on following page

EDGE-GRAIN TRIVET—From ½″ plywood, cut ¾″-wide strips. From strips, cut a ½″ length; lay down with edge-grain up. Around it glue three 1″ and one 1½″ length with white glue. Continue to add pieces of increasing lengths to form the 7″ square design. Sand all surfaces smooth; soak trivet well in vegetable oil.

GRADUATED DRILL-BIT HOLDER—Any scrap of pine lumber can be used to make this efficient bit organizer. Starting ½″ from the end, simply drill a hole with each bit, leaving ¼″ between bits. Saw block ½″ from the last hole and finish off with sandpaper.

WALL-HUNG TOOL BOARD—"A place for everything" is still the handy-man's dream, and our compact tool board is a step in the right direction. It's just big enough (16″x19″) to hold the tools you use frequently, and good-looking enough to hang out in full view. Just screw 15″x16″ pegboard to a 16″x19″ piece of ½″ plywood with ⅜″ spacers between to allow air space for the hooks. Glue ½″ pine shelf as shown; nail through the back.

PAINTBRUSH CLEANER RACK—Scrap lumber, coat hanger and tin can make a rack that won't bend bristles.

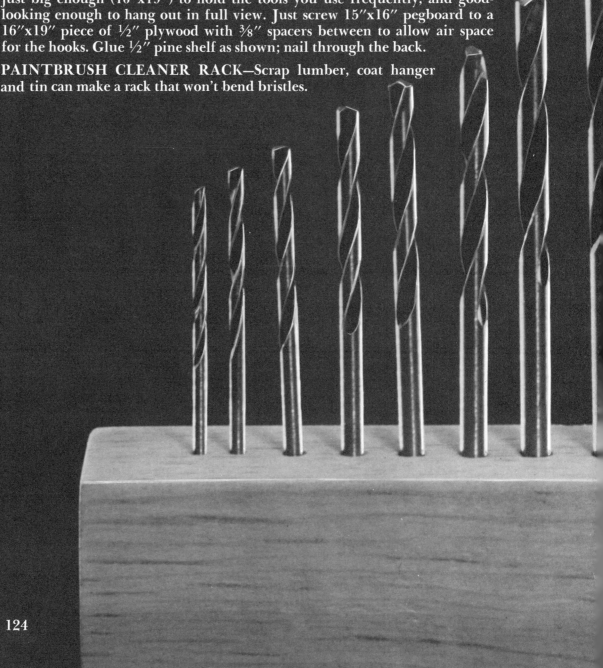

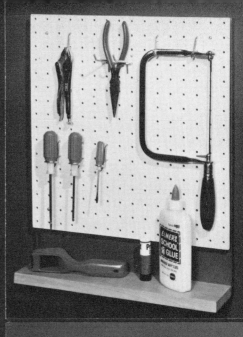

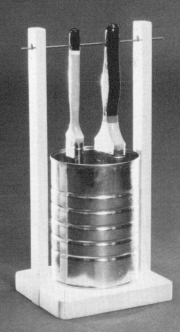

directions for this item appear on following page

continued

125

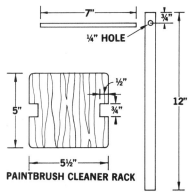

PAINTBRUSH CLEANER RACK

MATERIALS: Scrap of 1x6 clear or C pine; 2 feet parting strip or ½″x¾″ molding; plastic resin glue or white glue; wire coat hanger; 120-grit sandpaper; 1 lb. coffee can to hold paint solvent.

DIRECTIONS: To make the base, cut 1x6 pine 5″ long. Cut a ¾″-wide notch out of each side by sawing ½″ in, then chip each piece away with a chisel. Sand rough edges. Cut two 12″ lengths of parting strip to make side supports. Drill a ¼″ hole in the center of one end of each; sand. Glue into notches. Cut a 7″ length of wire from a coat hanger. Rotate ends over 120-grit sandpaper to remove burrs. Place can on base; suspend brushes in solvent from wire, held by side supports.

KITCHEN ORGANIZERS—Our wall-mounted **out box** is a handy holder to hang by the back door. Your good knives deserve a **rack:** Glue/clamp overnight two 2½″x16″x1″ pine with 2½″ square spacers of hardboard sandwiched flush at ends. Sand corners round. Drill 1″ holes ½″ from each end and insert 1″

dowels. Drill two holes in back and wall-mount. The portable **herb caddy** is made from scrap pine.

Wall-Hung Out Box—MATERIALS: 2′ of 1x12 pine; 1½″ of ½″ dowel; 5½″x11¼″ of ¹⁄₁₆″ acrylic plastic; four ⅜″ #4 flathead wood screws; white glue; 6d finishing nails; wood putty; polyurethane finish; stick-on lettering ("out"); two 2½″ Molly bolts.

DIRECTIONS: Cut an 11½″-high back from 1x12. Drill ⅜″ mounting holes 1″ in from each top corner; round the top corners to a 1″ radius, using a small jar top or juice glass for a template. Rip the remaining 1x12 to two 5″-wide pieces. Cut a 9¾″ bottom from one piece and two 5½″ sides from the other. Glue/nail sides to bottom, then glue/nail back flush with sides and bottom.

In the middle of one side, 1½″ from the bottom, drill a ½″-diameter, ⅜″-deep blind hole. Glue dowel in hole. Countersink all nails and fill holes with wood putty. Sand smooth and apply finish.

Along the short edges of the plastic, drill ⅛″ holes centered ⅜″ from the edges and 1″ from top and bottom. Screw plastic to front of box. Apply stick-on lettering. Mount on wall near door with Molly bolts (or mount on door itself with wood screws).

Portable Herb Caddy—MATERIALS: 40″ of 1x4 pine; white glue; 4d finishing nails; wood putty; polyurethane finish.

DIRECTIONS: Rip 1x4 to 2¾″ width. Cut two 17″ and two 2⅝″ lengths. With a 2″ hole saw, drill a series of six holes centered on one of the long pieces. The end holes should be centered 2¼″ from the ends. Other holes will occur at ½″ intervals. Glue/nail the two short pieces between and flush with the ends of the two long pieces. Countersink nails; fill holes with wood putty; sand smooth. Apply finish.

LACED LEATHER TRIVET AND NAPKIN RINGS—This leather trivet is easily made by interweaving leather straps and securing them around the sides with leather lacing. Napkin rings are made to match trivet.

MATERIALS: 1″-wide leather belting, twelve 9″ lengths; ³⁄₃₂″ leather lacings, about 2 yds. for trivet and one 7″ length for each napkin ring; ice pick.

DIRECTIONS: With ice pick, punch a hole ½″ from each end of all leather strips. On four strips, punch holes down the center, 1½″ apart. Using these as the border, weave strips together to make a square, with ½″ between strips, lining up the holes. With one end of the lacing, tie strips together through the holes at one corner, knotting the lacing in the back. Insert the lacing from back to front through the holes in the next strip-end. Bring lacing over the edge of the strip, down and under the lacing at the hole to anchor it, then on to the next hole. Continue around, taking two stitches through holes at each corner. Knot lacing ends at back of last corner. **Napkin Rings:** Lap ends of strips ½″. Insert lacing through holes and tie ends on wrong side.

REMINDER CHALK BOARD AND WALL-HUNG MATCH BOX—These handy items for the kitchen can be made of odds and ends of pine you have saved. **Reminder Board:** To make the blackboard, paint an 8″x10″ scrap of hardboard with blackboard paint. For the backing, trim corners from a piece of 1x12x14″ pine; sand cut edges into neat rounded corners. Onto backing piece, glue, then clamp, the painted blackboard and allow to dry. For the chalk shelf, cut a scrap of pine 1½″x6″ and nail a ⅜″x⅜″ lip to the top front edge. Paint. Glue to backing as shown, then nail through back into shelf. For the note pad, cut a strip of pine ¾″x¼″x3″ and paint. Use a ⅛″ hanger bolt with a wing nut to attach to backing.
Match Box—MATERIALS: 7″ of 1x6 pine; 12″ of 1x4 pine; 3½″x6½″ of ⅙″ acrylic plastic; 4d finishing nails; two ⅜″ #2 flathead wood screws; white glue; wood putty; polyurethane finish; stick-on lettering ("Matches"); 2″ L-shaped screw hook. DIRECTIONS: Following the directions in the METHODS chapter, enlarge the pattern and cut out. Trace onto 1x6 and cut. Drill ⅜″-diameter hole as shown. Rip 1x4 to 2¾″ width. Cut two 3½″ sides and one 5″ bottom. Glue/nail back to sides and sides to bottom; nail through back into bottom. Sink, fill and sand holes; apply finish. Drill a ³⁄₃₂″ pilot in the center of each short edge of the plastic, ⅜″ in from the edge. Fasten plastic to front of box with ⅜″ screws. Apply lettering. Hang box on hook driven into the wall.

TISSUE HOLDERS—These holders fit over standard-size boxes and are made of 8″ pine.
DIRECTIONS: From ½″x8″, cut two pieces ⅛″ wider than the ends of your cardboard tissue box and two pieces ⅛″ longer than the sides, plus 1″. With white glue and brads, fasten the four pieces into a box shape with the side pieces overlapping the ends. Trace the outside edge of the box shape on stock; cut out for box top. Cut the top from the *cardboard* tissue box. Center it on the pine top; tape in place and trace the opening. Remove cardboard top. Saw on the traced line to cut out the opening. With glue and brads, fasten top to box. Countersink brads and fill. Sand all surfaces. Leave wood natural, stain it, or finish with varnish or colored enamel.

"ETCHED" PLASTIC PLACEMATS—For each placemat you will need one piece of sheet acrylic, measuring 12″x18″. On one side, with an awl, draw vertical and horizontal lines, two inches apart, making 54 squares. In each square, scratch lines, alternating the directions, to create a basket weave design. Rub white paint into the scratches and the dividing lines. Use the "etched" side down.

BULLETIN BOARD TRAY—Any household can use an extra tray. Ours is made from a cork-face bulletin board With a mat knife, cut board as follows: 12″x18″ tray section, and four 2½″x12″ strips for handles and feet. Sand edges; stain edges with shoe polish. Glue together as shown. Weight the tray and dry overnight.

PATCHWORK PLACEMATS AND NAPKINS—For each mat, sew four 7″x7″ squares of gingham together and add 4″x13″ solid color rectangles along two sides using ½″ seams. With right sides together, stitch this to a 13″x19″ backing, leaving one side open. Clip seams; turn right side out. Press; topstitch ½″ all around. For napkins, cut 18″ squares of gingham and fringe edges all around.

SPICE SHAKERS—Use clear-plastic bouillon containers for these spice shakers. From cardboard, cut a pattern of the design shown or make up your own. Trace onto the back of self-adhesive vinyl. Cut out and press in place. Punch four, evenly spaced holes in top, ¼″ from the edge; add two more holes between each pair.

128

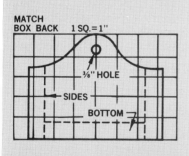

MATCH
BOX BACK   1 SQ. = 1"

⅜" HOLE

SIDES

BOTTOM

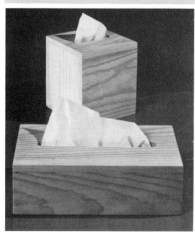

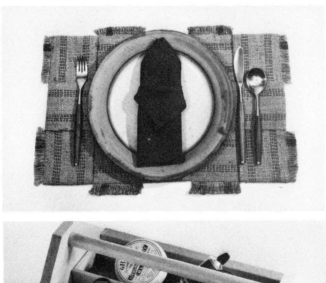

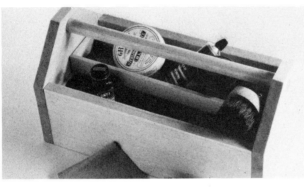

UPHOLSTERY WEBBING PLACEMATS—Even a child can make these no-nonsense placemats—from 3½ yards of jute upholstery webbing cut into three 19″ strips and five 12″ strips. Align 19″ strips horizontally and weave remaining strips through them. Turn under every other edge ½″; whipstitch to the strip underneath. Fringe the other edges, as shown.

SHOESHINE BOX WITH DRAWER—This 15½″x7⅞″ shoeshine box could also be used as a tool carrier. From 1x8, cut two 8″-wide ends with 5″ sides and 2″ at center top. Drill hole for ⅞″-dowel 1″ from top. Insert dowel. Glue/nail the assembly to 14″x6⅜″ bottom. Glue sides in place flush with outside edges of ends; nail sides through ends. Nail ⅝″x6⅜″ ledger strips inside the ends (*see photo*). *To make a brush drawer:* From hardboard cut 13⅞″x3¼″ bottom. Glue ¼″x1″x13⅞″ side pieces on bottom, side edges flush. Glue ¼″x1″x2⅝″ end pieces between side pieces.

SNACK BUCKETS—These servers stack and store easily. Glue or pin ribbons and trims to inexpensive styrofoam flower pots. Line pots with plastic or foil.

BATHROOM ORGANIZER—Cut three vinyl pieces: 18″x42″ backing, 32″x14″ and 32″x10″. Fold each in half crosswise; topstitch ½″ from all edges. Tape down pleats to form pockets in 32″ strips. Sew to backing. Add the dowel.

HERB "INLAID" TRAYS—Kitchen herb trays are made from dime-store plastic or metal trays. Fresh herbs are pressed and dried. Coat herbs on trays with découpage glue which dries clear—the *underside* on transparent trays, the *topside* on solid ones. Allow herbs to dry. Coat twice again with découpage glue; for

130

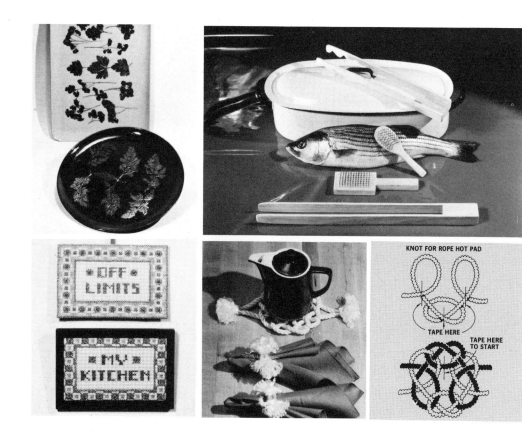

water-resistant surface, varnish when dry.

CROSS STITCH SIGNS—With seven-squares-to-the-inch gingham and scraps of embroidery floss you can make 5¼″x4¼″ cross-stitch signs. Tape 7″x11″ fabric to table and lighty mark evenly spaced border and legend, using fabric rows as guidelines. With two strands floss, stitch one cross per square; mount.

FUNCTION AND BEAUTY—**Short tongs:** Cut two 14″ lengths of ¼″x1⅛″ lattice. Sand to taper ends; cut ¾″x⅝″ notches. Glue to 1⅛″x1¾″x2½″ scrap lumber block.
Long tongs: Cut lattice 20″ long; wooden block, 1⅛″x1¼″x3¼″.
Square fish scaler: Cut one 2½″x8″ piece of 1x3 lumber. Saw end to form 1″x4″ handle. Sand well. Hammer ¾″ 18-gauge brads in 12 rows of 8 each.
Round scaler: Cut handle of wood food paddle to get 6¼″ *overall* length; add the brads. Spray all with clear plastic coating.

ROPE HOT PAD AND NAPKIN RINGS—Nylon rope is knotted and tied with dyed nylon twine.
MATERIALS: ⅜″ nylon rope (8 feet for the hot pad and 10″ lengths for as many rings as you want to make); 8 feet fine nylon twine; yellow dye; large-eye needle.
DIRECTIONS: To make *hot pad*, cut ⅜″ rope into two 4 foot lengths. Follow diagram to make knot, taping the first length (A) to work surface in three places, as shown. Tape the center point of other rope (B) and intertwine. To secure the ends, wind with nylon twine (dyed yellow); fringe rope ends. *To make napkin rings,* form 10″ of nylon rope into a circle, crossing the rope ends about 2″ from each end. With twine, take several stitches through the double thickness of rope, then wrap twine around rope ends in a figure "8." Secure twine ends; fringe rope ends.

131

FELT-APPLIQUÉD KITCHEN ACCESSORIES—These colorful accessories add color to any kitchen.

MATERIALS: Felt yardage of squares in various colors; white fabric glue.

DIRECTIONS: Following the directions in METHODS chapter, enlarge the patterns and cut out.

Picture Panels: Cut out felt vegetables, leaves and stems in colors and number you wish and apply to felt background, then frame.

Hot Mitt: Slipstitch felt appliqués to purchased hot mitt.

Apron—MATERIALS: ½ yd. each of solid and gingham fabric.

Cutting: *Apron* 18"x36" and *waistband* 4"x18" from solid color; *two pockets,* each 9½"x10½" and *two ties,* each 4"x36" from gingham.

DIRECTIONS:

1. Make narrow hems at all side edges and 2" hem at the bottom of the apron.

2. Stitch pocket pieces right sides together, leaving opening. Turn and press. Slipstitch opening. Iron felt appliqué to pocket over fusible webbing. Edgestitch pocket to apron about 3" from one side, at top of hem.

3. Turn under ½" at ends and one long edge of waistband. Sew gathering row at top of apron. Stitch it to raw edge of waistband, right sides together, pulling apron up to fit.

4. Make narrow hems on long edges and one end of ties. Pleat other end to 1½". Lap one at each end of waistband over wrong side near raw edge. Baste.

5. Fold waistband to wrong side. Pin ends together to enclose ties and place long folded edge over apron raw edges. Stitch ⅛" from all waistband edges.

Hot Pads: Buy an asbestos disc from dime or hardware store. Trace around it on felt, twice. Cut out on outer side of tracing line. Slipstitch appliqué to one circle. Whipstitch edges of the two circles together over asbestos.

Shopping Tote—MATERIALS: One yd. 39" fabric; felt appliqués.

DIRECTIONS: Cut bag 32"x21"; cut two straps, each 32"x9".

Sewing:

1. Fold bag piece in half matching 21" sides. Seam sides and stitch bottom fold.

2. *To square corners:* At seamed corner, pull back away from front, bringing seams together. Pin. Draw 3″ line across corner, perpendicular to the seams. Stitch on line. Repeat at other corner. Turn.

3. Fold bag vertically from each corner and edgestitch fold to top of bag to give appearance of boxing strip. Turn under and stitch 3″ hem at top.

4. Turn in one long edge of strap ½″ and press. Fold strap twice lengthwise, matching second fold to pressed edge for 3″ wide straps. Stitch large X from corner to corner through bag and strap.

5. Appliqué felt pieces with fusible webbing.

ELEGANT CANDLE HOLDERS—This charming **chandelier** is made with an assortment of cleverly assembled wooden knobs, dowels and finials. To make the **finial candle holders** simply drill candle-size holes in the tops, then paint. A pair of H-shapes, which overlap each other, becomes a **candle stand.**

Eight-Arm Chandelier—MATERIALS: (Note: Decorative finials are available in a wide variety of styles and sizes; check the millwork department of your lumberyard. Sizes given are approximate; diameters refer to base.) Eight 2½″-long, 1″-diameter finials; one 5″-long, 1½″-diameter finial; one 1¾″-long, 1½″-diameter finial; eight 2″-diameter flat wood knobs; 5½″ of 2x2 lumber; 18″ of 1¼″ dowel; 5′ of 5/16″ dowel; white glue; enamel in colors of your choice; polyurethane finish; 1″ screw eye; antique chain, length as needed; screw hook.

DIRECTIONS: Cut eight 1½″ lengths of 1¼″ dowel, and eight 7″ lengths of 5/16″ dowel. For each candle holder section glue a knob to one end of a 1¼″ dowel piece. Drill a ¾″ hole through the center of the knob to hold the candle. Drill the other end of the dowel to accommodate a 2½″-long finial; glue on finial. Paint as desired; also paint other finials.

Drill a 5/16″-diameter, ½″-deep blind hole centered ¾″ above the bottom of the dowel. Glue a length of 5/16″ dowel in the hole. Round the top and bottom corners of the 2x2 with sandpaper. Drill 5/16″-diameter, ½″-deep blind holes in each side of the 2x2, centered ½″ from one end. Drill similar holes at the same level in each corner. Drill the end of the 2x2 below these holes as necessary to accommodate the 5″ finial; glue in place. Drill other end of 2x2 and glue in 1¾″ finial. Glue arms into holes in side of 2x2. Apply polyurethane finish. Insert screw eye in top finial. Place chain through screw eye. Hang from ceiling hook driven into a joist or beam.

Four-Way Candle Stand—MATERIALS: 14″ of 5/4x6 pine; polyurethane finish.

DIRECTIONS: Cut as shown. Drill ¾″-diameter 1″-deep blind holes in top ends of each piece. Apply finish. Fit together as in photo.

KITCHEN APPLIQUÉS
1 SQ.=1″

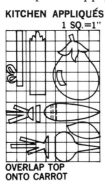

OVERLAP TOP ONTO CARROT

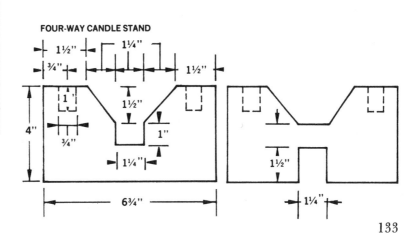

FOUR-WAY CANDLE STAND

1½″ 1¼″ 1½″
¾″
1″ 1½″
4″ ¾″ 1″
1¼″ 1½″
6¾″ 1¼″

LATTICE-TRIMMED BREAD BOARD AND DOWEL TRIVETS—Glue ¾″ strips of pine lattice to upright side edges of a 14″ square of ¾″ plywood, then on top, flush with the edges. Drive in and countersink ¾″ 18-gauge wire brads. Sand, stain and varnish all board surfaces. Glue ½″ slices of ¼″, ¾″ and 1½″ diameter dowels together as shown for **large trivet;** omit ¾″ size for the **small trivet.**

CALICO HOT PADS—Three strips of calico (each 2½″x8 yds.) are braided then stitched to make spiraled pads.

BIRCH BRANCH WHISK AND CARVED LATTICE SPATULAS—The **Whisk** is young, bark-stripped, 14″ birch branches tied as shown with nylon or wax cord. **Spatulas,** 5¾″ and 11¼″, are made from ¼″ lattice in 6″x1⅛″ and 12″x1⅜″ lengths. Draw knife shape with pencil; cut with utility knife. Bevel edge with sandpaper-wrapped block (use jar for curves); retain half of width of original edge to prevent its breaking.

COOKBOOK STAND—Make it in a hurry from scraps of plywood and pine and spray enamel.

MATERIALS: ¼″ plywood scraps (2 sq. ft.); ½x8 clear pine (3 ft.); ¼″ doweling (18″); white glue; 1″ and 1¼″ brads; Flecto Varathane Crystal Clear #90 Gloss varnish; Krylon spray enamel #1901 Royal Blue; ½″ masking tape; spackle or wood filler.

DIRECTIONS: Following directions in METHODS chapter, enlarge and cut out pattern. Cut plywood into two pieces. Trace pattern on wood. Fasten with brads at waste. Cut out ends simultaneously. Drill hole for page minder dowel in ends. Fill and sand ends for finishing. Trace center ½″ pine book-rest section on inside of end pieces. Place tape over these areas which will be glued later. Finish ends. From ½″ pine cut one piece 2″x16½″ and one piece 7¼″x16½″. Glue and nail (four 1¼″ brads) 2″x16½″ piece of pine to bottom edge of 7¼″x16½″ piece of pine, with edge flush at back and ends. Varnish this center section and 18″ length of doweling. (Avoid varnishing ends of center section.) When dry, remove tape from ends and glue and nail pieces together. Wrap newspaper around varnished center and touch up nails with spray enamel. (Nails may be countersunk and filled before touching up.)

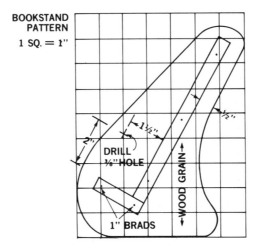

SELF-STRIPED CANISTERS—Clean 1-lb. shortening cans of labels, glue, etc. Affix two strips of ¾″ tape to make stripes. Turn can upside down. Spray four times with paint; let dry between coats. Remove tapes.

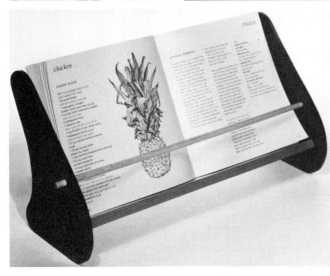

TWO-STEP LADDER—What home doesn't need a two-step ladder? Made from scraps of plywood and pine.
MATERIALS: ½″ plywood (4 sq. ft.); 1x3 clear pine (2 ft.); 1x6 clear pine (1 ft.); 1x8 clear pine (1 ft.); 4d finishing nails; white glue; wood filler; Flecto Varathane Crystal Clear #90 Gloss varnish; Flecto Varathane #100 Chinese Red; ¾″ masking tape.
DIRECTIONS:
1. Cut plywood into two pieces for ladder ends, using the dimensions in pattern.
2. Cut two 12″ lengths of 1x3 for step supports; cut one 12″ length of 1x6 for bottom step and one 12″ length of 1x8 for top step. Varnish steps (avoiding ends).
3. Glue and nail step supports at center of steps with two finishing nails; countersink and fill.

HOT MITTS FOR GOOD COOKS—The food gets barbecued without burning the cook. Use bulky yarn to crochet these heat-resistant, protective mitts as a welcome gift. Directions are given for a mitt which fits all sizes.
MATERIALS: Columbia-Minerva Washable Rug Yarn (1¾″ oz. Pull skeins): 1 skein each Navy and Scarlet, a few yards of White; Boye crochet hook, Size I, OR ANY SIZE HOOK WHICH WILL OBTAIN THE STITCH GAUGE BELOW; a brass button ¾″ in diameter.
GAUGE: 3 sc = 1″; 7 rows = 2″.
DIRECTIONS: **Palm:** Start at little finger edge with Navy, ch 22. *Row 1:* Sc in 2nd ch from hook, sc in each ch—21 sc. Ch 1, turn. *Row 2:* Sc in each sc. Ch 4 for finger tip, turn. *Row 3:* Sc in 2nd ch from hook, sc in next 2 ch, sc in 21 sc—24 sc. Ch 1, turn. *Rows 4 through 12:* Sc in each sc. Ch 1, turn. *Row 13:* Sk first sc, sc in each sc. Ch 1, turn. *Row 14:* Sc in 12 sc, ch 8 for thumb, turn. *Row 15:* Sc in 2nd ch from hook, sc in 6 ch, sc in 12 sc. Ch 1, turn. *Rows 16 and 17:* Sc in 19 sc. Ch 1, turn. *Row 18:* Sc in each sc to last 2 sc, sk next sc, sc in last sc. Fasten off.
Back: With Navy work same as Palm until 8 rows have been completed. Fasten off Navy. Attach Scarlet to last sc made, ch 1, turn and finish same as Palm. Leaving wrist edge open, sew edges of Palm and Back tog. *Cuff:* Attach Scarlet to little finger edge. *Row 1:* Ch 1, work 30 sc, evenly spaced, along entire wrist edge. *Do not join.* Ch 1, turn. *Row 2:* 2 sc in first sc, sc in each sc across—one sc increased at beg of row. Rpt Row 2 nine more times—40 sc. Fasten off.
Trim: With White make a 20″ chain. Fold chain in half and sew to wrist. Sew on button.
Barbecue Mitt with Heart—Directions are given for a mitt which fits all sizes.
MATERIALS: Columbia-Minerva Washable Rug Yarn (1¾ oz. pull skeins): 2 skeins Gold and a few yards of Scarlet; Boye crochet hook, Size I, OR ANY SIZE HOOK WHICH WILL OBTAIN THE STITCH GAUGE BELOW.
GAUGE: 3 sc = 1″; 3 rnds = 1″.
DIRECTIONS: Start at tip with Gold, ch 5. *Rnd 1:* 2 sc in 2nd ch from hook, sc in next 2 ch, 3 sc in last ch; working along opposite side of starting chain, make sc in 3 ch—10 sc. *Do not join rnds but mark beg of rnds for easy st counting. Rnd 2:* (2 sc in each of next 2 sc, sc in next 3 sc) twice—14 sc. *Rnd 3:* (2 sc in each of next 3 sc, sc in next 4 sc) twice—20 sc. *Rnd 4:* Sc in 2 sc, 2 sc in next 2 sc, sc in 8 sc, 2 sc in next 2 sc, sc in last 6 sc—24 sc. Work even until total length is 6½″. *Next Rnd:* 2 sc in next sc, ch 6 for thumb opening, sk 3 sc, 2 sc in next sc, sc in rem 19 sc—29 sts. *Cuff: Rnd 1:* Sc in 2 sc, sc in 6 ch, sc in 11 sc, 2 sc in next sc—mark this inc; sc in each rem sc—30 sc. *Rnds 2, 3 and 4:* Work even. *Rnd 5:* Sc in each sc making an inc directly in line with last marked inc—31 sc. Rpt Rnds 2 through 5 once more—32 sc. Work even until total length is 11½″. Fasten off; attach Scarlet and work 1 more rnd. *Thumb:* Attach Gold to a corner of thumb opening, ch 1 and work

For knit and crochet abbreviations box, see Methods (Chapter 11)

TWO-STEP LADDER DIMENSIONS

1 SQ. = 1"

1 x 8

1 x 3

GRAIN

1 x 6

1 x 3

4d FINISHING NAILS

12 sc evenly around opening. Work even for 2½″. *Next Rnd:* * Sk next sc, sc in next sc. Rpt from * around—6 sc. Fasten off leaving an 8″ end. Thread a needle with this end and draw tip-of-thumb sts tog. Fasten.

Heart: With Scarlet, ch 5. Work sc in 2nd ch from hook, hdc in next ch, dc in next ch, 5 tr in next ch, ch 3, sl st in same ch, ch 3, working along opposite side of starting chain make 5 tr in same ch, dc in next ch, hdc in next ch, sc in last ch, sl st in first sc. Fasten off. Sew to back of mitt.

DUSTMOP, WINDOW BLIND CLEANER AND "FEATHER" DUSTER—

When your old broom is worn down to a bunch of stubbly bristles—don't throw it away! Cut it off an even 6″ from the top, crochet a cover for it and add new "bristles" of yarn. Presto—a dustmop! Our dowel covered with yarn loops helps you reach window blinds. So does the gay green "feather" duster.

Dustmop—MATERIALS: Bear Brand Win-Knit Acrylic 4-ply knitting worsted (4 oz. skeins): 4 oz. Orange; 2 oz. each Bright Green and Green; crochet hook, Size K, OR ANY SIZE HOOK WHICH WILL OBTAIN THE STITCH GAUGE BELOW; a 3″ hairpin-lace loom; an old straw broom; small can of orange paint.

GAUGE: 2 sts = 1″.

DIRECTIONS: Leaving 6″ at top, cut off broom straws. Paint handle. **Cover:** *Side (make 2):* Start at top with one strand each of Bright Green and Green, ch 14 to measure 7½″. *Row 1:* Working loosely, dc in 4th ch from hook, dc in each ch across—12 dc counting ch-3 as one dc. Ch 2, turn. *Row 2:* Working loosely, dc in *front* loop of first dc—inc made; dc in front loop of each dc and in top of ch-3—13 dc. Rpt Row 2 until Side measures 6″. Matching ridges, sew side edges tog.

Mop: Wind 4 strands of yarn (1 each Green and 2 Orange) around hairpin lace loom. Slide strands up to create bulk and machine stitch strands tog 1″ from one leg of loom. Sliding the stitched part off the loom as the work progresses, make 3 yds in all of stitched loops. Fold in half to form double layer of loops and, starting at lower edge of Cover, sew doubled loops along edge being sure to keep measurement of edge; then continue sewing loops around just above last rnd of loops until all loops are used up. Cut loops. Slip Cover over broom. With 2 strands of Orange make a 20″ chain; run through sts at top of Cover; tie.

Window Blind Cleaner—MATERIALS: 18″ of ⅜″ dowel; Bear Brand Win-Knit acrylic 4-ply knitting worsted, 4 oz. yellow, #476; orange paint; 3″ hairpin lace loom; staple gun; one decorative screw-on hanger.

DIRECTIONS: Paint dowel. Following package directions, wind loom with yarn, slide up to form thick layer. Stitch down center to form fringe. Keep sliding loom out of stitched fringe, continue winding and stitching until you have 4 yds. of fringe. Using a double layer of fringe, staple an 11″ strip along dowel. Take care to include all yarn ends. Repeat three more rows, distributing strips around dowel. Clip long threads and screw hanger to end.

"Feather" Duster—MATERIALS: 12″ of ½″ dowel; Bear Brand Win-Knit acrylic 4-ply knitting worsted, 4 oz. Bright Green, #448, about 10 yds. Yellow #476; one piece of heavy cardboard, about 7″ square; one decorative screw-on hanger; glue; orange paint; twine.

DIRECTIONS: Paint dowel. Wind cardboard with all of the Green yarn. Slip triple strand of yarn through one end and tie loosely. Slip yarn from cardboard. Apply glue to 3″ on end of dowel and wrap yarn around end. Tie with yarn slipped through top. Wind twine around yarn and dowel about 1″ from top of yarn. Tie tightly. Wind a double strand of Yellow yarn over twine. Attach screw to end of dowel.

TERRIFIC TOTES

*Easy-to-make bags in all
sizes from clutch,
to carryall, to carry-on*

If there's one thing you can always use one more of, that thing is a tote bag. In fact, the tote bag has become the one sure-fire gift that's right for anybody, for any occasion. When in doubt give a tote. Or in this instance, make a tote. Even novice sewers should be tempted to try their hand at the 36 totes shown on these pages, because their construction is primarily a series of straight seams. For those with a yen to do something more elaborate there's a needle-point knapsack, and shoulder bags with colorful crewel embroidery.

directions for items shown above appear on following page

STENCILED BRUSHED DENIM TOTES—To make brushed denim tote bags: Cut **Lunch** bag 12″x21″, straps (2) 15″x6″; **Etc.**, 16″x30″, (2) 15″x6″; **School**, 36″x16″, (2) 18″x6″; **Market**, 45″x20″, (2) 16″x6″. *To sew:* Halve bag fabric crosswise and press fold; stitch ¼″ side seams. Turn under top edge ¼″, then 1″; edgestitch. **To square corners:** Center side seam on pressed fold. From corner point, measure 1½″ for Lunch and draw line across point from fold to fold (measure 2″, 2½″ and 3″ for remaining sizes). Stitch on line and cut off points leaving ¼″ seam. Quarter straps lengthwise, raw edges in; topstitch four times. Sew to bag. Using 1″-letter stencils, trace words on bag. Embroider (satin stitch) with 6-strand floss.

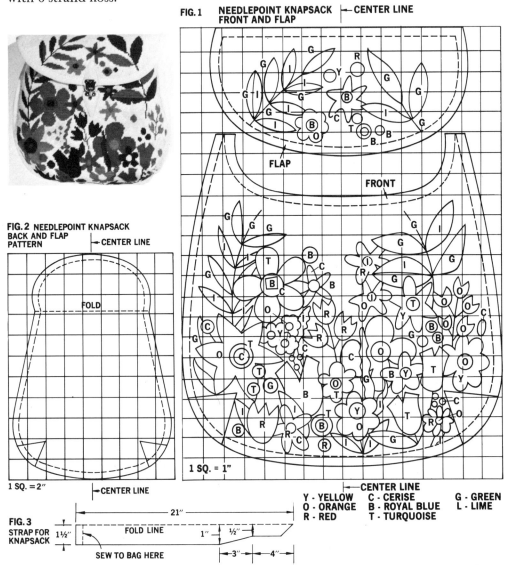

FIG. 1 NEEDLEPOINT KNAPSACK FRONT AND FLAP ←CENTER LINE

FLAP

FRONT

FIG. 2 NEEDLEPOINT KNAPSACK BACK AND FLAP PATTERN ←CENTER LINE

FOLD

1 SQ. = 2″ ←CENTER LINE

1 SQ. = 1″

Y - YELLOW	C - CERISE	G - GREEN
O - ORANGE	B - ROYAL BLUE	L - LIME
R - RED	T - TURQUOISE	

←CENTER LINE

FIG. 3 STRAP FOR KNAPSACK 1½″ FOLD LINE 1″ ½″ 21″ SEW TO BAG HERE 3″ 4″

A KNAPSACK IN NEEDLEPOINT—A needlepoint knapsack is a natural for cycling and shopping. Our design is a spray of field flowers on a white background. MATERIALS: Off-white cotton canvas or duck, 1¼ yds.; one piece No. 10 mono canvas, 27″x28″; two buckles for 1″-wide belt; belt closure or kiltie tab, available at notions counters; 4-ply knitting worsted (or 3-strand Persian yarn): 8 yds. yellow,

9 yds. orange, 6 yds. red, 9 yds. cerise, 6 yds. royal blue, 10 yds. turquoise, 14 yds. green, 12 yds. lime, and 80 yds. off-white; 2½ yds. folded double-knit edging in off-white; white thread; artist's stretcher bars, 18" and 24" (one pair each); tapestry needle; *waterproof* felt pen in two colors—one black and one neutral or medium tone; stapler; eight eyelets and eyelet-fastener tool.

DIRECTIONS:

1. When copying the pieces in FIG. 1, place the bag front and flap exactly as they are shown. To enlarge FIGS. 1 and 2 see METHODS chapter.

2. Mark guidelines at the center top and bottom of the canvas. Place the enlarged pattern underneath the canvas and tape it, matching center lines. If you used a black pen to enlarge the design on paper, it will show through the canvas (if it doesn't, tape the pieces to a window). Trace the pattern (flap and bag front) onto the canvas, using a waterproof felt-tip pen in a neutral color, or in the color(s) of the yarn you will be using. Also trace the outer broken and the solid lines and then trace the corner darts.

3. Place the canvas in the stretcher bars and staple. Work the pattern in Half Cross Stitch (*see* METHODS chapter), the background in off-white and the flowers and leaves as indicated by the color key in FIG. 1. Work a couple of meshes beyond the traced broken lines. When needlepoint is complete, remove from stretcher bars and cut out the bag front and flap on the solid lines. Set aside.

4. **Bag Back and Lining:** Place knapsack back pattern on the cotton canvas; mark corner darts and cut out around solid line to make lining. Now, to make knapsack back, cut one more back pattern from canvas, omitting the flap portion, but allowing ½" for seam allowance beyond the broken horizontal line; mark corner darts. Using the front pattern, cut another piece of canvas for the front lining; mark corner darts.

5. **Sewing:** Seam allowance is ½" throughout. Pin and stitch embroidered knapsack front to front lining around edge. Enclose top edge with double-knit edging and sew with zigzag stitch. Now sew the embroidered flap to the back canvas piece without a flap; press seam open. Pin and stitch seamed back piece to back lining around edge.

6. **Shoulder Straps and Buckle Tabs:** Make a pattern for the straps (*see the diagram in* FIG. 3) using paper 21"x3", folded to measure 21"x1½", tapering as indicated in diagram. Cut out pattern and open flat; then cut four canvas straps. With right sides together, pin and stitch each of two together on long sides and the narrower end; clip corners and turn to right side. Turn in seam allowance on open end and topstitch. Center three eyelets in the narrow end, about ¾" apart.

7. With narrow end of the strap falling away from you over the flap, pin wide end to upper corners on right side of knapsack back, 1½" from sides, on strap dotted line (*see* FIG. 3), flush with seamline where back joins embroidered flap. Topstitch to back on dotted line, then on other strap edges.

8. **For Buckle Tabs:** Cut two pieces canvas 3"x5". Fold each lengthwise and press; sew on one short and one long side. Clip corners; turn to right side.

9. Turn in seam allowance and topstitch. Center one eyelet in each tab. Slip the prong of the buckle through the eyelet. Sew the tab ends together just below the prong. Pin tab ends to bag above bottom corners (inside the *points* of the darts) and parallel with the flap seam. Topstitch to bag.

10. Position and sew down lower half of front closure to knapsack front.

11. With wrong sides together, pin and baste bag front to back. Remove pins. Starting and ending at knapsack bottom, enclose knapsack edges with a continuous strip of double-knit edging. Pin, then baste the edging to keep it perfectly even all around. Remove pins. Now sew with a zigzag stitch close to the edge. Position and sew upper half of closure on flap.

142

VINYL PATCHWORK SHOPPING BAG—A spacious Patchwork Shopping Bag is made of vinyl fabric patches sewn together. Colorful patches in assorted washable fabrics are also used to make a variety of **pockets** for teenagers to sew onto jeans. Cut floral motifs out of other fabric scraps and appliqué to the pockets. For a three-dimensional quilted effect, slip a little fiberfill beneath the stitched edges when you are three quarters of the way around—then complete the stitching.
MATERIALS: Vinyl patches, seamed together to make piece 18″x42″ and strap 3″x44″; ½ yd. 42″-wide fabric for lining.
Sewing (Seams are ½″ throughout):
1. **Bag:** Seam patches of vinyl to make piece 18″-wide x 42″-long. Fold in half crosswise, right sides together. Stitch side seams. Turn right side out. Turn in ½″ hem at top and baste.
2. **Straps:** Seam strips of vinyl to make piece 3″x44″. Turn in ¾″ along one side. Turn in ½″ along other side and fold it to center, making a 1″-wide strap. Top-stitch along fold.
3. Pin and stitch each end of strap 4″ below top of bag, whipping over the side seams.
4. **Lining:** Fold lining (18″x42″) in half crosswise, right sides together. Stitch side seams. Turn ½″ hem to outside and baste. Place lining inside bag, wrong sides together. Pin top edges together and edgestitch.

PLACEMAT ENVELOPE BAG—Would you believe this elegant bag is a placemat folded as shown, then stitched along both sides?

SCARF NEEDLEWORK BAG—You can make this handy needlework bag from a 27″ scarf.
MATERIALS: 27″ scarf; 13″x27″ piece bonded batting; pair 8″ rods and knobs; 1½ yds. velvet cord.
DIRECTIONS:
1. Pin together two sides of scarf and seam. Press seam open and turn. Center the seam. Slide bonded batting inside tube.
2. Fold 1¾″ at short ends to right side and pin. At ¾″ from fold, stitch through all layers for ruffle. Trim batting to stitching. Turn under raw edge and edge-stitch, for casing.
3. Fold bag in half, right sides together, ruffles and sides matching. Stitch narrow side seams stopping 6″ from bottom.
4. Turn. Insert rods. Cut two 27″ cords and tie one end at each end of rod, for handle.

QUILTED CLUTCH—to wear day or night.
MATERIALS: Chintz, ¾ yd.; striped twill for lining, ¾ yd.; ⅞″ bias foldover tape, 1 package; thin polyester quilt batting, 16″x27″.
DIRECTIONS—**Cutting:**
1. From chintz, lining and quilt batting cut one each of the following: 11¼″x 14¾″ flap-and-back piece; 11¼″x7¼″ front piece; 2¾″x25¼″ gusset. Cut 6″x9″ inside pocket *from lining only*.
2. For back, front and gusset—layer batting between chintz and lining. Pin securely at edges. Quilt in rows, 1″ apart, parallel with the long edges.
3. Turn raw edges of pocket under ½″; press. Turn raw edge at top of pocket under again ¼″; edgestitch. Center pocket on lining of back of bag 1″ from bottom edge. Whipstitch in place.
4. Stitch gusset around side and bottom edges of front. Bind these raw edges first, then bind raw edges across top of front and gussets.
5. Stitch gusset around side and bottom edges of back and flap. Bind all raw edges.

QUILTED BIRDWATCHER SHOULDER TOTE AND QUILTED INDIAN PRINT TOTE—We quilted our totes on the fabrics' obvious design lines.

Quilted Birdwatcher Shoulder Tote—MATERIALS: ½ yd. each of firm fabric for lining and bonded batting; two fabric pictures each about 9″x10″ plus ¼″ seams (for bag front and back); 1 Velcro®fastener.

DIRECTIONS: Cut two pieces batting and lining fabric same size as front. Cut two fabric and one batting strip, each 3″x54″, for boxing and strap.

Sewing:

1. Place front and back over batting. Quilt, outlining print motifs. Additional stuffing in certain areas may be pushed through small slits in the batting.
2. With right sides together, stitch lining to top edge of front and back. Trim batting, then turn lining to inside and press open.
3. Baste batting to wrong side of a strap. Pin straps, right sides together. Stitch middle 23″ of strap with ¼″ seams at each side. Turn; press. Stitch ½″ seam at ends.
4. With right sides together, match seamed end of strap to bottom center of front and back. Stitch panels to strap squaring corners. (*Do not stitch lining.*)
5. Turn under ¼″ at lining edges and slipstitch over boxing seams.
6. Topstitch top edges. Sew Velcro fastener to inside at centers.

Quilted Indian Print Tote (10″ *square*)—MATERIALS: ⅜ yd. of 36″ or wider firm

fabric; ⅜ yd. each of 36″ lining and batting.

DIRECTIONS: Centering design of fabric cut 13″x29″ pieces for bag from fabric, batting and lining; cut two pieces each 3″x10″ for handles from fabric.

Sewing (½″ *seam allowance*):

1. Place fabric over batting and quilt, stitching around motifs in the print.
2. Seam 13″ sides together. Trim batting and press seam open. Fold bag, *so seam is at center back matching design.* Seam bottom edges. Trim and press open.
3. At lower corners, pull front away from back, forming a triangle with the bottom seam in the center. Stitch across corners 1½″ from points.
4. Sew lining same as bag. Turn bag right side out. From each bottom corner, fold bag straight to the top. Edgestitch to form the appearance of boxing.
5. Cut 10″x1″ batting strip for each handle. Center batting on wrong side of handle and baste each edge. Turn up one edge of fabric, then the other. Turn under and slipstitch the lapped edge. Edgestitch strap edges.
6. Stitch straps to bag, right sides together and raw edges matching, with outside edge of strap 2″ from stitched "boxing" fold.
7. Turn under top edge of bag and lining and press. Slip lining, wrong side out, into bag. Pin top edges, matching center back seam, and edgestitch.

TOTES AND TAGS—The cigarette case and tags are made of two layers of fabric with a fusible material between. For calico cigarette case, make a 3″x4½″ pocket;

sew flap to top edge. Sew on Velcro®dots for flap closures. Add loop at bottom to hold a lighter. The baggage straps of heavy braid have regulation "overall" hooks sewed to ends. The ID tag of felt with stenciled initials and the ribbon keyholder have hole punched in end for the chain.

Burlap Tote Bag (*Finished Size:* 15"x15"x6")—MATERIALS: ⅜ yd. each 54" burlap and 44" iron-on interfacing; cardboard, 5½"x15".

DIRECTIONS—**Cutting:** Using the dimensions shown in the diagram, cut one piece of burlap for bag front and one for bag back; also cut two pieces of interfacing to bag dimensions *minus the 2" hem*. Cut two burlap straps, each 4½"x22½".

Sewing: Seam allowance is ½". Stitch all seams with fabric right sides together.

1. Press interfacing to wrong sides of front and back, up to the hemline. Stitch front and back together down both sides and across the bottom, omitting the short corner edges. Press seams open. On bag bottom, topstitch ¼" each side of seam, through all thicknesses.

2. Pin corner edges together, matching side and bottom seams; stitch across. Press seam. Topstitch ¼" from seam through all thicknesses. Hem the top edge. Topstitch ¼" from side seams through all thicknesses, down the entire length.

3. Turn bag right side out. Crease the fabric 3" from each side of bottom and side seams. Press, then edgestitch crease to form boxing.

4. Fold each strap in half lengthwise. Fold raw edges in to meet at the fold; edge-

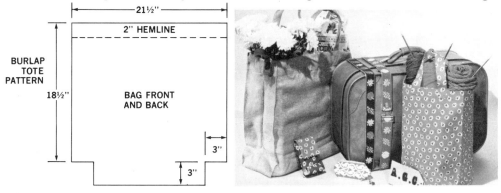

stitch. Pin 2" of the strap ends to the inside of the bag top edge; inner edge of the straps should be 2½" from the center. Edgestitch all around strap ends; stitch across from corner to corner.

5. Drop in cardboard to stiffen bottom.

Red Print Tote Bag—MATERIALS: ⅔ yd. each of two 36"-wide cotton fabrics, print for the outer bag and solid color for lining; thread to match fabrics; 1 yd. of 18"-wide fusible webbing iron-on interfacing (referred to as FW in directions below).

DIRECTIONS—**Cutting:** For *Sides,* cut two 6"x16" pieces from each fabric; cut two 6"x14" pieces from FW. For *Front* and *Back,* cut two 9"x16" pieces from each fabric; cut two 9"x14" pieces from FW. For *Bottom,* cut two 6"x9" pieces from fabrics *and* FW. For *Straps,* cut two 3"x14" pieces from print *and* FW. Cut 2" strips FW to fuse hems.

Fusing and Sewing: (Follow manufacturer's directions for **Fusing.**)

1. Make top hem in Side, Front and Back pieces in both fabrics by folding one short end 2" to wrong side; fuse in place. Fuse the print and lining fabrics for each bag section.

2. With right sides together, stitch Sides to Front and Back in ⅝" seams. Stitch Bottom to all sides, squaring the corners as you sew.

3. Turn under ½" hem on ends of Straps; fuse in place. Fold strap long edges to center; fuse. Pin 1" of strap ends to bag top edge, right side, with center of straps 2¼" from side seams; fuse in place.

CREWEL BAGS—The crewel bags shown above, with a folk-art, hearts-and-flowers motif, are embroidered on felt with an adjustable strap. You can wear them at either shoulder or handbag length. Stitches include Lazy Daisy, Satin Stitch, French Knot and Chain Stitch. Both bags are constructed the same way.

146

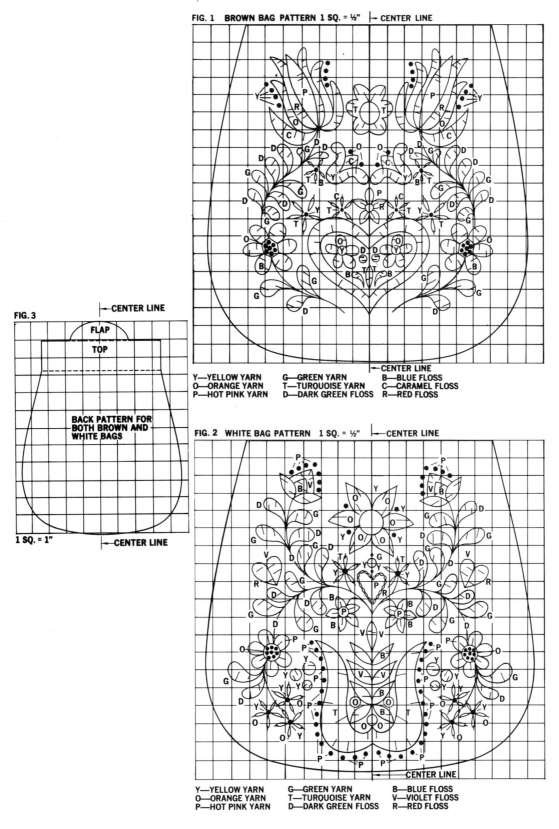

FIG. 1 BROWN BAG PATTERN 1 SQ. = ½" ⊢CENTER LINE

⊢CENTER LINE

Y—YELLOW YARN   G—GREEN YARN   B—BLUE FLOSS
O—ORANGE YARN   T—TURQUOISE YARN   C—CARAMEL FLOSS
P—HOT PINK YARN   D—DARK GREEN FLOSS R—RED FLOSS

FIG. 3

⊢CENTER LINE

FLAP

TOP

BACK PATTERN FOR
BOTH BROWN AND
WHITE BAGS

1 SQ. = 1"   ⊢CENTER LINE

FIG. 2 WHITE BAG PATTERN 1 SQ. = ½" ⊢CENTER LINE

CENTER LINE

Y—YELLOW YARN   G—GREEN YARN   B—BLUE FLOSS
O—ORANGE YARN   T—TURQUOISE YARN   V—VIOLET FLOSS
P—HOT PINK YARN   D—DARK GREEN FLOSS R—RED FLOSS

directions for these items appear on following page   147

MATERIALS: **White bag:** ½ yd. white felt; Persian yarn, 24″ lengths of each: 2 yellow, 5 orange, 5 hot pink, 5 green and 5 turquoise; 6-strand embroidery floss, 1 skein each: Dark green, blue, red and violet.
Brown bag: ½ yd. brown felt; Persian yarn, 24″ lengths of each: 2 yellow, 6 orange, 5 hot pink, 3 green and 2 turquoise; 6-strand embroidery floss, 1 skein each: Dark green, blue, red and caramel.
Both bags, each: Buckram, 1½ yds; buttons with chain (one set); 2 buttons to match each set; crewel needles (one for yarn, one for floss); 10″ embroidery hoop; tracing wheel and dressmaker's carbon.
Note: If edge of bag is whipstitched with yarn (*see photo*), five 24″-lengths should be allowed in desired color.
DIRECTIONS:
1. To enlarge the design in FIG. 1 or FIG. 2 see METHODS chapter. Then copy the embroidery design and outline of bag pattern around it, drawing freehand, one square at a time, plus center guidelines. Cut out bag pattern. Repeat for bag back pattern (Fig. 3).
2. Cut two pieces of felt 3″ larger all around than the bag patterns; draw a 3″ line at the exact center at top and bottom of each. Draw a light lengthwise pencil line to mark the center on two pieces of dressmaker's carbon, cut the same size as the enlarged patterns for bag front and back. Tape the carbon to the felt, matching center lines. Place the enlarged pattern over the carbon, again lining up center lines and tape to the felt. *For front,* trace pattern outline and design with wheel, using the tip of a hard pencil for fine detail. *For back,* trace outline *only.*
3. Place felt front in embroidery hoop. Embroider the design—using 3 strands of the embroidery floss, and 2 strands of the Persian yarn (following the stitch code and color key with FIG. 1 or 2). Remove from hoop. Cut out bag on pattern outline. Steam-press to remove creases made by hoop. Cut out bag back on pattern outline.
4. **Lining:** Using the same enlarged patterns, cut one more felt, front and back.
Strap-Gusset: Cut two strips of felt, each 1¾″x53″.
5. **Interlining:** From buckram cut one strap-gusset strip 1¾″x53″, one bag back and one front. Cut buckram back into three pieces on the pattern's broken lines (this makes flap "bendable").
6. **Assembling the pieces:** For the front, sandwich the buckram between the two felt pieces. Sew together on the machine, close to the edge, using zigzag stitch. Repeat for back, inserting the three buckram pieces in their original order. Assemble the strap-gusset pieces. Stitch edges as for bag front.
7. **Sewing bag:** Using matching thread, overcast the strap-gusset to the bag front with one end of the strap even with the top edge of the bag at the right front. Overcast all around, up to the other top edge. Let the rest of the strap hang loose. Then attach bag back the same way. Whipstitch the edges of the bag and strap with yarn in a contrasting color, if desired.
8. Sew one button to the top of the gusset, one to the gusset center-bottom and another to the bag front in the middle of the upper center embroidered flower.
9. Sew the button-with-chain to the center of the flap. Make a buttonhole in the end of the strap; slip it over the bottom button. Make a second buttonhole where the strap covers the top-gusset button. To use as a handbag, button the strap to the bottom button; for a shoulder length strap, button strap to the top button. If the chain on the chain-button is too long, loop it around the flap-button.

WOMAN'S CARRY-ON GARMENT BAG AND TWO-POCKET DUFFLE—
A traveling lady would love this carry-on garment bag and two-pocket duffle.
Woman's Carry-on Garment Bag—MATERIALS: 1⅜ yds. 44″ quilted fabric; 3 strips ribbon, each 45″ long; 30″ zipper.
DIRECTIONS: Make paper pattern for upper end, following diagram. Extend sides

148

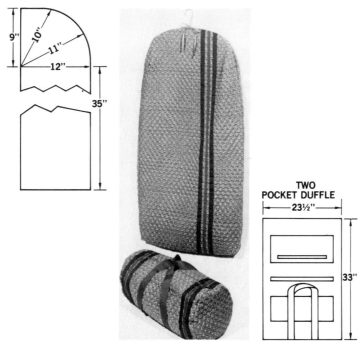

on fabric with a yardstick to measure 35″ sides. With pattern crosswise on fabric, cut front and back.

Sewing:

1. Edgestitch ribbons to front, parallel to side edges.
2. Starting 5″ above lower edge, stitch side edges of front and back to zipper.
3. Open zipper. Pin front to back, right sides together. Stitch remaining sides except 2½″ each side of center top for opening.
4. Turn in top opening edges and whipstitch.
5. *To square corners:* Pull front away from back, to match side and bottom seams. Stitch across point 2″ from point, perpendicular to seam.

Woman's Two-Pocket Duffle—MATERIALS: ⅞ yd. 45″-wide quilted fabric to match CARRY-ON GARMENT BAG; two ribbons and two lengths of stiff tape, each 1½″x39″ for straps; four ribbons, each 33″x1″ and two ribbons, each 33″x⅝″ for trim; 18″ top zipper and 14″ pocket zipper.

DIRECTIONS: Cut *one bag* 23½″x33″; *two ends*—11½″ diameter circles; *two pockets*—8″x18″ each.

Sewing:

1. *Pockets:* Turn under ½″ on all edges and press. On open pocket topstitch top edge. On zippered pocket, centered and 1½″ from top, draw ½″ wide rectangle the length of the zipper *teeth*. Within rectangle, draw a center line ending in a diagonal clip to each corner. Cut on that line, turn under on rectangle, and press. Baste opening over zipper and edgestitch.
2. Mark crosswise center on bag. Center and apply zipper as you did on pocket.
3. Center pockets on bag, with top edges 4″ from zipper. Edgestitch, except top edge of open pocket.
4. Edgestitch tapes to straps. At each end of bag, loop a strap—8″ from each side and ends flush with bag edges. Edgestitch both sides of ribbon up to pockets. Pin ribbon trim to bag so outside ribbon meets the ends of the zipper opening. Turn under other ribbon ends at zipper. Edgestitch.
5. Fold bag right sides together and stitch bottom seam. Open bag zipper. Pin ends to bag. Stitch. Turn through zipper.

149

QUILTED TEA COZY PATCHWORK BAG—Leave off the handle and you have a clutch or tea cozy.

Tea Cozy/Shoulder Bag—MATERIALS: ¾ yd. 35″ fabric; ½ yd. 35″ contrasting fabric; 11″ trouser zipper; synthetic batting; 4″ piece of ¼″-wide ribbon.

DIRECTIONS—**Pattern:** To make a diamond-shaped pattern for the bag bottom, quarter a 16″x6″ piece of paper. Mark, then cut along dotted line (*see* FIG. 1), then mark "center" on the 6″ line (*see* FIG. 2).

Cutting—Following the Cutting Layout in FIG. 3: From larger piece of fabric cut 8 patches, each 9″x7″; 1 bottom; 1 strap, 27″x8″. From smaller piece of fabric cut: 8 patches, each 9″x7″; 1 bottom.

Sewing (seam allowance is ½″ throughout):

1. Machine baste pairs of matching patches, *wrong* sides together, leaving 2″ open at end of one long side.

2. Pin two contrasting Left Front patches together along long edge with openings at top and bottom. Stitch. Repeat for Right Front, reversing color positions.

3. **Darts:** Fold each *top* patch in half lengthwise. On Center Front edges mark 1″ below fold. Then mark 4″ from Center Front edges along fold. Join the marks with a straight line to form dart. Stitch.

4. Join patches at Center Front, matching darts and seams, with seams open and darts facing in opposite directions.

5. Make Darts in lower patches, as in Step 3, but start them at outside edges.

6. Repeat Steps 2 through 5 for Back, reversing color positions.

7. Seam Front to Back at sides.

8. Machine baste pair of Bottoms, wrong sides together, leaving 2″ open each side of "center" to correspond with the four openings in lower patches. Stitch across 6″ "center" (as indicated on pattern piece).

9. Seam Bottoms to sides as far as openings.

10. Stuff all patches. Baste patch edges together.

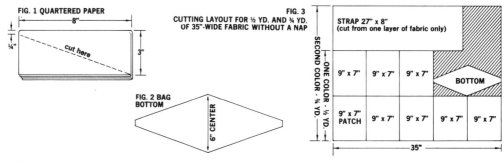

FIG. 1 QUARTERED PAPER

8″

¼″

3″

cut here

FIG. 2 BAG BOTTOM

6″ CENTER

FIG. 3
CUTTING LAYOUT FOR ½ YD. AND ¾ YD. OF 35″-WIDE FABRIC WITHOUT A NAP

STRAP 27″ x 8″ (cut from one layer of fabric only)

SECOND COLOR · ¾ YD.
ONE COLOR · ½ YD.

9″ x 7″ 9″ x 7″ 9″ x 7″

BOTTOM

9″ x 7″ PATCH 9″ x 7″ 9″ x 7″ 9″ x 7″ 9″ x 7″

35″

11. Whip side patches to Bottom at openings.

12. Center the zipper at Bag Top edges. Turn in seam allowance on one side and pin to zipper tape. Hand sew securely. Sew other side (*with zipper open*).

13. **Handle:** Fold Handle in half lengthwise, right sides together. Seam long side. Turn right side out. Center the seam on wrong side and pin it for 7″ in the middle. Stitch through seam to make two channels at the top of the Handle. Stuff Handle, using knitting needle.

14. Turn under and baste each end at an angle—1½″ on the seam side and ½″ at opposite side. Close Zipper. Set Handle ends over corners of Bag. Pin seams at zipper. Sew rest of ends to Bag, at a slant, pulling down over the Bag corners.

15. Pull ribbon through opening in zipper tab, and tie.

Clutch Bag—Assemble same as Shoulder Bag through Step 12, omitting 8, 9 and 11. Whip sides together at Bottom, turning in seam allowance.

Tea Cozy—Assemble same as Clutch, omitting zipper (Step 12). Turn raw edges under and whipstitch narrow hem to inside. Set over teapot.

CROCHETED CARTRIDGE BAG—Even a novice crocheter can make this spacious round handbag. Bag measures 10″ across and approximately 18″ around.

MATERIALS: Rug yarn: 8 ozs. of desired color; crochet hook, Size J, OR ANY SIZE HOOK WHICH WILL OBTAIN STITCH GAUGE BELOW; one matching zipper, 7″ long; 2 circles of buckram, each 5½″ in diameter.

GAUGE: 5 sts = 2″.

End Circle (*Make 2*): Start at center, ch 4. Join with sl st to form ring. *Rnd 1:* 8 sc in ring. Do not join rnds, but carry a contrasting color strand up between last and first st of each rnd to indicate beg of rnds. *Rnd 2:* 2 sc in each sc around—16 sc. *Rnd 3:* * Sc in next sc, *2 sc in next sc*—**inc made**; rpt from * around—8 incs made. *Rnd 4:* Sc in each sc around—24 sc. *Rnd 5:* * Sc in each of next 2 sc, 2 sc in next sc; rpt from * around—32 sc. *Rnd 6:* Rpt Rnd 4. *Rnd 7:* Inc 8 sc evenly spaced around, sc in each sc—40 sc. *Rnd 8:* Inc 4 sc evenly spaced around, sc in each sc—44 sc. Sl st in each of next 3 sc. Break off and fasten. Sew a buckram circle to wrong side of each end circle, leaving top edge of crochet free.

Main Section: Start at one side edge, ch 45; this chain should fit around outer edge of end circle. *Row 1 (right side):* Sc in 2nd ch from hook and in each ch across—44 sc. Ch 1, turn. *Row 2:* Sc in first sc, * ch 1, draw up a lp in each of next 2 sc, yarn over hook and draw through all 3 lps on hook; rpt from * across to within last sc, ch 1, sc in last sc. Ch 1, turn. *Row 3:* Sc in first sc, ch 1, draw up a lp in each of next 2 ch-1 sps, yo and draw through all 3 lps on hook, * ch 1, draw up a lp in same sp as last lp of last st, draw up a lp in next ch-1 sp, yo and draw through all 3 lps on hook; rpt from * across, end with ch 1, sc in last sc. Ch 1, turn. Rpt last row until length is 10″ from beg or desired length. Fasten off.

Join End Circles: With wrong sides of a circle and main section together, pin starting chain edge of Main Section along outer edge of circle; with circle toward you and working through back lp only of each st, sl st through both edges, matching sts around. Join. Break off and fasten. Join other circle to opposite edge.

Handle (*Make 2*): Make a chain the desired length of handle. Sl st in 2nd ch from hook and in each ch across; working along opposite side of starting chain, sl st in each ch st across. Break off and fasten.

Finishing: Line bag, if desired. Starting from end circles, sew 1½″ seam at each end of top opening. Sew ends of handles firmly to top seam at each end of bag. Sew zipper in top opening, between ends of handles.

APPLIQUÉD CALICO SHOULDER TOTE—Halve 6″x65″ strip cotton lengthwise; seam ¼″. Turn; press. Lap ends 1″; stitch to form boxing strip/shoulder band. Stitch 14″x15″ panels to band *opposite each other* to form bag. Appliqué with contrasting calico. Line; bind top.

TEN STURDY AWNING-CLOTH TOTES—Choose the cheerful lightweight bags that fit your needs most and make them yourself in just a few hours—at a fraction of the price you'd pay in stores. The bold-color fabric is durable, weather proof awning cloth (plain or striped), and there is a size and shape for every occasion.

1. Bike Pack 2. Sunny Shopping Bag (small) 3. Multi-pocketed Backpack 4. Rounded and Zippered Flight Bag 5. Roomy Carryall 6. Sunny Shopping Bag (medium) 7. Makeup Case 8. Roll-up Beach Mat 9. Super-Sized Striped Tote 10. Sunny Shopping Bag (large)

directions for these items start on following page

153

GENERAL INFORMATION:

● When cutting pockets, flaps and straps, take care to match the strips with those on the bag section where they will be sewed. Our Cutting Diagrams show where to cut each piece to obtain a match. These diagrams, however, are based specifically on the use of 30″-wide striped canvas. Therefore, if a *different* fabric is used, extra allowance may be necessary to match the stripes.

● Dimensions of all pieces are given in the Cutting Diagrams for each bag.

● Sewing Procedures used throughout are described below. Each one is numbered and is referred to by that number in parentheses in the Directions for each bag.

● Seam allowances are ¼″ and hem allowances 1″ unless otherwise specified.

● We recommend zigzagging all exposed raw edges.

● Use polyester or cotton-wrapped polyester thread and a large (size 18) sewing machine needle.

SEWING PROCEDURES (*A number in parentheses refers to another Sewing Procedure*):

1. **Topstitching**—When topstitching is called for, make two rows, the first as close as possible to the edge and the second ¼″ from the first row of stitching (unless otherwise specified).

2. **Exposed Zipper Application**—At the zipper location indicated on the bag section, draw a rectangle ½″ wide and as long as the zipper teeth (*not* the tape). Cut the fabric as shown (*see* FIG. 1) and fold under. Press the folded edges. On the wrong side of fabric, lay the zipper, face down, centering the teeth in the opening; tape zipper in place. On the right side, topstitch (1) all around the zipper teeth. Remove the tape.

3. **Zippered Pocket**—Insert zipper (2). Fold under and press seam allowance on all edges of pocket. Topstitch (1) pocket in place along all edges.

4. **Plain Pocket** (*no zipper, no pleat*)—Turn under and press the hem allowance on the top edge. Stitch with two rows, 1″ apart. Turn under and press seam allowance on the other edges. Topstitch (1) pocket in place along bottom and side edges.

5. **Expansion Pocket** (*with pleat*)—Turn under and press the hem allowance on the top edge. Do not stitch. Attach a gripper snap (8) in the exact center of the top edge, ¾″ from the folded edge. Fold under and press side seam allowances; fold pocket on pleat lines. Stitch across the pocket ⅛″ from the bottom edge, through all thicknesses, to hold pleats in place. Fold under and press the bottom seam allowance. Topstitch (1) pocket in place along bottom and side edges.

6. **Pocket Flaps**—Fold flap on fold line with right sides together. Stitch and trim side seams. Turn right side out; press. Zigzag raw edges. With the underside of flap up, and the zigzagged edge about ¼″ from the pocket top, pin the flap in place; topstitch (1). Fold the flap down; press.

7. **Straps and Handles**—Turn under and press seam allowance on all edges. Fold strip in half lengthwise; topstitch (1) along all edges. Position straps or handles where shown in Cutting Diagram. Stitch as shown (*see* FIG. 2).

8. **Snaps, Grommets, Eyelets**—Follow the manufacturer's directions supplied with the attaching tool.

1. Bike Pack—MATERIALS: Canvas, 1 yd.; one 6″ zipper; two buckles, 1″ wide x 1¾″ long; 10 eyelets; attaching tool; thread.

DIRECTIONS (*Note:* Numbers in parentheses refer to Sewing Procedures):

1. Cut the required pieces (*see* FIG. 3 *for dimensions*). Mark fold lines, as shown.

2. Construct pocket (3) and stitch to pack front.

3. Construct straps (7). Attach eyelets (8) where indicated. Two inches from other strap-end make ⅜″ buttonhole for buckle prong. Attach buckle; secure strap-end by a double row of stitching. With right sides together, position straps; stitch (7).

4. With right sides together, fold pack piece on fold line; stitch side seams.

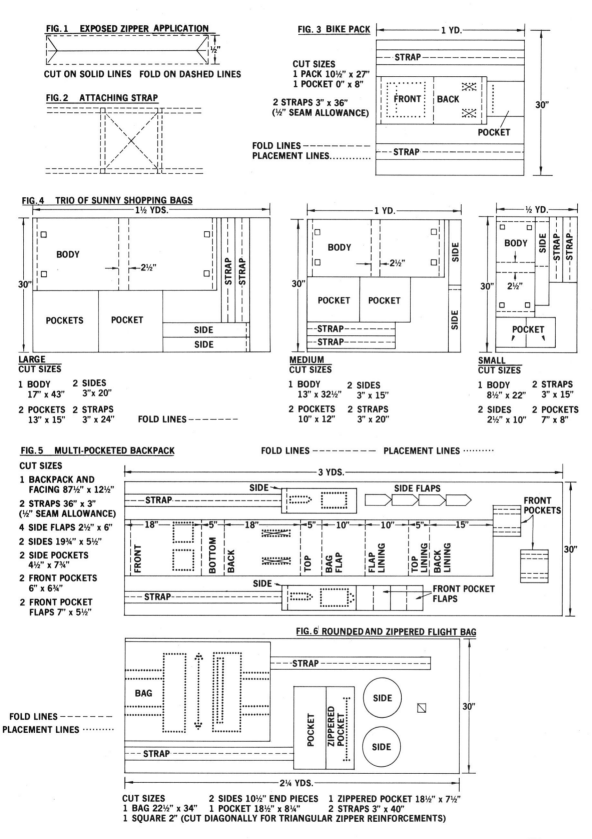

FIG. 1   EXPOSED ZIPPER APPLICATION

½"

CUT ON SOLID LINES   FOLD ON DASHED LINES

FIG. 2   ATTACHING STRAP

FIG. 3 BIKE PACK

1 YD.

STRAP

CUT SIZES
1 PACK 10½" x 27"
1 POCKET 0" x 8"

2 STRAPS 3" x 36"
(½" SEAM ALLOWANCE)

FOLD LINES – – – – –
PLACEMENT LINES............

FRONT   BACK

POCKET

STRAP

30"

FIG. 4   TRIO OF SUNNY SHOPPING BAGS

1½ YDS.

30"

BODY

2½"

STRAP   STRAP

POCKETS   POCKET

SIDE
SIDE

LARGE
CUT SIZES

1 BODY	2 SIDES
17" x 43"	3" x 20"
2 POCKETS	2 STRAPS
13" x 15"	3" x 24"

FOLD LINES – – – – –

1 YD.

30"

BODY

2½"

SIDE

POCKET   POCKET

SIDE

STRAP – – – – –
STRAP – – – – –

MEDIUM
CUT SIZES

1 BODY	2 SIDES
13" x 32½"	3" x 15"
2 POCKETS	2 STRAPS
10" x 12"	3" x 20"

½ YD.

30"

BODY   SIDE   STRAP   STRAP

2½"

POCKET

SMALL
CUT SIZES

1 BODY	2 STRAPS
8½" x 22"	3" x 15"
2 SIDES	2 POCKETS
2½" x 10"	7" x 8"

FIG. 5   MULTI-POCKETED BACKPACK

FOLD LINES – – – – – –   PLACEMENT LINES ··········

CUT SIZES

1 BACKPACK AND
FACING 87½" x 12½"

2 STRAPS 36" x 3"
(½" SEAM ALLOWANCE)

4 SIDE FLAPS 2½" x 6"

2 SIDES 19¾" x 5½"

2 SIDE POCKETS
4½" x 7¾"

2 FRONT POCKETS
6" x 6¾"

2 FRONT POCKET
FLAPS 7" x 5½"

3 YDS.

STRAP

SIDE

SIDE FLAPS

FRONT
POCKETS

18"   5"   18"   5"   10"   10"   5"   15"

FRONT   BOTTOM   BACK   TOP   BAG FLAP   FLAP LINING   TOP LINING   BACK LINING

STRAP

SIDE

FRONT POCKET
FLAPS

30"

FIG. 6 ROUNDED AND ZIPPERED FLIGHT BAG

FOLD LINES – – – – –
PLACEMENT LINES ··········

BAG

STRAP

STRAP

POCKET   ZIPPERED POCKET

SIDE

SIDE

30"

2¼ YDS.

CUT SIZES   2 SIDES 10½" END PIECES   1 ZIPPERED POCKET 18½" x 7½"
1 BAG 22½" x 34"   1 POCKET 18½" x 8¼"   2 STRAPS 3" x 40"
1 SQUARE 2" (CUT DIAGONALLY FOR TRIANGULAR ZIPPER REINFORCEMENTS)

155

5. Clip seams at the hem fold line. Fold hem under 1½″; press and topstitch (1).

6. Turn pack right side out; press.

2., 6. and 10. Trio of Sunny Shopping Bags—MATERIALS: Canvas, ½ yd. for small size, 1 yd. for medium and 1½ yds. for large; matching thread; dark green thread for topstitching.

DIRECTIONS FOR ALL SIZES (*Note:* Numbers in parentheses refer to Sewing Procedures):

1. Cut the required pieces (*see* FIG. 4 *for dimensions*). Mark fold lines as shown.

2. Construct two plain pockets (4) with three rows of topstitching (1) on top edge and in large X shape across the pocket center. Position on bag and stitch with triple topstitching on bottom and side edges.

3. With right sides together, and matching thread, stitch side pieces to front and back, squaring the corners to shape the bottom.

4. Hem top edge with three rows of topstitching.

5. Construct and attach straps (7).

3. Multi-pocketed Backpack—MATERIALS: Canvas, 3 yds.; 2 buckles 1″ wide x 1¾″ long; 16 eyelets; 5 gripper snaps; attaching tool for snaps and eyelets; two 1″ metal curtain rings; 4″ of 1″ wide black twill tape; 4¾″x11¾″ cardboard; thread.

DIRECTIONS (*Note:* Numbers in parentheses refer to Sewing Procedures):

1. Cut the required pieces (*see* FIG. 5 *for dimensions*). Mark fold lines, as shown.

2. Construct two front pockets (5) and flaps (6).

3. Attach the top half of a snap (8) to each flap and the bottom half to each pocket.

4. Topstitch (1) pockets (5) and flaps (6) just above bottom fold line on bag front.

5. Construct two side pockets (4). With a 1″ loop of twill tape, attach a curtain ring to the center of the bottom edge of each pocket. Position pockets on each bag side and stitch (4) sewing through the twill tape at the same time.

6. With the right sides together, stitch two side strap sections together along both long edges and the pointed end. Trim seams. Turn right side out. Fold top edge under ¼″. Press. Topstitch (1) all edges. Attach the top half of a snap to the point of the strap. Position straps on bag side and stitch (7). Attach bottom half of snap to bag side in correct position.

7. Hem (1½″) top edge of front.

8. Fold pack on fold line. With right sides together, stitch the side seams from the fold down to the X mark. At X, snip the seam almost to the stitching line. Below X, machine-baste the lining to the bag back edges.

9. Beginning at the top front, stitch the sides to the bag, squaring the corners to shape the bottom.

10. Turn bag to right side, pushing out the corners of the flap. Topstitch (1) all flap edges.

11. Construct back straps. Attach eyelets (8) at one end as shown. Two inches

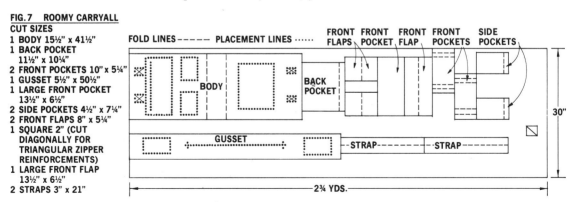

FIG. 7   ROOMY CARRYALL
CUT SIZES
1 BODY 15½″ x 41½″
1 BACK POCKET
  11½″ x 10¼″
2 FRONT POCKETS 10″ x 5¼″
1 GUSSET 5½″ x 50½″
1 LARGE FRONT POCKET
  13½″ x 6½″
2 SIDE POCKETS 4½″ x 7¼″
2 FRONT FLAPS 8″ x 5¼″
1 SQUARE 2″ (CUT
  DIAGONALLY FOR
  TRIANGULAR ZIPPER
  REINFORCEMENTS)
1 LARGE FRONT FLAP
  13½″ x 6½″
2 STRAPS 3″ x 21″

from other end, make a ⅜″ buttonhole for the buckle prong. Attach buckle, securing strap end with a double row of stitching. With right sides together, position straps on back; stitch (7).

12. Insert cardboard in bag bottom for shaping.

4. Rounded and Zippered Flight Bag—MATERIALS: Canvas, 2¼ yds.; thread; one 18″ green zipper; one 14″ green zipper.

DIRECTIONS (*Note:* Numbers in parentheses refer to Sewing Procedures):

1. Cut the required pieces (*see* FIG. 6 *for dimensions*). Mark fold lines, as shown.

2. Construct zippered pocket (3) using 14″ zipper and plain pocket (4); topstitch (1) pockets to bag in positions shown.

3. Insert 18″ zipper (2) in the center of the bag piece, as shown. Press under ¼″ on the edges of the triangular reinforcements and topstitch (1) to the bag at the zipper ends.

4. Construct handles (7). Attach a handle in a loop to each end of the bag, with the handle ends 6½″ apart and the edges even with the bag edges. Topstitch (1) the side edges of the handles up to the bottom edge of each pocket.

5. Open the 18″ zipper. Turn bag wrong side out. With right sides together, pin and stitch the circular side pieces in place, making sure that the stripe is running in the same direction at both ends.

5. Roomy Carryall—MATERIALS: Canvas, 2¾ yds.; two brass gripper snaps and attaching tool; one 24″ orange zipper; one 12″ orange zipper; thread.

DIRECTIONS (*Note:* Numbers in parentheses refer to Sewing Procedures):

1. Cut the required pieces (*see* FIG. 7 *for dimensions*).

2. Construct the two expansion pockets (5) and two pocket flaps (6) for the lower half of the front. Attach snaps (8) where shown. Position pockets and flaps and stitch (5 and 6).

3. Construct one large front pocket (3) and one flap (6) for upper half of front. Position pocket and flap (with raw edge under pocket top edge) and stitch (3).

4. Construct side and back pockets (4). Position pockets were shown and stitch (4).

5. Insert zipper, centered (2) in the center of the gusset. Press under ¼″ on all edges of the triangular reinforcements and stitch the triangles at the zipper ends.

6. Open the zipper in the gusset (so you can turn the bag right side out later). With right sides together, stitch gusset to the body of the bag, squaring corners to shape the bottom.

7. Construct straps and stitch (7) to bag.

7. Makeup Case—MATERIALS: Canvas, 1 yd.; one 22″ zipper; four zippers for pockets.

Note: The zipper opening in the pockets is 3½″ long. Buy zippers as close to this size as possible and shorten to correct size as follows: Measure off the correct length on the metal part (*not the tape*). At this point, whipstitch 5 or 6 times

FIG. 8   SHORTENING A ZIPPER

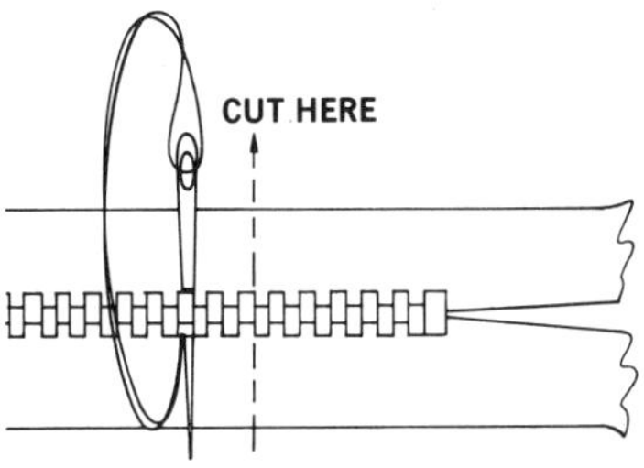

CUT HERE

FIG. 9   MAKEUP CASE

FOLD LINES - - - - - - - -
PLACEMENT LINES ··········

2½″   ZIPPERED POCKETS

BAG

ZIPPERED GUSSET

30″

CUT SIZES
1 BAG 21″ x 14″
4 POCKETS 5″ x 6½″
1 GUSSET 3″ x 28½″
2 STRAPS 3″ x 16″

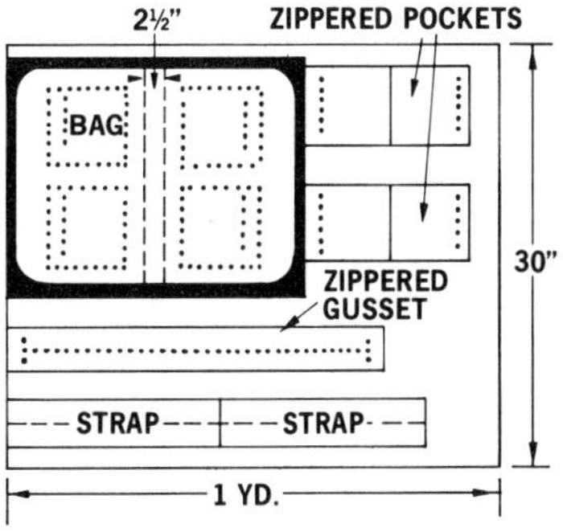

— STRAP — — STRAP —

1 YD.

over the teeth with doubled button thread (*see* FIG. 8). Secure thread ends. Cut off the zipper ½″ below this. (Your scissors *will not* be damaged since you cut the tape only, *between the teeth*.)

DIRECTIONS (*Note:* Numbers in parentheses refer to Sewing Procedures):

1. Cut the required pieces (*see* FIG. 9 *for dimensions*), rounding the corners, as shown. Mark fold lines, as shown.
2. Construct four zippered pockets (3); topstitch (1) to bag.
3. Sew the 22″ zipper, centered, in the gusset (2). Open the zipper (so you can turn the bag right side out later).
4. Fold the bag on the fold lines, with right sides together. Beginning at the bottom, with right sides together, stitch the gusset to the bag, squaring the corners to shape the bottom.
5. Construct and attach straps (7).

8. Roll-up Beach Mat—MATERIALS: Canvas, 2¾ yds.; thread; 1″ twill tape, black, 1 package; one #1 bag polyester fiberfill.

DIRECTIONS (*Note:* Numbers in parentheses refer to Sewing Procedures):

1. Use the full length of the fabric, trimming the ends to straighten, if necessary. Mark fold lines, as shown (*see* FIG. 10).
2. Turn under and press ¼″ of each end.
3. Turn under and press hem allowance at bottom edge, as shown.
4. Fold tape in half and insert folded end into the center of the hem. Topstitch (1) all edges of hem, reinforcing at tape with an X.
5. To form pillow, fold other end on fold line. Topstitch (1) two long edges and one short edge.
6. Stuff pillow with fiberfill. Topstitch the open short edge.

9. Super-size Striped Tote—MATERIALS: Canvas, 2¾ yds.; thread.

DIRECTIONS (*Note:* The numbers in parentheses refer to Sewing Procedures):

1. Cut the required pieces (*see* FIG. 11 *for dimensions*). Mark fold lines as shown.
2. Following Sewing Procedure (4), construct front, back and side pockets and stitch to tote as shown.
3. With right sides together, sew sides to front and back, squaring the corners to shape the bottom.
4. Hem the top edge.
5. Construct straps (7) and stitch (7) to tote, as shown.

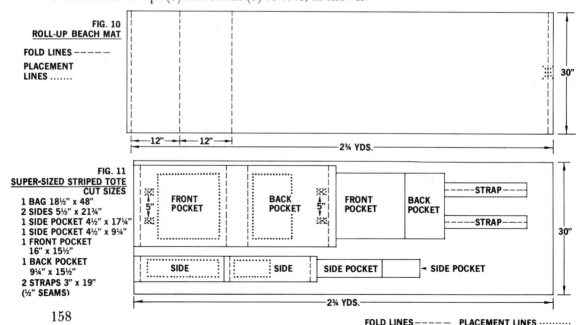

FIG. 10
ROLL-UP BEACH MAT

FOLD LINES -----

PLACEMENT LINES ....

30″

12″   12″   2¾ YDS.

FIG. 11
SUPER-SIZED STRIPED TOTE
CUT SIZES
1 BAG 18½″ x 48″
2 SIDES 5½″ x 21¾″
1 SIDE POCKET 4½″ x 17¼″
1 SIDE POCKET 4½″ x 9¼″
1 FRONT POCKET
    16″ x 15½″
1 BACK POCKET
    9¼″ x 15½″
2 STRAPS 3″ x 19″
(½″ SEAMS)

FRONT POCKET   BACK POCKET   FRONT POCKET   BACK POCKET   STRAP   STRAP

SIDE   SIDE   SIDE POCKET   SIDE POCKET

30″

2¾ YDS.

FOLD LINES ----- PLACEMENT LINES ....

*Big savings on wonderful
clothes and gifts
that children will love*

Where children are concerned, there's more to gift-giving than toys. Into this chapter fall 32 unique ideas for children's clothing and child's room accessories that you'd never be able to find in a store. Like the rest of the gifts in this book, the designs are in good taste and easy to make. In fact, the children themselves would enjoy making many of the simpler items like the yarn-wrapped desk accessories, the crêpe paper party balls and the painted frames that glorify their very own art. Mommy and Daddy can make the rest.

directions for item shown above appear on following page

159

CHAPTER 9

APPLE CHALKBOARD

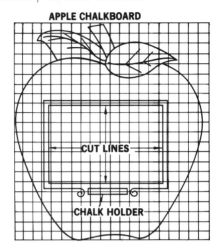

APPLE CHALKBOARD—Apple is cut from insulation board with a small coping saw and sanded. Surface is prepared with gesso; apple design painted with acrylics. Small blackboard is glued in place. Chalk holder is molding.

MATERIALS: Saber saw or coping saw; 1 piece of insulation board 20″x22″; 4″ molding strip; 1 chalkboard 8¼″x12¼″; Xacto knife; red, green, brown and black acrylic paint; paintbrush; sandpaper; 1 pint gesso (a white liquid sealer); epoxy cement; picture hanger.

DIRECTIONS: Enlarge apple pattern following directions in METHODS chapter. Trace pattern onto insulation board and cut out with saw. Sand edges. Center the chalkboard and trace around it. With Xacto knife gouge out the insulation board inside traced lines, to a depth of ⅟₁₆″. Coat the surface with gesso sealer and allow to dry. Paint the design with acrylic paints. Glue chalkboard and chalk holder in place. Attach picture hanger to back.

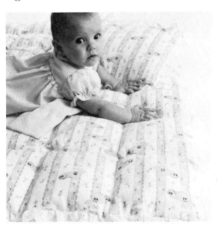

BABY'S RUFFLED QUILTED CRIB SET—Baby-soft **reversible** crib set is made with soft cotton flannel, striped on one side, plain on other. **Quilt** (36″x48″): Cut fabric and polyester batting 37″x49″. With right sides facing, pin quilt pieces together with pre-gathered 1½″ eyelet ruffling (5 yds.) between, all raw edges even. Stitch ½″ seams around three sides and four corners. Turn right side out and insert batting. Whipstitch opening. Machine-quilt four evenly spaced rows lengthwise and five crosswise. Cut pink satin ribbon into 13″ lengths and make bows to trim the quilt squares. **Pillow** (11″x16″): Cut fabric and batting 12″x17″. You'll need 1⅔ yds. of ruffling. Join same as for quilt.

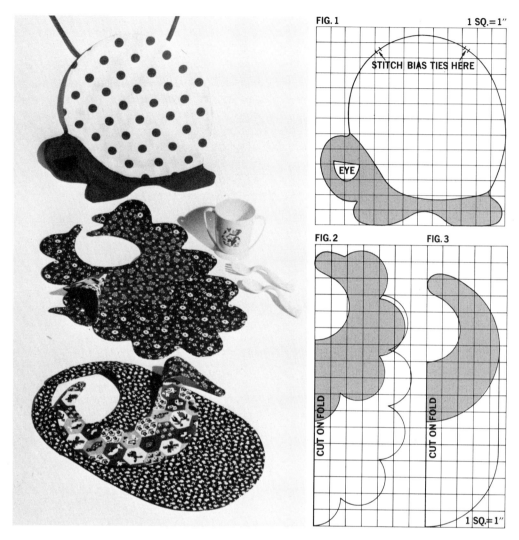

FIG. 1   1 SQ.=1"

STITCH BIAS TIES HERE

EYE

FIG. 2   FIG. 3

CUT ON FOLD

CUT ON FOLD

1 SQ.=1"

BABY BIBS—The mothers of infants who need burping or who are "on solids" will welcome practical, reversible bibs.

Turtle Bib—DIRECTIONS: Following directions in METHODS chapter, enlarge the pattern in FIG. 1; cut out. Cut two polka dot pieces for the whole pattern, two red pieces for shaded body area, and one brown eye. From bias fold tape, *or* red fabric, make two ties, ¼"x10". Appliqué a brown eye in place on each red body piece. Pin the red pieces to bottom front and back of polka dot pieces, trimming as needed so edges match exactly. Zigzag edges of red piece with close machine stitch. With right sides facing, pin pieces together with the ties between (*see* FIG. 1). Stitch a ½" seam around the edges, leaving a 3" opening on bottom edge. Turn right side out; press, turning in raw edges of the opening. Slipstitch opening.

Reversible Bibs—DIRECTIONS: Follow directions in METHODS chapter to enlarge the patterns (FIGS. 2, 3) for the full size bibs and collar-like over-bibs. Cut each pattern *twice* from fabric, using coordinated but different prints. With right sides together, stitch front and backing pieces together in a ½" seam, leaving a 3" opening on the bottom edge. Turn right side out; press, turning in raw edges of opening. Slipstitch opening. Sew snap fasteners to the neck tabs, or attach gripper fasteners, following manufacturer's directions.

161

CHILDREN'S DESK ACCESSORIES—With a little yarn and
embroidery floss you can turn giveaway pens and frozen orange juice cans
into children's desk accessories. Smear items with transparent cement
and wind covering tightly, concealing ends. If repeating a color, let the
tail end hang as you overlap with the next color, then pick up tail and
continue. Our pine desk organizer is made with overlapping construction.
Glue/screw 3½"x3" sides to 17½"x3"x1". Glue in three 2½"x2¼"
dividers at 2" intervals. Screw 3"x17½" clear plastic to front.

RECYCLED OVERALL JUMPER—Cut off overall legs 1″ longer than desired jumper length. Open the inseams to bottom of the fly. In both front and back, overlap the curved crotch seams; topstitch same as the other seams. Cut fabric appliqués; arrange as shown. Zigzag the edges or bond in place, using fusible webbing.

CROCHETED APPLIQUÉ FOR MITTENS—Grape Cluster is crocheted in a popcorn stitch and then clustered on ready-made angora mittens.
MATERIALS: Bucilla Crewel Wool, 1 card each of colors A and B; crochet hook, Size F; tapestry needle.
Grapes (make 11): With F hook and color A, ch 4. Work 4 dc in 4th ch from hook, drop loop from hook, insert hook in top of beg ch, pick up dropped loop and draw through, ch 1 to fasten. Break off. Sew grapes on mittens and embroider leaves and stem. Repeat for second mitten.

BABY'S EMBROIDERED SHIRT—Split Stitches in 6-strand floss outline inner edges of this purchased shirt's appliqué calico block.

BABY'S EMBROIDERED JACKET—The striped embroidery design is worked on the jacket's ribs with alternate rows of Chain and Detached Chain Stitches, with French Knots on the snaps (see stitch diagrams in METHODS chapter).

COLD WEATHER CAP FOR GIRLS OR BOYS—We used rows of double crochet to make up this cold-weather cap in bulky acrylic yarn. One size fits all. Directions are given for Berella Bulky yarn. Changes for the Krysta yarn are in parentheses.
MATERIALS: Bernat Big Berella Bulky (4 oz. balls): 2 balls OR Bernat Krysta (2 oz. skeins): 3 skeins; Bernat Aero crochet hook, Size K(J) OR ANY SIZE HOOK, WHICH WILL OBTAIN THE STITCH GAUGE BELOW.
GAUGE: 5 sts = 2″; 1 row:= 1″; (3 sts = 1″; 3 rows = 2″).
DIRECTIONS—Ch 38(46) to measure 15½″. *Row 1:* Dc in 4th ch from hook, dc in each ch across—36(44) dc counting ch-3 as one dc. Ch 3, turn. *Row 2:* Sk first dc, dc in back loop of each dc across, dc in top of ch-3—36(44) dc. Rpt 2nd row 18(22) times more. Fasten off. Sew back loop of each st of last row to corresponding ch st of starting chain to form a tube. Run a strand of yarn through every other st at one end of tube, draw tog tightly and fasten securely. Turn up lower edge to form cuff.

SUPER LUNCH BOX AND FANCY MUK-LUKS—Dress up a lunch box with ribbon—a good way to use up scrap lengths. Cut ribbon to fit and glue on. Do the same thing for children's muk-luks, as shown. Treat with soil-retardant spray.

CRÊPE PAPER PARTY BALLS—Make a generous assortment of bright crêpe paper wrapped balls for holiday parties. As you unwind the colorful layers, miniature toys (or more extravagant surprises for a loved one) drop out. A conversation piece for all ages that keeps everyone guessing until the very end.

SANTA APRON AND PILLOW TOY—Santa Claus is coming (*see page* 166) on an apron and a pillow toy, made from remnants of white piqué and red polyester/cotton. If you stuff the pillow with polyester fiberfill, it can be tossed into the washing machine when Santa gets soiled from too much loving.
Santa Apron—MATERIALS: ½ yd. red fabric; scraps of blue, flesh and white fabric; 3½ yds. double-fold white tape.

DIRECTIONS: Following the directions in METHODS chapter, enlarge pattern and cut out (*1 sq. = 2″*). Make paper pattern of apron, following diagram, tracing facial appliqués separately on transparent paper.

Cutting: *Red*—apron and lining (from entire shape), pocket, nose and mouth; *flesh*—face; *white*—beard and moustache; *blue*—eyes.

Sewing:

1. *Ties:* Cut two 18″ pieces of tape. Fold in half lengthwise and stitch edges. With raw edges matching, stitch ties to apron front piece, 2″ each side of center.

2. Pin apron to lining, right sides together (ties between). Stitch bib; clip and turn. Pin remaining raw edges together.

3. Bind top edge of pocket. Stitch to lower edges of apron. Topstitch 4″ from each end to make three pockets.

4. Bind side and lower edges of apron.

5. Bind each upper raw edge of apron (Santa's shoulders) with a 20″ piece of tape, letting tape extend at side for ties. Fold and stitch edges together.

6. Position beard, face, mouth, moustache, nose and eyes as shown—zigzagging raw edges in place with matching thread.

Santa Pillow Toy—MATERIALS: ½ yd. 36″ red fabric; 16″ square white fabric; scraps of blue and flesh fabric; 1½ yds. rickrack; polyester stuffing.

DIRECTIONS: Enlarge same pattern, head only (*1 sq. = 4″*). Extend seam allowance all around head and use full outline for front and back. Trace facial appliqués separately onto transparent paper.

Cutting: Cut *red* front, back, nose and mouth. Cut *flesh* face, *blue* eyes, *white* beard and moustache.

Sewing:

1. Stitch appliqués to face. Stitch center of rickrack to front seamline.

2. With right sides together, stitch front to back, leaving opening for stuffing.
3. Clip inside curves and corners. Turn. Stuff. Slipstitch opening closed.

RUFFLED CARRIAGE SET–Appliqué our pigeon-toed gingham bear on your baby's carriage or bassinet set. The coverlet is interlined with washable, quilted coat lining for extra warmth.
MATERIALS: 42″-wide white cotton fabric, 1 yd.; 44″-wide gingham, 1¼ yds.; 39″-

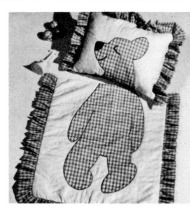 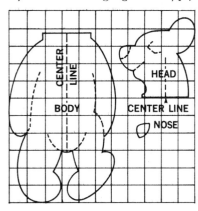

wide flannel or quilted coat-lining fabric, 1¼ yds.; scrap of pink flannel; thread to match fabrics; wrapping paper; dressmaker's carbon and tracing wheel; 12″x16″ pillow.

DIRECTIONS: Following directions in METHODS chapter, enlarge bear pattern pieces including all markings. Cut out patterns.

Cutting: From *both* white cotton and padding fabric, cut two coverlet pieces, each 21″x23″ and two pillow pieces, each 17″x13″; from gingham, cut five 6″x44″ pieces for ruffle, and one bear's head and body. Cut nose from pink scrap. Using dressmakers' carbon and tracing wheel, on fabric right side, transfer bear's features to gingham head piece and inner outline of arms to bear's body piece. Mark center line on each appliqué with a pin.

Sewing:
1. Matching straight edges and center lines, on fabric right side, pin gingham head to one pillow section and body to one coverlet section; edgestitch in place. With widest satin stitch, zigzag edges and inner-arm outline on gingham appliqués. Pin nose appliqué in place. Edgestitch, then zigzag around edges. With black thread, zigzag over mouth and eye markings.
2. Pin padding to wrong side of appliquéd pillow top and coverlet top. With a straight stitch, sew the two layers together around the appliqué edges and ⅜″ from raw edges; trim padding within the seam to the stitching line.
3. Seam together three ruffle sections for the coverlet and two for the pillow. Fold each stitched piece in half lengthwise, with wrong sides together; pin raw edges together. Stitch two rows of machine gathering stitches ⅛″ and ¼″ from the raw edge, starting and stopping at each seam. Pull up gathering stitches until coverlet ruffle measures 86″ and pillow ruffle, 42″. Tie ends of gathering threads securely. Distribute gathers evenly.
4. Starting ½″ from the top edge, pin ruffle to right side of coverlet along side and bottom, with raw edges even and folded edge of ruffle toward center. Stitch ⅜″ from edge. In the same way, stitch ruffle to pillow top.
5. Pin backs to coverlet and pillow tops, with right sides together, edges even and ruffles in between. Stitch together on ruffle stitching line. Turn right side out.
6. Turn in raw edges of coverlet ½″; slipstitch. Insert pillow into case. Turn in raw edges of case ½″; slipstitch.

167

CROCHETED CHRISTENING COAT AND CAP—This lacy crocheted christening set will become a family heirloom.

Infant size.

MATERIALS: Coats & Clark's "Red Heart" Knitting Worsted, 4 Ply (4 oz. "Tangle-Proof" Pull-Out Skns): 12 ozs. No. 1 White; crochet hook, Size F OR ANY SIZE HOOK WHICH WILL OBTAIN THE STITCH GAUGE BELOW; 3½ yds. white ribbon, ½" wide.

GAUGE: 9 sts (including ch sts) = 2"; 4 rows = 1¾".

FINISHED MEASUREMENTS:	
BACK WIDTH AT UNDERARM:	12¼"
EACH FRONT WIDTH AT UNDERARM:	6"

Coat: Back: Start at lower edge, ch 70 to measure, without stretching, 17". *Row 1:* Dc in 6th ch from hook and in each of next 2 ch, *ch 1, sk next ch, *dc in each of next 3 ch—**3-dc group made;** rpt from * across to within last 2 ch, ch 1, sk next ch, dc in last ch—16 3-dc groups. Mark this row for right side of pat. Ch 3 to count as 1 dc; turn. *Row 2:* 2 dc in first ch-1 sp, *ch 1, sk next 3 dc, 3 dc in next ch-1 sp; rpt from * across to within last 3 dc, ch 1, sk 3 dc, 2 dc in turning chain sp, dc in next ch of same turning chain—17 3-dc groups, counting ch-3 as 1 dc. Ch 4; turn. *Row 3:* Sk first 3 dc, *3 dc in next ch-1 sp, ch 1; rpt from * across, end with sk last 2 dc, dc in top of turning chain. Last 2 rows form pat. Ch 3; turn. *Rows 4 through 9:* Rpt Rows 2 and 3, 3 times. At end of last row, ch 3; turn. Always count the ch-3 as 1 dc. *Row 10:* Dc in first sp, ch 1, *sk next 3 dc, 3 dc in next ch-1 sp, ch 1; rpt from * across to within turning chain sp, dc in turning chain sp, dc in next ch of same turning chain—1 dc dec at each end. Ch 3; turn,

 For knit and crochet abbreviations box, see Methods (Chapter 11)

Row 11: Sk first 2 dc, *3 dc in next ch-1 sp, ch 1; rpt from * across; at end of row *do not* ch 1, sk last dc, dc in top of turning chain. Ch 4; turn. *Row 12:* Sk first 4 dc, *3 dc in next ch-1 sp, ch 1; rpt from * across to within last 3 dc, sk last 3 dc, dc in top of turning chain—15 3-dc groups. Ch 3; turn. *Rows 13 through 21:* Rpt Rows 2 and 3 alternately 3 times, then rpt Rows 10, 11 and 12 once—14 groups on Row 21. *Rows 22 through 25:* Rpt Rows 2 and 3 alternately twice. *Rows 26, 27 and 28:* Rpt Rows 10, 11 and 12—13 groups on last row. Rpt Rows 2 and 3 alternately until total length is about 15″, end with Row 3. At end of last row, ch 21 for sleeve; drop yarn and loop from hook; attach a separate strand to 3rd ch of ch-4 at beg of same row and ch 19 for other sleeve. Break off and fasten this strand. Pick up dropped loop; turn.

Sleeves and Yoke: *Row 1:* Dc in 4th ch from hook and in next ch, (ch 1, sk next ch, dc in each of next 3 ch) 4 times; across last row make (ch 1, 3 dc in next sp) 14 times; ch 1, dc in each of first 3 ch on next chain; (ch 1, sk next ch, dc in each of next 3 ch) 4 times—24 dc groups. Ch 4; turn. *Rows 2 through 7:* Rpt Rows 3 and 2 of Back alternately 3 times. There are 23 dc groups on Rows 2, 4 and 6 of sleeves and yoke. Ch 4; turn.

Neck: *Row 1:* Work in pat across until the 9th 3-dc group has been completed; ch 3, sl st in next ch-1 sp. Break off and fasten. Sk next 3 ch-1 sps; attach yarn to following ch-1 sp, ch 3, make 3 dc in next ch-1 sp, ch 1 and complete row in pat. Break off and fasten.

Right Front: Start at lower edge, ch 38 to measure about 8½″. *Row 1:* Rpt Row 1 of Back—8 3-dc groups. Mark right side of this row for right side of pat. Ch 3; turn. *Rows 2 through 9:* Rpt Rows 2 and 3 of Back alternately 4 times. Ch 3; turn. **This is front edge.** *Row 10:* 2 dc in first sp, *ch 1, sk next 3 dc, 3 dc in next ch-1 sp; rpt from * across to within turning chain sp, ch 1, dc in turning chain sp, dc in next ch on same turning chain—1 dc dec at side edge. Ch 3; turn. *Row 11:* Sk first 2 dc, *3 dc in next ch-1 sp, ch 1; rpt from * across, end with sk last 2 dc, dc in top of turning chain. Ch 3; turn. *Row 12:* 2 dc in first sp, *ch 1, 3 dc in next ch-1 sp; rpt from * across to within last 3 dc, ch 1, sk 3 dc, dc in top of turning chain. Ch 3; turn. *Rows 13 through 18:* 2 dc in first sp, *ch 1, 3 dc in next ch-1 sp; rpt from * across to within last 2 dc, ch 1, sk last 2 dc, dc in top of turning chain. Ch 3; turn. End of last row is at side edge. *Row 19:* Dc in first sp, (ch 1, 3 dc in next sp) 7 times; ch 1, sk last 2 dc, dc in top of turning chain. Ch 3; turn. *Row 20:* 2 dc in first sp, (ch 1, 3 dc in next sp) 7 times; do not ch 1, dc in top of turning chain. Ch 4; turn. *Row 21:* Sk first 4 dc, (3 dc in next sp, ch 1) 7 times; sk last 2 dc, dc in top of turining chain. Ch 3; turn. *Rows 22 through 25:* Rpt Rows 2 and 3 twice. Ch 3; turn. *Rows 26, 27 and 28:* Rpt Rows 10, 11 and 12 of Front. Ch 3; turn. Now rpt Row 13 until total length is about 15″, end at side edge. At end of last row, ch 21 for sleeve; turn.

Sleeve and Yoke: *Row 1:* Dc in 4th ch from hook and in next ch, (ch 1, sk next ch, dc in next 3 ch) 4 times; ch 1, sk next st, (3 dc in next sp, ch 1) 7 times; sk last 2 dc, dc in top of turning chain. Ch 3; turn. *Rows 2 through 6:* 2 dc in first sp, (ch 1, 3 dc in next ch-1 sp) 11 times; ch 1, dc in top of turning chain. Ch 3; turn. End of last row is at sleeve edge.

Neck: *Row 1:* 2 dc in first sp, (ch 1, 3 dc in next sp) 9 times; dc in next ch-1 sp. Do not work over rem sts. Ch 3; turn. *Row 2:* Sk first 4 dc, make 3 dc in next sp; complete row in pat. Break off and fasten.

Left Front: Work same as for Right Front until Row 9 has been completed. Ch 3; turn. This is side edge. *Row 10:* Dc in first sp, *ch 1, 3 dc in next sp; rpt from * across to within turning chain, ch 1, 2 dc in turning chain sp, dc in next ch of same turning chain. Ch 4; turn. *Row 11:* Sk first 3 dc, *3 dc in next ch-1 sp, ch 1; rpt from * across to within last dc, do not ch 1, dc in top of turning chain. Ch 4; turn. *Row 12:* Sk first 4 dc, 3 dc in next sp; complete row in pat. Continue to work to correspond with Right Front, reversing shaping until total length is 15″, end last row at front edge; drop yarn and loop from hook; attach a separate strand of yarn to 3rd ch of turning chain at beg of last row; ch 19 for sleeve. Break off and fasten this strand. Pick up dropped loop at end of row; ch 4; turn.

Sleeve and Yoke: *Row 1:* (3 dc in next sp, ch 1) 7 times; dc in each of first 3 ch on ch-19, (ch 1, sk next ch, dc in each of next 3 ch) 4 times. Ch 4; turn. *Rows 2 through 6:* (3 dc in next ch-1 sp, ch 1) 11 times; 2 dc in turning chain sp, dc in next ch of same turning chain. Ch 4; turn. At end of last row omit the ch-4, turn.

Neck: *Row 1:* Sl st in each st to within 2nd ch-1 sp, sl st in next sp, ch 3, (3 dc in next ch-1 sp, ch 1) 9 times; 2 dc in turning chain sp, dc in next ch of turning chain. Ch 4; turn. *Row 2:* Work in pat until the 9th 3-dc group has been completed; ch 3, sl st in the ch-3 sp of previous row. Break off and fasten.

Finishing: Block pieces to measurements. Sew side and underarm seams. Sew top of sleeve and shoulder seams. *Border:* Working along opposite side of starting chains at lower edge, with right side facing, attach yarn to lower right front corner. *Rnd 1:* Sc in each ch st across lower edge to next corner, 3 sc in corner st; being careful to keep work flat, sc evenly along entire outer edge of coat, making 3 sc in same st at each corner and having a number of sts divisible by 4. Join with sl st to first sc. Ch 1; turn. *Rnd 2:* Sc in each of next 4 sc; *ch 3, sc in next 4 sc; rpt from * around, end with ch 3. Join to first sc. Ch 1; turn. *Rnd 3:* Make 3 sc in each ch-3 loop and sc in each sc around. Join. Break off and fasten. **Sleeve Borders:** With right side facing, attach yarn to end of underarm seam at lower edge of sleeve. *Rnd 1:* Ch 1, being careful to keep work flat, sc evenly along lower edge of sleeve, having a number of sts divisible by 4. Join to first sc. Ch 1; turn. *Rnds 2 and 3:* Rpt Rnds 2 and 3 of Coat Border. Break off and fasten. Press borders. Cut 6 pieces of ribbon, each 14″ long. Make half of a bow at one end of each 14-inch piece. Leaving 3 inches free between bows and having first bow at neck, sew the bow-end of 3 ribbons along each front edge.

Cap: Start at front edge, ch 54 to measure about 11½″. Work same as for Back of Coat until Row 8 has been completed, having 12 3-dc groups on first row and on all uneven rows. At end of Row 8, break off and fasten. Turn. *Back Section:* Sk first 5 3-dc groups on last row made; attach yarn to next ch-1 sp; ch 3, 2 dc in same sp where yarn was attached, (ch 1, 3 dc in next sp) 3 times. Do not work over rem sts. Ch 4; turn. *Rows 10 through 17:* Rpt Rows 3 and 2 of Back of Coat 3 times; then rpt Row 3 once more. Break off and fasten. *Finishing:* Working through back loop only of sts, sew free edges of Row 8 of front section to corresponding side edges of back section, adjusting to fit. *Border:* With right side facing, attach yarn to left corner st at lower edge. *Rnd 1:* Working along lower edge of cap, make 3 sc in corner st, sc evenly along left side edge of front section; make 10 sc evenly spaced across last row of back section, continue to sc evenly along outer edge of cap, making 3 sc in same st at corner and having a number of sts divisible by 4. Join with sl st to first sc. Ch 1; turn. *Rnds 2 and 3:* Work same as Rnds 2 and 3 of Coat Border. Break off; fasten.

COVER-UP PLAY APRONS FOR BOYS AND GIRLS—Children's work and play aprons are made from fabric remnants.

Boy's Play Apron—MATERIALS: 16 patches 6½″x7½″ (½″ seam and hem allowance included); 1½″x18″ for strap; 1½″x42″ for ties.

Sewing:

1. **Strap and Ties:** Turn in ⅜″ along one side. Turn in ¼″ along other side; fold to center. Topstitch along center through all thicknesses.

2. **To Make Apron Skirt:** Stitch 2 rows each of 4 patches, joining on the longer edges. Right sides together, join the rows and press open.

3. **For Bib:** Seam 2 patches together on the longer edges. To slant sides of Bib

top, mark 1″ from each corner on top edge of Bib. With ruler, draw line joining that mark with lower corner of Bib. Cut along lines. Turn under ½″ hem at sides and top of Bib. Stitch. Sew each end of Strap to Bib top corners, wrong side.

4. Center and join Bib to Skirt.

5. **Pockets:** Turn under ½″ at top of 4 patches and stitch. Turn under and baste other 3 edges. Edgestitch pockets over center patches of top row, then over end patches of bottom row.

6. Hem upper, side and lower edges of Skirt.

7. Cut Tie fabric in half crosswise and sew end of one to each corner of Apron Skirt.

Girl's Play Apron—MATERIALS: Fabric: 1 piece 21″x12″ for skirt, 1 piece 6″x15″ for pocket, 1 piece 10″ square for bib; ⅓ yd. 44″ fabric for straps, trim and binding; two gripper snappers.

DIRECTIONS—**Cutting:** Fold bib fabric in half. At top edge, measure and mark 3″ from fold. Draw line from the mark to the bottom corner. Cut on line through both layers. Also cut: 2 straps, 4″x18″; bib binding, 1½″x24″; skirt binding and trim, 2″x42″; pocket binding, 2″x15″.

Sewing:

1. Bind pocket top edge. Make ½″ pleat in center of pocket and 2″ from each end. Stitch across bottom edge of pleats. Turn under and baste ½″ at side and lower edges of pocket. Center pocket on skirt; pin. Edgestitch on basted edges. Topstitch across pocket 4″ from each end to make 3 pockets.

2. Make a ½″ pleat 2″ from each end of skirt. Stitch across top of pleat. Bind 4½″ at each end of skirt top edge. Turn under and press long edges of skirt—trim ½″. Edgestitch on skirt bottom. Hem (½″) skirt side edges.

3. Hem (2″) top edge of bib. Bind bib side edges, turning binding ends in ½″.

4. With right sides together, center bib on skirt, waist edges even. Baste. Fold bib up. Topstitch across skirt and bib on both edges of binding.

5. Fold each strap in half lengthwise, right side out. Stitch ½″ from long raw edge. Trim seam. Stitch one end in a point. Turn right side out. Fold in raw edge at end ½″. Topstitch. Topstitch pointed strap ends to corners of bib top.

6. Attach gripper snappers to straight end of straps and to back corners of skirt.

 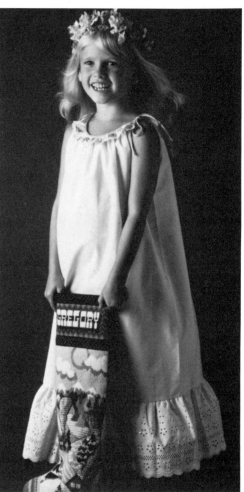

BOY'S TURTLENECK PULLOVER—A combination of Ribbing and Stockinette Stitch worked in stripe pattern.

Directions are given for Size 1–2. Changes for Size 3–4 are in parentheses.

MATERIALS: Bear Brand, Fleisher's or Botany Winsom (2 oz. skein): 2(2) skeins Color A; 1(2) skeins Color B; knitting needles, 1 pair each No. 5 and No. 7, OR ANY SIZE NEEDLES WHICH WILL OBTAIN THE STITCH GAUGE BELOW; 2 stitch holders; tapestry needle.

GAUGE: No. 7 needles: 11 sts = 2"; 15 rows = 2".

FINISHED MEASUREMENT:	SIZES:	1–2	3–4
	CHEST MEASUREMENT:	22"	25"

Back: Starting at lower edge with No. 7 needles and A, cast on 61(69) sts. Change to No. 5 needles. *Row 1:* P 1, * k 1, p 1. Rpt from * to end of row. *Row 2:* K 1 * p 1, k 1. Rpt from * to end of row. These 2 rows establish ribbing. Rpt Rows 1 and 2 alternately until length is 1¼(1½)". Change to No. 7 needles and work stripe pat in stockinette stitch as follows: *Row 1 (right side):* With A, k across. *Row 2:* With A, p across. Drop A, pick up B. *Row 3:* With B, k across. *Row 4:* With B, p across. Drop B, pick up A. Rpt Rows 1–4 for stripe pat throughout. *Note:* Carry picked up colors loosely along edge. Work in strip pat until total length is 6½(8)″ ending with a p row. Keeping continuity of stripe pat, work as follows:

Raglan Shaping: *Row 1:* K 1, decrease by k 2 tog; k in each st across until 3 sts rem on left-hand needle; decrease as follows: Sl 1, k 1, psso; k last st—2 sts dec. *Row 2:* P across. Rpt Rows 1 and 2 alternately until 23(25) sts rem. Slip these 23(25) sts onto a stitch holder for back of neck.

Front: Work same as Back.

Sleeves: Starting at wrist with No. 7 needles and A, cast on 35(39) sts. Change to No. 5 needles and work in ribbing same as Back for 2½(3)″. Change to No. 7 needles and work in st st stripe pat same as Back until total length is 3½(4)″ ending with a p row. Keeping continuity of stripe pat throughout, work as follows: *Next Row:* Inc in first st; k in each st across until 2 sts rem on left-hand needle, inc in next st, k last st—2 sts increased. *Following 3 Rows:* P 1 row, k 1 row, p 1 row. Rpt last 4 rows 6(7) times more. There are 49(55) sts on needle. Work even until total length is 11(13)″ ending with a p row and with same stripe as Back before Raglan Shaping.

Raglan Shaping: Work same as Raglan Shaping on Back until 11 sts rem. Slip these 11 sts onto a safety pin for side of neck.

Finishing: Block pieces. Matching stripes, sew raglan shaping of right sleeve bet raglan shaping of Front and Back. Sew left sleeve to Front only.

Turtleneck Collar: With right side facing, slip sts from holders and safety pins onto No. 5 needle in the following order: Left Sleeve, Front, Right Sleeve, Back. There are 68(72) sts on needle. With wrong side facing and A, p across. Then work in k 1, p 1 ribbing for 2″. Change to No. 7 needles and continue until Collar measures 4″ in all. Purling the p sts and knitting the k sts, bind off loosely. Sew rem seam. Sew collar seam, having seam on wrong side when collar is turned to right side as shown. Sew side seams.

PILLOW-SLIP NIGHTIE—This darling nightie is made from a ruffled case. MATERIALS: One ruffled pillowcase; ½ yd. 1″-wide ruffled trim; 1 package regular bias tape.

DIRECTIONS: Following diagram, draw neck and armhole edges at closed end of pillowcase. Cut on drawn lines, through both layers.

Sewing:

1. Bind armholes with bias tape.
2. Sew two gathering rows across front and back necklines. Gather each to 7½″, or to fit.
3. Sew ruffle trim over gathering.
4. Cut two 24″ strips of bias tape. Center one at each neck edge. Trim and bind seams. With tape folded lengthwise, continue stitching to end to form ties.

PILLOW-SLIP NIGHTIE

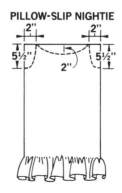

VICTORIAN VEST—Our quickly made Victorian vest gives a simple blouse and skirt a festive look for Christmas Day. It is made of self-lined velveteen, and hooks at the waist, in girl's sizes Small (7–8) and Medium (10–12).

MATERIALS: 44″-wide red velveteen (Crompton Veltessa), ⅞ yd. for Small Size, 1 yd. for Medium; pearl and gold trim, 2 yds. for Small, 2¼ yds. for Medium; thread to match velveteen; white thread for trim; hook and eye; wrapping paper.

DIRECTIONS: Following directions in METHODS chapter, enlarge pattern pieces, using the solid lines for Medium Size and dotted lines for Small. Making sure that the nap is running the same way on all pieces, cut fabric as follows for both vest *and* lining: Front, *one pair* each; Back, cut one each with fold line on fabric fold.

Sewing: Seam allowance is ½″. Unless otherwise directed, stitch seams with fabric right-sides together.

1. Stitch side seams in vest and lining. On lining, press under ⅝″ on shoulder edges; trim to ¼″.

2. With right sides together, pin lining to vest, matching centers and seams, with raw edges even. Seam all edges *except shoulders, leaving a 5″ opening in bottom edge at center back.* Trim seams and corners; clip curves. Turn vest right side out through opening in bottom edge. Press. Slipstitch opening.

3. Stitch vest shoulder seams, being careful not to catch in the lining; press seams. Slip seams under lining edges; slipstitch lining edges together.

4. Pin trim to all edges except armholes. Machine stitch inner edge with zipper foot; hand stitch outer edges. Sew hook and eye closure on lower front edges.

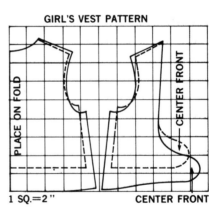

GIRL'S VEST PATTERN

PLACE ON FOLD

CENTER FRONT

1 SQ.=2″   CENTER FRONT

RAIN SLICKERS FOR GIRL AND DOG—Use our patterns and sewing instructions for slickers to protect a girl and her dog.

Girl's Rain Cape (*One Size:* 8–14)—MATERIALS: 55-wide vinyl, 2 yds.; 45″-wide lining fabric, 2⅓ yds.; thread to match fabrics; 24″ separating zipper; wrapping paper; dressmaker's carbon and tracing wheel.

DIRECTIONS: Following directions in METHODS chapter, enlarge the pattern pieces, including all markings. Cut out. From both vinyl and lining fabric, cut one Back; cut *one pair* of Front, Side Front, Side Back and Hood. With dressmaker's carbon and tracing wheel, on Side Front pieces, mark *cut-off* line at neck edge and circles on side edges; mark circles also on Front pieces. Trim Side Front pieces on *cut-off* line.

Sewing—*General Information:* Seam allowance is ½″. Stitch all seams with fabric right sides together. Clip curves in seams. Finger-press vinyl seams open; steam-press lining seams.

1. Matching circles, seam vinyl cape Front to Side Fronts, leaving seam open between circles, Seam Back to Side Backs. Stitch side seams to join front and back.

2. Seam the Hood sections along top and back edges. With right sides together, pin Hood to neck edge, with edges even, matching back seams, with notch on Hood at side seam of cape; stitch seam.

3. Following directions on package, stitch separating zipper to cape front edges.

4. Assemble lining as you did the vinyl cape and hood. With right sides together and edges even, pin lining to cape, matching seams. Stitch around hood. With zipper foot, stitch the front edges together; trim bottom of seam on a slant. Turn cape right side out.

5. Slipstitch lining neck seam to cape. Turn armslit edges ½″ in; slipstitch lining to cape all around slit.

6. Press lining away from zipper. On the inside, topstitch ¼″ from the edge of hood and front opening. Hem bottom edge of cape and lining separately, making the lining a little shorter.

Dog's Rain Cape (*for neck size up to 9″*)—MATERIALS: Flannel-backed vinyl, ⅜ yd.; ½″-wide single-fold cotton bias tape, 3¼ yds.; one 1″ buckle; one button, ⅝″ in diameter; wrapping paper; dressmaker's carbon and tracing wheel.

DIRECTIONS: Following directions in METHODS chapter, enlarge and cut out the

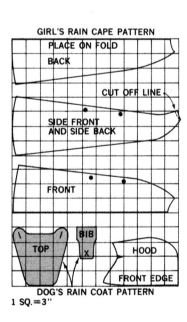

GIRL'S RAIN CAPE PATTERN
PLACE ON FOLD
BACK
CUT OFF LINE
SIDE FRONT AND SIDE BACK
FRONT
BIB
TOP
X
HOOD
FRONT EDGE
DOG'S RAIN COAT PATTERN
1 SQ. = 3″

shaded patterns. From vinyl, cut one each: Top, Bib and Strap, 24″x1″. On Top wrong side, mark buttonholes. On Bib right side, mark position of button, shown by X on pattern.

Sewing: Bind edges of all pieces with bias tape. Slip buckle over one end of strap; fold strap under and stitch across. Lap strap ½″ over straight edge of Bib, 3″ from the buckle edge; stitch in place. Sew on button. On the wrong side of the Top, zigzag along each side of marked buttonholes. Cut vinyl on marked lines.

Buckle the strap around dog's neck as shown in photo with the Bib under his throat. Wrap top piece around neck; put button on Bib through both holes.

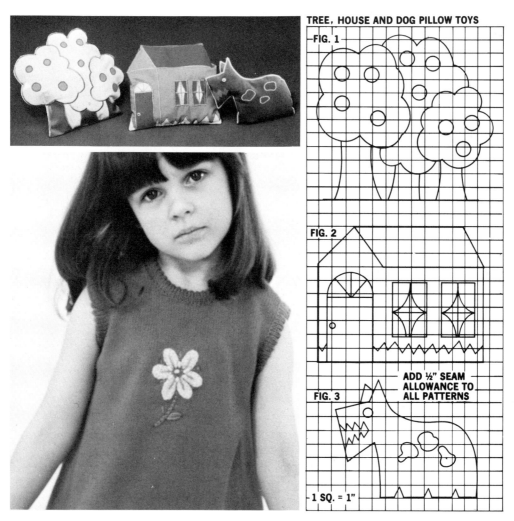

TREE, HOUSE AND DOG PILLOW TOYS

FIG. 1

FIG. 2

FIG. 3

ADD ½" SEAM ALLOWANCE TO ALL PATTERNS

1 SQ. = 1"

TREE, HOUSE AND PUPPY PILLOWS—Children's Pillows will delight the small fry. They're easy to do, with simple pattern shapes. Each is cut from two pieces of fabric for front and back. Details on the front are machine-appliquéd, using decorative machine stitches in contrasting colored thread. The eyes of the dog and the doorknob on the house are buttons.

MATERIALS: Permanent press fabric, ½ yard each turquoise, lime and pink; scraps of red, yellow and olive green; turquoise, red and lime thread; polyester pillow fill; ½" buttons, 1 yellow, 1 blue; iron-on backing (optional).

DIRECTIONS: Enlarge patterns (*see* FIGS. 1, 2 and 3) following directions in METHODS chapter. Trace *all* lines of each pattern onto top layer of a double thickness of fabric of the desired color for each. Cut around the traced outline, adding ½" seam allowance on all edges. Remove patterns. Trace, then cut each appliqué (windows, apples, etc.) from the correct color fabric. (*Optional:* Back all pieces with iron-on backing.) Pin appliqués to corresponding section on each pillow front. With contrasting color thread, use a satin-stitch setting to zigzag on all marked lines and edges of appliqués. Sew on yellow button for dog's eye and blue button for door knob. With right sides together sew pillow top and back as close as possible to embroidered outline, on all edges, leaving 4" opening in bottom edge. Trim seam; clip curves. Turn pillow covers right side out. Stuff to desired plumpness. Slipstitch bottom opening.

176

CHILD'S RED A-LINE DRESS—A folded band of knitted ribbing forms a picot edge around the neckline and armholes of this knitted A-line dress (sizes 2, 4 and 6), with crocheted flower tacked at the bodice.

Directions are given for Size 2. Changes for Sizes 4 and 6 are in parentheses.

MATERIALS: Coats & Clark's "Red Heart" Wintuk Sock and Sweater Yarn, 3 Ply skeins: 5(7,8) oz. of No. 905 Red, 2 oz. of No. 645 Shamrock; a few yards each of Orange and Yellow for flower appliqué; knitting needles, 1 pair each of No. 2 and No. 3, OR ANY SIZE NEEDLES WHICH WILL OBTAIN STITCH GAUGE BELOW; crochet hook, Size F; tapestry needle, No. 18; one small button; stitch holder.

GAUGE: St st: 7 sts = 1"; 10 rows = 1".

FINISHED MEASUREMENTS:			
SIZES:	2	4	6
CHEST:	23"	25"	27"
WIDTH ACROSS BACK OR FRONT AT UNDERARM:	11½"	12½"	13½"
LENGTH OF SIDE SEAM:	11"	13"	15"
LENGTH FROM SHOULDER TO LOWER EDGE:	15½"	18"	20½"

Back: Starting at lower edge with Red and No. 3 needles, cast on 126(136,146) sts. P 2 rows, then work in st st (k 1 row, p 1 row) for 1". Dec one st at both ends of next row and every 6th row 3(11,17) times in all; then dec one st at both ends of every 4th row 20(13,9) times—80(88,94) sts rem. Work even until total length is 11(13,15)" ending with a p row.

Armholes: Bind off 5(6,6) sts at beg of next 2 rows—70(76,82) sts. Dec one st at both ends of every other row 4 times—62(68,74) sts rem. Work even until 2" from first row of armhole shaping. Inc one st at both ends of every 4th row 3(4,4) times—68(76,82) sts.

Neck Shaping: Work across 27(30,32) sts. *Slip these last sts worked onto a stitch holder.* Bind off next 14(16,18) sts for back of neck, complete row. Work over the last 27(30,32) sts only, shaping neck and armhole edges *simultaneously* as follows: Continue to inc one st at armhole edge every 4th row, as before, until 6(7,7) sts in all have been increased on armhole edge—**at the same time**—dec one st at neck edge on every row 7(8,8) times—23(25,27) sts rem. Work even until 4½(5,5½)" from first row of armhole shaping, ending at armhole edge.

Shoulder Shaping: At armhole edge, bind off 6(6,7) sts on every other row 3 times; at same edge bind off rem 5(7,6) sts. *Slip sts from holder onto needle;* attach yarn at neck edge and work other side to correspond reversing shapings.

Front: Work same as Back.

Finishing: With right sides facing, baste Back and Front tog close to all edges. Then block, following measurements. Pin to a padded surface. Cover with a wet Turkish towel and allow to dry thoroughly. When dry, remove bastings, sew side and right shoulder seams. Sew left shoulder seam from armhole edge to within 1½" of neck edge. With Red and crochet hook, work sc evenly along shoulder opening.

Neckband: Starting at outer edge with Shamrock and No. 2 needles, cast on 122 (130,138) sts. Work in k 1, p 1 ribbing for 6 rows. **Eyelet row:** * Yo, p 2 tog. Rpt from * across. **Following row (right side):** *K 1, p 1. Rpt from * across. Work 5 rows of ribbing as before; bind off in ribbing. Starting at left shoulder, fold Neckband over neck edge, having eyelet row extend beyond neck edge. Pin evenly, curving the cast-on and bound-off edges so that they lie flat on both right and wrong sides of neck edge. Sew in place. Close shoulder opening with button and crocheted loop.

Armbands: With Shamrock and No. 2 needles, cast on 74(84,94) sts. Work same as Neckband; then pin and stitch to armholes in same way.

Flower Appliqué: Starting at center with Orange and crochet hook, ch 4. Join with sl st to form ring. **Rnd 1:** Ch 1, * sc in ring, ch 6, sc in 2nd ch from hook, sc in next 4 ch, sc in same ring. Rpt from * 5 more times. Join to first sc—6 spokes with 2 sc between spokes. Fasten off. **Rnd 2:** Attach Yellow to same place where last joining sl st was made, * sc in each of 6 ch sts of next spoke, 3 sc in back loop of next sc, sc in back loop of each of next 4 sc, skip next sc, sl st in next sc. Rpt from * around ending with sl st in same place where yarn was attached—6 petals. **Rnd 3:** Working in back loops only, * sc in 6 sc, 3 sc in next sc, sc in next 6 sc, sl st in next sl st. Rpt from * around. Fasten off. Pin flower in position on front of dress. Sew in place. With double strand of Yellow, work four ½" straight sts loosely across center of flower to form a "puff st." Make "puff sts" between petals around center. With double strand of Shamrock, embroider stem in Chain St and leaves in Lazy Daisy st as shown; then work ½" of Chain St from top of each "puff st" to complete flower.

RAINBOW PICTURE FRAMES—Let children frame their art in unfinished wood frames. Add thin coat of clear plastic coating, then paint with permanent nylon-tipped markers. Finish with several layers of plastic coating until glossy.

SOCK DOLLS TO MAKE IN A JIFFY—Christmas just isn't Christmas unless your child finds a doll under the tree (even though he or she may have 10 already). For the price of a pair of tube socks from your local supermarket, you can make *two* cute 10-inch bunny dolls. Dig into your scrap bag for pink felt (for ear linings) and some yarn for a woolly tail. Follow our sketches to make the bunny's body and head from a 10-inch toe portion of the sock; cut ears from the remainder. Fill firmly with any washable stuffing and sew on a smiling face and two bright eyes with bits of embroidery floss.

Fine foods from your kitchen—
when only the best
is good enough for your friends

If you are looking for the unusual in food gifts (at a fraction of the price you'd pay in a fancy gourmet shop) we've got 74 delicious ideas for you. Aside from a wondrous assortment of cookies and candies, consider our piquant relishes and sauces, the pâtés, cheese mold and nibbles perfect for parties, the shimmering wine jellies, the fruits cooked into chutnies, jams and condiments. Those short on time will like the no-bake and no-cook quickies, including the festive gingerbread house that kids can make from a milk carton.

recipes for foods shown above start on following page

CHAPTER 10

International Food Gifts for Connoisseurs

If you're searching for the unusual in food gifts, try these exotic recipes gathered from the four corners of the earth. They'll be enjoyed long after the holidays are over! Shown on page 179: **Ginger Figs in Port Wine**—a traditional treat in Portugal; **Andalusia Relish** from Spain—green olives layered with pimiento and mushrooms in a piquant marinade; **Herbed Vinegars** (basil and tarragon)—a secret the French country women have known for years and the staple of gourmet shops; **Brandied Apricots and Raisins**—a good example of the way the peoples of the Middle East team spices with fruit to make delicious sauces; **Parslied Vermouth Jelly** from Italy—the perfect accompaniment to platters of cold meat, and it only takes one half hour to make. Plus **Spiced Walnuts**—a Mexican trick of blending chili and oil with walnuts and roasting until mellow; **Curried Popcorn Nibbles**—the result of Yankee influence on the curried nut nibble eaten in Bombay; and **Orange Spiced Tea**—one of the delightful teas originally sold in wooden boxes with brass screws in the little tea shops in Dublin; and more!

GINGER FIGS IN PORT WINE (Portugal)

Makes 1½ cups.

The zest of ginger enhances the mellow flavor of the figs.

1. Drain syrup from figs into measuring cup, reserving 1 cup (use remaining syrup for a fruit punch).
2. Combine the 1 cup fig syrup, sugar, ginger and lemon rind in a medium-size saucepan. Slowly bring to boiling over medium heat; lower heat; simmer 5 minutes, or until mixture becomes syrupy. Add figs; simmer an additional 5 minutes. Remove rind; add port.
3. Pack into two small jars; add a lemon slice to each. Store in refrigerator. (Allow flavors to develop for 1 week.)

2 jars (1 pound, 1 ounce each) whole figs in syrup
½ cup sugar
½ cup chopped preserved ginger
1 four-inch strip fresh lemon rind
¼ cup white port
2 lemon slices

HERBED VINEGARS (France)

Makes 2 pint bottles.

A gift of aromatic herbed vinegar to make a simple salad just superb.

1. Wash 2 bottles and stoppers, about 2 cups each, in hot soapy water and rinse thoroughly.
2. Fill bottles almost to the top with vinegar and add a sprig of fresh herbs and/or several shallots or cloves of garlic; insert stoppers.
   Note: If fresh herbs are not available, you can substitute 1 tablespoon dried tarragon, basil, rosemary or chives for each bottle.

1 bottle (32 ounces) cider or wine vinegar
Fresh tarragon, basil, rosemary or chives
Shallots or garlic

BRANDIED APRICOTS AND RAISINS (Middle East)

Makes 3½ cups.

A rich, fruity sauce to spoon over ice cream.

1. Combine apricots, raisins and water in a medium-size saucepan; let stand 10 minutes for fruit to soften.
2. Stir in sugar, add cinnamon. Bring to boiling over medium heat; simmer 5 minutes, or until apricots are soft but not mushy. Add brandy.
3. Pack into decorative containers. Store in refrigerator for a week. (Mixture will thicken on standing.)

1 package (8 ounces) dried apricots
½ cup golden raisins
1½ cups water
1 cup sugar
1 three-inch piece stick cinnamon
½ cup brandy
Vanilla ice cream

ANDALUSIA RELISH (Spain)

Makes 3 cups.

Colorful and piquant, a good companion for a cold meat platter.

1. Arrange olives, pimiento strips, mushrooms and capers in small jars.
2. Combine garlic, olive oil, lemon juice, salt, pepper, chervil and tarragon in a bowl. Mix until blended with a fork or wire whip. Pour over mushrooms in jars, dividing equally. Seal; refrigerate.

1 jar (4 ounces) pitted green olives, drained
1 can (4 ounces) pimientos, drained and sliced
2 cans (4 ounces each) whole mushrooms, drained
1 tablespoon drained capers
1 clove garlic, chopped
½ cup olive oil
5 tablespoons lemon juice
¼ teaspoon salt
⅛ teaspoon pepper
½ teaspoon leaf chervil, crumbled
½ teaspoon leaf tarragon, crumbled

PARSLIED VERMOUTH JELLY (Italy)

Makes 5 half pints.

A sprightly, flavorful jelly, just right for an important dinner party.

1. Combine vermouth and sugar in top of a double boiler. Place over boiling water; cook, stirring constantly, until sugar is dissolved. Continue cooking until very hot, about 5 minutes; skim off foam on top.
2. Remove from heat; stir in liquid fruit pectin and parsley; mix well. Allow to stand 5 minutes.
3. Ladle jelly into hot sterilized jars or glasses; seal, following manufacturer's directions. Label and date.

2 cups dry vermouth
3 cups sugar
1 bottle (6 ounces) liquid fruit pectin
½ cup chopped parsley

CURRIED POPCORN NIBBLES (India)

Makes 18 cups.

The popcorn is American but the subtle curry flavor is the gift of India.

1. Pour half the oil into a large heavy skillet with a tight-fitting lid; sprinkle ½ cup popping corn over; cover skillet.
2. Heat slowly; start shaking skillet gently as soon as you hear the first pop. Continue shaking until popping stops.
3. Pour popped corn into a very large bowl and repeat with remaining oil and popping corn. (Or follow manufacturer's directions, if you have an electric corn popper.)
4. Heat butter or margarine with curry powder and salt in a small saucepan until butter or margarine bubbles, but does not brown.
5. Add nuts to popcorn in bowl; drizzle curry mixture over and toss until well-coated.
6. Gift-giving idea: Pack a pretty glass storage container with nibbles.

6 tablespoons vegetable oil
1 cup popping corn
¼ cup (½ stick) butter or margarine
2 teaspoons curry powder
1 teaspoon salt
1 can (12 ounces) mixed nuts

ORANGE SPICED TEA (Ireland)

Bake at 250° for 10 minutes.
Makes 3 gifts.

A delicate china cup and saucer makes a perfect container for this fragrant gift.

1. Remove thin bright-colored rind from each orange with a vegetable peeler or sharp knife (no white); cut into thin strips. Spread out on cookie sheet.
2. Heat in very slow oven (250°) 10 minutes, or just until rind is dry.
3. Toss loose tea with orange rind, cinnamon and whole cloves in a medium-size bowl; cover bowl; allow to stand in a dark place for 1 week to develop flavors. Spoon into 3 teacups, if you wish, for gift-giving.

3 large navel oranges
1 package (8 ounces) loose tea leaves
1 three-inch piece stick cinnamon, broken
2 teaspoons whole cloves

CHEDDAR-ALE CHEESE SPREAD (England)

Makes 2 balls about 4 inches in diameter.

Cheese and ale complement each other in this hearty spread.

1. Beat Cheddar and cream cheese and butter or margarine in large bowl with electric mixer until smooth. Gradually beat in ale, mustard and crushed red pepper. If mixture is very soft, refrigerate until firm enough to hold its shape.
2. Divide mixture in half and shape into 2 balls. Press a 3-inch round of wax paper onto top of each ball. (To keep area free for decorating.) Combine walnuts and parsley on a sheet of wax paper. Roll cheese balls in nut mixture to cover completely. Place on serving plates or boards; remove paper rounds.
3. Cut pimiento into petal shapes; arrange on uncoated part of cheese to resemble a full-blown rose; add a sprig of parsley as the stem. Cover with a cheese cover or plastic film. Refrigerate. Keeps well for several weeks. Do not roll in nuts or decorate until ready to serve.

6 cups shredded Cheddar cheese (1½ pounds)
1 package (3 ounces) cream cheese
4 tablespoons soft butter or margarine
¾ cup ale or beer
1 teaspoon dry mustard
¼ teaspoon crushed red pepper
½ cup finely chopped walnuts
½ cup chopped parsley
Pimiento
Parsley

"DIJON" MUSTARD (France)

Makes 2 cups.

A mustard with a good hot tang for those discriminating gourmets on your gift list.

1. Combine wine, onion and garlic in a small saucepan; heat to boiling; lower heat; simmer 5 minutes.
2. Pour mixture into a bowl; cool. Strain wine mixture into dry mustard in a small saucepan, beating constantly with a wire whip until very smooth.
3. Blend honey, oil, salt and pepper seasoning into mustard mixture in saucepan. Heat slowly, stirring constantly, until mixture thickens; cool.
4. Pour into a container (not metal); cover; chill at least 2 days to blend flavors.
5. Gift-giving idea: Spoon mustard into a tiny bean pot, with instructions to keep refrigerated.

2 cups dry white wine
1 large onion, chopped (1 cup)
2 cloves garlic, minced
1 can (4 ounces) dry mustard
2 tablespoons honey
1 tablespoon vegetable oil
2 teaspoons salt
Few drops bottled red-pepper seasoning

SPICED WALNUTS (Mexico)

Makes 3 cups.

Spicy nut nibbles for the cocktail hour.
Bake at 300° for 10 minutes.

1. Combine oil, chili powder, cumin, turmeric and cayenne in a skillet. Heat over low heat until oil is quite hot (do not let oil smoke). Remove from heat.
2. Add walnuts to oil; stir until coated. Spread walnuts in a paper towel-lined shallow baking pan.
3. Bake in slow oven (300°) 10 minutes, or until crisp. Sprinkle with salt. Cool; pack in fancy jars; seal.

¼ cup vegetable oil
2 teaspoons chili powder
½ teaspoon ground cumin
½ teaspoon ground turmeric
 Pinch cayenne
3 cups walnuts
½ teaspoon salt

FLOWERPOT FRUITCAKE (United States)

Bake at 325° for 1 hour.
Makes 3 flowerpot cakes.

For those dedicated gardeners on your list, a cake to eat and a flowerpot for spring.

1. To prepare flowerpots for baking: Use new clay pots (*do not use plastic*) that are 4 inches wide at the top (inside rim) and 4½ inches in depth. Pull off a 12-inch square of heavy-duty aluminum foil. Turn clay pot over and press foil as smoothly as possible over bottom and up sides of outside of pot. Remove shaped foil; then turn clay pot over and carefully press foil down into pot firmly and smoothly against insides of pot. (This is important to prevent cake from getting into cracks during baking.) Press extra foil out over rim of pot for easy lifting later. Grease bottom and side of foil; then dust with flour.
2. Combine pound-cake mix, cinnamon and nutmeg in a large mixing bowl.
3. Pour ½ cup apple juice (to replace water in package directions) into a 1-cup measure; add brandy to the ⅔ cup mark.
4. Add apple juice mixture to pound-cake mixture with two eggs. Stir until ingredients are thoroughly moistened. Then beat 3 minutes on medium speed of electric mixer or 450 strokes by hand.
5. Toss raisins with the flour; stir into cake mixture. Divide batter among the 3 pots. Sprinkle slivered almonds equally over the tops of the cakes, pressing them into the top of the batter.
6. Place flowerpots on baking sheet; place on middle rack in oven.
7. Bake in a pre-heated slow oven (325°) 1 hour, or until cake tester inserted in center comes out clean. Carefully remove cakes to wire racks; let cool 10 minutes. Loosen cakes from clay pots by pulling up on the foil. Let cool thoroughly in foil in the pots.
8. To decorate: Remove cakes from pots; remove foil; brush tops with heated corn syrup, decorate with whole blanched almonds, candied cherry halves and angelica or citron. Wrap cakes in clear plastic. Wash and dry pots. Put wrapped cakes back in pot for gift-giving.
Note: Cake may be baked in a 9x5x3-inch loaf pan which has been generously greased and floured. Follow package directions for temperature and time.

1 box (1 pound) golden
  pound cake mix
½ teaspoon ground cinnamon
½ teaspoon ground nutmeg
½ cup apple juice
 Brandy
2 eggs
½ cup golden raisins
1 tablespoon flour
½ cup slivered almonds,
  optional
 Corn syrup
 Candied red cherries
 Angelica
 Whole almonds

COOKIE CHRISTMAS CARDS (Scandinavia)

Bake at 350° for 12 minutes. Makes about ten 4- to 6-inch cookies.

It is a lucky person who receives your gift and can eat the gift card, too!

1. Sift flour, baking soda, cinnamon, cloves and nutmeg onto wax paper.
2. Combine honey, sugar and butter or margarine in a small saucepan; bring just to boiling, stirring constantly. Pour into a large mixing bowl; cool, stirring often, 10 minutes. Stir in fresh lemon rind and juice, orange peel and almonds. Gradually work in flour to make a stiff dough. Chill.
3. Roll out dough, one quarter at a time, to 1/4-inch thickness, on lightly floured surface. Cut into shapes with floured 4- to 6-inch cookie cutter, or cut around your own cardboard patterns with a small knife. Place 1 inch apart on lightly greased cookie sheet.
4. Bake in moderate oven (350°) 12 minutes, or until golden. Remove from cookie sheet to wire racks.
5. Combine 10X sugar with water to make a thin glaze; stir until smooth; brush over cookies while hot; cool.
6. Decorate with ROYAL FROSTING.

4½ cups *sifted* all-purpose flour
1 teaspoon baking soda
1 teaspoon ground cinnamon
¼ teaspoon ground cloves
¼ teaspoon ground nutmeg
1 cup honey
1 cup sugar
4 tablespoons butter or margarine
1½ teaspoons grated lemon rind
¼ cup lemon juice
½ cup finely chopped candied orange peel
1 cup finely chopped almonds
Whole almonds
1 cup 10X (confectioners') sugar
2 tablespoons water
Royal Frosting (*recipe page 211*)
Assorted food colorings

PÂTÉ MAISON (France)

Bake at 300° for 1 hour 45 minutes. Makes 5 small pâtés or one large 6-cup pâté.

An easy and very Continental way to say bon appétit.

1. Place chicken livers, onion and garlic in container of electric blender. Whirl at high speed until smooth, about 30 seconds; turn into a large bowl.
2. Add pork and eggs; beat until well-combined. Stir in flour, salt, allspice, pepper and cloves. Add cream and brandy, beating until smooth; stir in nuts.
3. Spoon pâté mixture into 5 well-greased 10-ounce custard cups or oven-proof dishes, or spoon onto one large 7- or 8-cup baking dish. Place 1 or 2 bay leaves on top of each; cover with foil.
4. Place baking dishes in a large roasting pan on oven shelf. Pour boiling water into outer pan to depth of about 1½ inches.
5. Bake in slow oven (300°) 1 hour 45 minutes, or until juices run clear when pâté is pierced in center with a small knife; remove from water; peel off foil. Place a clean piece of foil on top. Place a weight on each pâté (an unopened 8- to 10-ounce can is about right). Chill overnight.
6. Make BEEF ASPIC. Pour in enough aspic in each dish to cover and fill to the rim. Chill until firm; cover with plastic wrap. Serve as appetizer on crackers, melba toast or party rye. Refrigerate; will keep well

1 pound chicken livers
1 medium onion, peeled and quartered
1 clove garlic
1¼ pounds ground pork
2 eggs
⅓ cup flour
2 teaspoons salt
½ teaspoon ground allspice
¼ teaspoon pepper
⅛ teaspoon ground cloves
⅔ cup light cream
⅓ cup brandy
¼ cup chopped pistachio nuts
Bay leaves
Beef Aspic (*recipe follows*)

about a week.

BEEF ASPIC—Combine 1 envelope unflavored gelatin and 1 can condensed beef broth in a small saucepan; heat slowly, stirring constantly, until gelatin is completely dissolved. Remove from heat; add 2 tablespoons brandy (*optional*). Cool; chill until slightly syrupy.

No-Cook Food Gifts: just measure, mix and give

Homemade food gifts can be hasslefree—made with plenty of thoughtfulness but very little work.

To prove the point, we've collected 9 unusually delicious recipes that don't require cooking. (One involves dissolving some gelatin, but that's not really cooking.) Just measure, mix, chop a little and spoon or pour the mixtures into glass containers. Tie a ribbon around each and, in the twinkling of an eye, you're out of the kitchen.

The gifts can be made ahead of time too, and stored on a cupboard shelf or in the refrigerator. They include fondue sauces, herb blends, beverages, a salad dressing, chutney, relish and dessert sauce—a little something for all and a great big carefree gift for yourself.

CREAMY CURRY FONDUE SAUCE
Makes 2½ cups.

Serve as a dipping sauce for beef fondue, shrimp, fruit, chips or crackers; as a salad dressing for fruit; or as an accompaniment to chicken salad.

Combine mayonnaise or salad dressing, sour cream, chutney, curry powder, orange rind and pecans in a medium-size bowl; stir until well-blended. Pack into glass jars or fancy containers; seal, label and chill until ready to give as a gift. (Will keep for about a week.)

1 cup mayonnaise or salad dressing
1 cup dairy sour cream
½ cup chopped chutney
1 teaspoon curry powder
1 teaspoon grated orange rind
½ cup finely chopped pecans

SPICY TOMATO FONDUE SAUCE
Makes 3 cups.

Good as a dipping sauce for beef, chicken or shrimp fondue; on hamburgers and franks; or to heat and serve over spaghetti or veal parmigiana.

Combine tomato sauce, green chilies, garlic and olives in electric-blender container; whirl at top speed until smooth and well-blended. Pack into glass containers; seal, label and chill until ready to give. (Will keep for about a week.)

1 jar (21 ounces) tomato sauce
  OR: 2½ cups of prepared spaghetti sauce with mushrooms
1 can (4 ounces) sweet green chilies, drained
2 cloves garlic
½ cup drained pitted ripe olives

ITALIAN HERB BLEND

Makes 1⅔ cups.

This easy-to-make bouquet of flavors can be used to season any food that needs an Italian character—from salad dressings and pasta sauces to meat loaves, roast meats, and eggplant.

Combine oregano, basil, sage, seasoned salt, lemon pepper and garlic powder in a small bowl and stir until well-blended. Pack into small crocks, jars or clear plastic containers; seal and label. Store in a cool, dry place.

- ½ cup leaf oregano
- ½ cup leaf basil
- 2 tablespoons leaf sage
- 1 jar (3¼ ounces) seasoned salt
- 2 tablespoons lemon pepper
- 2 tablespoons garlic powder

FRENCH HERB BLEND

Makes 2⅓ cups.

Use to season meats, poultry, salad dressings and vegetables. (Note: When using, you may also want to add salt and pepper to food being seasoned.)

Combine tarragon, chervil, sage, thyme, rosemary, chives, orange rind and celery seed in a medium-size bowl and stir until well-blended. Pack into crocks or small jars; seal and label. Store in a cool, dry place. Crumble in hand when using.

- ½ cup tarragon
- ½ cup chervil
- 2 tablespoons leaf sage
- ½ cup thyme
- 2 tablespoons rosemary
- 5 tablespoons freeze-dried chopped chives
- 2 tablespoons dehydrated orange rind
- 2 tablespoons ground celery seed

HOT MOCHA MIX

Makes 6½ cups.

Just add boiling water to this mix and serve in coffee mugs (the milk and cream are included).

1. Combine cocoa, sugar, milk powder, coffee creamer, instant coffee and vanilla bean in a large dry bowl; stir until well-blended.
2. Pack into jars, making sure a piece of vanilla bean is in each jar. Seal and label. Store in the refrigerator at least a week before using to allow vanilla flavor to be absorbed into the mix.
3. For drinking, use 3 level tablespoonfuls for every 6 ounces of boiling water. Top with a marshmallow or whipped cream.

- 1 cup unsweetened cocoa
- 2 cups sugar
- 2 cups nonfat dry milk powder
- 2 cups dry non-dairy coffee creamer
- ½ cup instant coffee
- 1 vanilla bean, cut into quarters

CELERY RELISH

Makes 4½ cups.

Serve on hamburgers, frankfurters, fried fish fillets or as an accompaniment to broiled meats.

1. Put celery, onion and pimiento into electric-blender container; reserve.
2. Mix gelatin and salad dressing in small saucepan. Stir over low heat just until gelatin is dissolved.
3. Pour gelatin mixture on vegetables in blender. Cover; whirl at low speed until ingredients are coarsely chopped.
4. Pour mixture into a bowl and chill until thick. Spoon into jars; seal, label and chill until ready to give as a gift. (Will keep for about a week.)

- 4 cups sliced celery
- 1 large onion, cut into sixths
- 1 jar (4 ounces) pimiento, drained
- 1 envelope unflavored gelatin
- 1 bottle (8 ounces) Italian salad dressing

186

ZESTY SALAD DRESSING

Makes 2⅔ cups.

This is more than a salad dressing, it's also delightful as a basting sauce for broiled chicken and fish!

Combine oil, vinegar, garlic, herb blend, cheese, sugar, salt and pepper in a large bowl; beat with wire whisk until thick and well-blended. Pack into three ½-pint jars; seal and label. Store in refrigerator. Beat or shake well before using.

- 2 cups vegetable oil
- ⅔ cup red wine vinegar
- 2 cloves garlic, chopped
- 2 tablespoons Italian Herb Blend (*see previous page*)
- ¼ cup grated Parmesan cheese
- 1 tablespoon sugar
- 1 tablespoon salt
- 1 teaspoon cracked pepper

APPLE CHUTNEY

Makes 6 cups.

Serve as an accompaniment to beef, poultry or ham, and with curries and other spicy foods.

Combine the apple butter, mincemeat, relish, onion and red-pepper seasoning in a large bowl; stir until well-blended. Spoon into glass jars, seal tightly and label. Store in refrigerator up to two weeks.

- 3½ cups apple butter (one 28-ounce jar)
- 2 jars (14½ ounces each) prepared mincemeat (about 3½ cups)
- 1 jar (9¾ ounces) sweet pickle relish, undrained (about 1¼ cups)
- ¼ cup instant minced onion
- ¼ teaspoon liquid red-pepper seasoning

HOLIDAY FRUIT SAUCE

Makes about 6 cups.

Spoon this sweet sauce over cake squares, vanilla ice cream and fresh fruit; or use as a filling between cake layers.

Combine apple-pie filling, pineapple, marmalade, cherries and ginger in a large bowl; stir until well-blended. Pour into glass containers; seal, label and chill until ready to give as a gift.

- 1 can (1 pound, 5 ounces) apple-pie filling
- 1 can (1 pound, 4 ounces) crushed pineapple, drained
- 1 jar (12 ounces) orange marmalade
- 1 cup chopped maraschino cherries (from an 8-ounce jar)
- ⅓ cup chopped crystallized ginger

Gifts for Food Lovers—with a Dividend

Delicacies you make or bake are thoughtful for all occasions, but they are doubly enchanting when they come in pretty containers that can be enjoyed once the goodies are gone. **Balls**, *(left, top)* are chocolate rounds with the spirited flavor of bourbon. **Peanut-Popcorn Clusters** are for the nutty-crunchy-munchy set on your list. They're ensconced in plastic flower pots (for African violets later) and sprout perky gingham flowers to bring cheer during the winter months. The **Cherry-Almond Braid**, a savory coffee cake redolent of almonds and cherries, is tucked inside a plastic-lined gingham tote bag. **Candied Fruit Basket** is a pleasant surprise—candied orange peel nestles in a candied grapefruit shell along with dates stuffed with blanched almonds. The clay pot beneath is perfect for holding potted plants. **Neapolitan Ribbons** are a dream. Ever-so-thin layers of easy-do pound cake are sandwiched with apple jelly and lavishly coated with chocolate and pistachio nuts. The fanciful tray is actually an inexpensive picture frame lined with gingham fabric.

TOTE OR TRAVEL BAG (*for Cherry-Almond Braid*)—Pretty and useful too— plastic-lined drawstring bags can be used for travel or as summer handbags. To make **Pink bag**—Cut 9″x24″ fabric of medium check for bag, 5″x24″ of small check (for trim) and 2½″x17″ of large check (for casing). For trim, turn under lengthwise edges of 5″x24″ strip, pin strip to center of bag and stitch. Stitch rickrack over stitching as shown. With right sides together, stitch side seams of bag with ½″ seams. Stitch casing strip to top of bag with ½″ seam, turning raw ends under ½″ at side seam. Trim seams; fold casing to outside; turn raw edges

188

under ¼″ and topstitch. Draw ribbon through casing (1 yard pink grosgrain, 1″ wide). For plastic lining, cut 8″x23″ strip of clear plastic, fold crosswise and stitch side seams. (Plastic may be stitched more easily if you stitch through tissue paper, then pull paper away when seam is stitched.) Trim closely. Turn top edges under ¾″ and topstitch. Insert lining in bag.

CHERRY-ALMOND BRAID

Bake at 350° for 25 minutes.
Makes 3 braids.

Tender, sweetly almondy and brimming with nuts and cherries, these coffee cakes make gifts for three.

	¾ cup milk
	½ cup sugar (for dough)
	1 teaspoon salt
	½ cup (1 stick) butter or margarine
	1 envelope active dry yeast
	¼ cup very warm water
	4 eggs
	5¼ cups *sifted* all-purpose flour
	1 container (8 ounces) candied red cherries, chopped
	1 can (8 ounces) almond paste
	2 tablespoons sugar (for filling)
	1 cup sliced blanched almonds
	½ cup 10X (confectioners') sugar
	2 tablespoons water
	¼ teaspoon almond extract

1. Combine milk, ½ cup sugar, salt and butter or margarine in a small saucepan. Heat slowly, until butter or margarine melts; cool to lukewarm.
2. Sprinkle yeast into very warm water in a large bowl. ("Very warm water" should feel comfortably warm when dropped on wrist.) Stir until yeast dissolves, then stir in milk mixture and 2 eggs.
3. Beat in 2 cups of flour until smooth; beat in 3 cups more flour to make a soft dough.
4. Turn out onto lightly floured pastry board; knead until smooth and elastic, adding only enough of remaining ¼ cup of flour to keep dough from sticking.
5. Place in a greased large bowl; turn to coat all over with shortening; cover with a clean towel. Let rise in a warm place, away from draft, 1½ to 2 hours, or until double in bulk.
6. Punch dough down; knead a few times on lightly floured pastry board; return to bowl; cover again; let rise again ½ hour, or until double in bulk.
7. While dough rises, crumble almond paste in a small bowl; stir in 1 egg and 2 tablespoons remaining sugar until smooth.
8. Divide dough into 3 even pieces. Roll each piece into an 8x10-inch rectangle; spoon ⅓ cup filling in a narrow strip down middle of dough almost to ends. Sprinkle with ⅓ cup cherries.
9. Cut dough on each side from outer edge just to filling in 1½-inch-wide strips with scissors or knife; fold strips, alternating from side to side, across filling at an angle; repeat with remaining 2 pieces of dough. Place on greased cookie sheets; cover.
10. Let rise again in a warm place, away from draft, 40 minutes, or until double in bulk.
11. Beat remaining egg with 2 tablespoons water; brush on braids; sprinkle with sliced almonds.
12. Bake in moderate oven (350°) 25 minutes, or until golden and coffee cake gives a hollow sound when tapped. Remove to wire racks; cool slightly.
13. Combine 10X sugar, almond extract, and 2 tablespoons water in a cup; blend until smooth and easy to pour from a spoon. Drizzle over braids. Garnish with additional red and green candied cherries, if you wish.

    For gift-giving: Put each plastic-wrapped braid into the pink TOTE OR TRAVEL BAG. Place in gift box (from variety store), if you wish. Wrap; tie; decorate.

CHECK-A-BLOOM FLOWERS (*for Bourbon Balls and Peanut-Popcorn Clusters*)—A gift for a nature lover—new see-through plastic flowerpots blooming with bright fabric flowers. For fabric "rose," cut 9"x12" strip of small-checked fabric and 6"x12" strip of medium-checked fabric for flower center. Starch strips stiffly; and iron dry. For flower center, fold strip in half lengthwise and roll loosely to form a rosebud; tack lightly to secure and set aside. For flower, fold strip in half crosswise and seam together. Then fold (so seams are inside) to form a double-thickness circlet. With machine-basting stitch, stitch bottom raw edges together, leaving thread ends long. Gather bottom evenly. Glue flower center to flower with white glue and let dry. For stem, stitch a 14" length of ½" green folded bias tape lengthwise to form casing and insert length of clothes-hanger wire into casing. Attach flower to stem by wrapping green fabric tape securely around flower bottom and stem. Cut green leaves from felt; stitch "veins" on sewing machine. Glue leaves to stem. For "peony," cut 10"x15" strip of medium-checked fabric and 6"x15" strip of small-checked fabric. Stitch each according to directions for flower above, omitting those for flower center. Glue 2 gathered circlets together, one inside the other, as shown. Gather a small square of plain pink fabric around a wad of cotton, tack and glue in position for flower center. Finish flower as described above. For an extra-thoughtful gift with the flower pots, you may wish to give a lovely amaryllis or hyacinth bulb to be planted and to burst out in color in spring. You will find bulbs at your local garden supply store.

BOURBON BALLS
Makes 3 dozen confections.

No baking, no bother, for these deep, dark chocolate confections made merry with just a touch of mellow bourbon.

1. Melt chocolate pieces in top of a double boiler over simmering water; remove from heat. Blend in corn syrup and bourbon; stir in sugar, vanilla wafer cookies and pecans until well-combined.
2. Roll mixture, a rounded teaspoonful at a time, into balls between palms of hands. Roll balls in chocolate sprinkles to coat generously, pressing firmly as you roll. Place in a jelly-roll pan; cover; chill several hours.
   For gift-giving: Fill clear plastic flowerpots with confections. Put a pink flower in pot. Place filled pot on clear plastic wrap. Bring wrap up and around pot, with flowers and leaves unwrapped. Tie with pink grosgrain ribbon.

1 package (6 ounces) semisweet chocolate pieces
3 tablespoons light corn syrup
¼ cup bourbon
½ cup sugar
1¼ cups crushed vanilla wafer cookies (about 36)
1 cup finely chopped pecans
1 container (4 ounces) chocolate decorating sprinkles

PEANUT-POPCORN CLUSTERS
Makes about 2½ dozen.

For TV snacking here is a nutty gift for the whole family to munch and crunch.

1. Combine sugar, molasses, corn syrup, butter or margarine and lemon juice in a large skillet. Heat slowly, stirring constantly, just until sugar dissolves; remove from heat.
2. Stir in popcorn and peanuts; toss until evenly coated. Cook, stirring constantly, over medium heat, 5 minutes, or until mixture is very sticky.
3. Spoon out onto wax paper. Let stand a few minutes until cool enough to handle, then shape into 2-inch clusters. Let stand until coating is firm and dry. Wrap individually in plastic wrap. Store in a loosely covered container.

⅓ cup sugar
3 tablespoons molasses
3 tablespoons dark corn syrup
1 teaspoon butter or margarine
1 teaspoon lemon juice
4 cups freshly popped corn
1 can (6½ ounces) cocktail peanuts

continued

190

For gift-giving: Fill clear plastic flowerpots with confections. Put a pink flower in pot. Place filled pot on clear plastic wrap. Bring wrap up and around top of pot, leaving flowers and leaves unwrapped. Tie with pink grosgrain ribbon.

PICTURE-FRAME TRAY (*for Neapolitan Ribbons*)—Another variety-store find —an inexpensive picture frame becomes a tiny tray. To make it, take frame elements apart, setting glass aside. Cover cardboard backing with fabric, gluing fabric to back. Insert glass in frame, then fabric-covered cardboard, then plain cardboard for backing. Tape all around to secure.

NEAPOLITAN RIBBONS

Bake at 350° for 15 minutes.
Makes 2 cakes,
2 inches by 9 inches.

Bright thin layers of easy-do pound cake sandwiched with tangy apple jelly and lavishly coated with dark chocolate

1. Grease and line three 9x9x2-inch pans with wax paper and then dust with flour, tapping out excess.
2. Prepare pound cake mix with eggs and liquid, following label directions.
3. Measure 1 cupful of batter in a small bowl; tint a bright yellow with a few drops yellow food coloring; pour into one of the prepared pans. Repeat with remaining batter, tinting pink and green with food coloring.
4. Bake layers in moderate oven (350°) 15 minutes, or until cake springs back when lightly pressed with fingertip. Cool in pans for 10 minutes. Loosen layers around edges with sharp knife and turn out layers onto wire racks; peel off wax paper and cool completely.
5. Trim cake layers to square off edges. Cut each layer into 4 even strips, about 2 inches wide.
6. Combine apple jelly and crème de cacao in a small saucepan. Heat slowly until jelly melts.
7. To make each cake: Place 1 yellow strip on cookie sheet. Brush apple syrup over cake with a pastry brush. Top with a green strip and brush, then with pink strip and brush. Repeat with 3 more strips of cake. Brush sides with syrup.
8. Combine butter or margarine, corn syrup and water in a small saucepan. Heat to boiling. Remove from heat. Stir in chocolate pieces until melted. Beat mixture until stiff enough to spread on cakes (about 3 minutes).
9. Frost cakes with chocolate and sprinkle with chopped pistachio nuts.
   For gift-giving: Place cake on the decorated picture frame. Place frame with cake in gift box (from variety store) without cover. Wrap box, if you wish, in wide plastic wrap, for a see-through effect. Tie with wide ribbon.

1 package pound cake mix
2 eggs
  Liquid as label directs
  Yellow, red and green
    food coloring
1 jar (10 ounces) apple jelly
4 tablespoons crème de cacao
2 tablespoons butter or
    margarine
3 tablespoons light corn syrup
¼ cup water
1 package (6 ounces)
    semisweet chocolate
    pieces
  Chopped pistachio nuts

CANDIED FRUIT BASKET

*Makes 1¼ pounds,
or 1 filled basket.*

*Give a double gift—zesty orange peel and stuffed dates
to nibble, then start on the grapefruit basket.*

1 large grapefruit
3 large oranges
4 cups sugar
2 tablespoons light corn
    syrup
2 cups water
2 packages (3 ounces each)
    orange-flavor gelatin
    Yellow sugar crystals
    Pitted dates
    Blanched almonds

1. Cut a slice from top of grapefruit. (For a pretty edge, use a 25-cent piece for a pattern to make scallops.) Remove the pulp from the grapefruit, using a grapefruit knife or a small sharp paring knife and being careful not to break through the shell. Scrape out remaining pulp and membrane.
2. Peel rind from oranges in quarters; cut rind into ¼-inch-wide strips.
3. Place grapefruit and orange peel in a large saucepan. Cover with cold water; heat to boiling; lower heat and simmer 15 minutes. Drain peel. Repeat cooking with fresh water, and draining two more times. Scrape off as much white membrane as possible.
4. Combine sugar, light corn syrup and water in same saucepan. Cook, stirring until sugar dissolves. Add grapefruit and orange peel.
5. Simmer, uncovered, turning often with a wooden spoon, until syrup registers 230° on a candy thermometer. (Or until syrup will spin a 2-inch thread when dropped from spoon.)
6. Remove saucepan from heat and let fruits stand in syrup overnight. Weight down, if necessary, to keep fruit covered with syrup.
7. Return saucepan to heat and cook until syrup reaches 238° on a candy thermometer. Remove fruits from syrup and invert grapefruit shell over a glass. Separate orange peel and place on wax paper. (Remaining syrup makes a delicious topping for French toast or ice cream.)
8. Sprinkle orange-flavor gelatin on wax paper. Roll orange peel strips on all sides to coat. Place in a single layer on a cookie sheet to dry.
9. Sprinkle yellow sugar crystals all over outside of grapefruit shell. Allow to dry completely.
10. Stuff date with almonds. Arrange candied orange peel and dates in grapefruit shell.
    For gift-giving: Place on new clean flowerpot saucer. Wrap in plastic wrap.

CHAMPAGNE JELLY

Makes 6 half pints.

For the ultimate gift from the preserving kettle—tangy, sparkly CHAMPAGNE JELLY. *Just the right go-with for the holiday meat platter.*

1 bottle (4/5-pint size)
    champagne (1⅔
    cups)
1⅓ cups reconstituted frozen
    tangerine juice
4½ cups sugar
1 bottle (6 ounces) liquid
    fruit pectin

1. Combine champagne, tangerine juice and sugar in top of a double boiler. Place over boiling water; cook, stirring constantly, until sugar is dissolved. Continue cooking until very hot, about 5 minutes; skim off foam on top.
2. Remove from heat; stir in liquid fruit pectin. Mix well.
3. Ladle jelly into hot sterilized jars or glasses; seal, following manufacturer's directions. Label and date. Wrap festively.

**SUPER GOOD
CHRISTMAS COOKIES
AND CANDIES**
Cookies in jar (from top):
Lemon-Nutmeg
Meltaway Cookies,
Sugar-crusted Choco-
late Pretzels, Almond-
Orange Confections,
Coconut Gingeroons.
Candy (top, right and
clockwise): Old-
fashioned Sponge
Candy, Molasses
Chips, Peanut Butter
Fudge, Molasses
Coconut Chews.
Cookies on tree:
Speculaas.

Recipes start on page 197

193

**INTERNATIONAL FOOD GIFTS
FOR CONNOISSEURS**
From right to left: Cheddar-Ale Cheese
Spread; Pâté Maison; Flowerpot
Fruitcake; "Dijon" Mustard.

Recipes for International Food Gifts
start on page 180

194

GOURMET FOOD GIFTS
YOU'LL BE PROUD TO GIVE

From top, counter clockwise: Crêpes au Grand Marnier, Glazed Walnuts, Olives Jerez, Chocolate Sauce Supreme, Brandied Butterscotch Sauce, Mustard Trio, Carioca Pastries, Ten-minute Pâté, Vin Rosé Jelly, Vin Chablis Jelly, Fruits aux Rhum and Banana Bread.

Recipes for Gourmet Food Gifts start on page 206

195

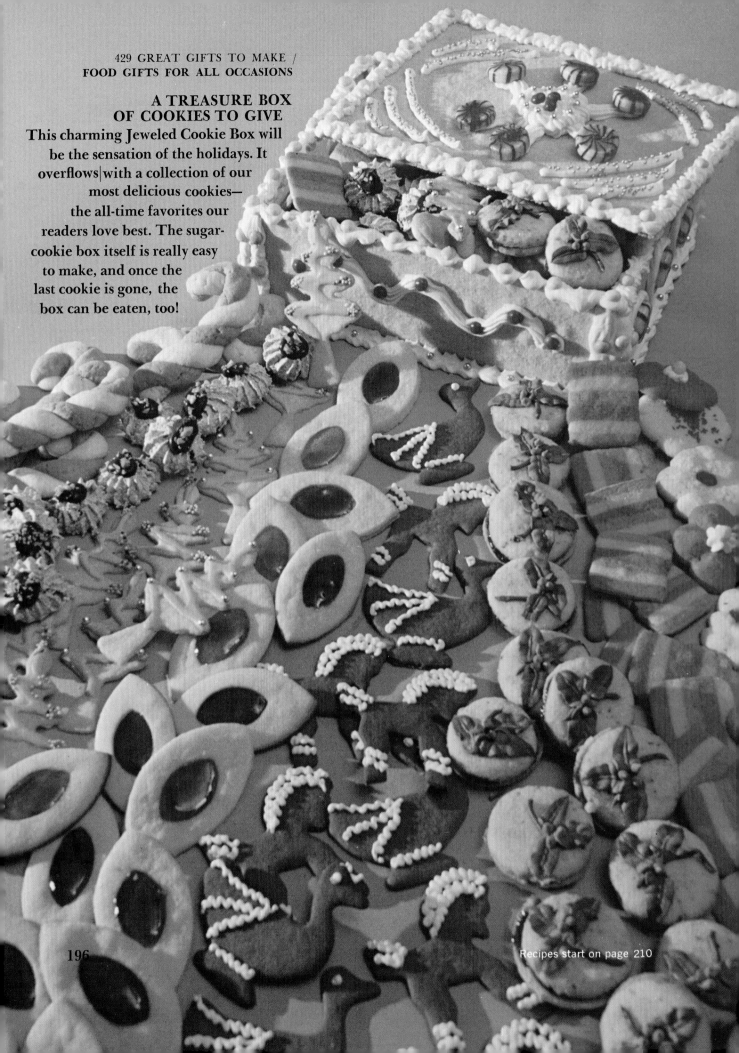

A TREASURE BOX
OF COOKIES TO GIVE

This charming Jeweled Cookie Box will
be the sensation of the holidays. It
overflows|with a collection of our
most delicious cookies—
the all-time favorites our
readers love best. The sugar-
cookie box itself is really easy
to make, and once the
last cookie is gone, the
box can be eaten, too!

196

Recipes start on page 210

Super Good Christmas Cookies and Candies

The season wouldn't seem right without cookie-baking, that's for sure. But this happy occupation will be even more fun if you can tackle it before the onset of the Christmas countdown. That's a special asset of this wonderful cookie collection—these actually improve with age. What's more, these cookies won't require space in your refrigerator or freezer; you just pack them in plastic containers or tins. You can even ship these mouthwatering goodies without their crumbling. These candies will also keep for a few weeks, so you can make them early too.

LEMON-NUTMEG MELTAWAY COOKIES

Bake at 325° for 15 minutes. Makes 64 single cookies or 32 double cookies.

Truly melt-in-the-mouth delicacies, with a fragile lemony aroma.

1. Sift flour, cornstarch, salt and nutmeg onto wax paper.
2. Beat butter, sugar and lemon rind in a medium-size bowl with electric mixer until light and fluffy.
3. Add sifted dry ingredients to butter mixture. Beat on low speed, scraping bowl, until mixture is smooth. Roll dough by measuring teaspoonfuls into balls. Place on ungreased cookie sheet; flatten slightly to 1¼-inch circles with bottom of glass dipped in 10X sugar.
4. Bake in a slow oven (325°) for 15 minutes or until cookies have turned a very pale golden-brown around the edges.
5. Cool 2 minutes on the cookie sheet, then transfer to a wire rack and cool completely. Pack into airtight containers and store up to 1 week.
Note: Cookies can be put together in pairs as follows: Cook ½ cup apricot preserves with 1 tablespoon sugar in a small saucepan for 2 minutes, stirring constantly. Cool, then spread just enough of the mixture between pairs of cookies to hold firmly.

1 cup *sifted* cake flour
½ cup cornstarch
¼ teaspoon salt
½ teaspoon ground nutmeg
10 tablespoons (1 stick plus 2 tablespoons) unsalted butter or margarine, softened
½ cup 10X (confectioners') sugar
2 teaspoons grated lemon rind

CANDIED FRUIT AND NUT RUSKS

Bake at 400° for 25 minutes, then at 300° for 40 minutes. Makes about 28 rusks.

These crisp biscuits are delicate and colorful and a graceful complement to after-dinner coffee or an afternoon tea.

1. Sift flour, baking powder and salt onto wax paper. Toss 2 tablespoonfuls of the mixture with fruit, nuts and anise seeds into a small bowl.
2. Beat butter, sugar, almond extract and eggs in a medium-size bowl with electric mixer at high speed until light and fluffy.
3. Stir remaining flour mixture and the fruit mixture into the butter mixture. Cover bowl; chill at least 2 hours.
4. Turn dough out onto floured surface; halve. Roll each half with floured hands to a cylinder 9 to 10 inches long. Place on large foil-covered cookie sheet, spacing loaves well apart.

2½ cups *sifted* all-purpose flour
2 teaspoons baking powder
¼ teaspoon salt
½ cup candied mixed fruit, chopped
½ cup whole almonds
1½ teaspoons anise seeds
6 tablespoons unsalted butter or margarine, softened
¾ cup sugar
½ teaspoon almond extract
3 eggs

continued

5. Bake in a hot oven (400°) for 25 minutes or until loaves are firm and golden.
6. Cool loaves on cookie sheet for 5 minutes, then transfer to wire rack to cool completely.
7. Cut each loaf into 13 or 14 about-½-inch-thick diagonal slices with a serrated knife. Put slices on a large cookie sheet.
8. Bake slices in a slow oven (300°) for 20 minutes. Turn over and bake 20 minutes longer. Cool on wire racks. Pack in airtight containers and store up to 2 weeks.

SPECULAAS

Bake at 350° for 12 minutes.
Makes about 7 dozen.

These crisp, buttery spice cookies take marvelously to designing: Press in blanched almonds or candied fruit before baking; when cooled, glaze or pipe on fanciful designs with decorator's icing. Use your imagination to form new shapes, new icing combinations. Hang the cookies on the tree or use them as room ornaments or personalized Christmas-present tags.

1. Sift flour, baking powder, cinnamon, ginger, cardamom, allspice, anise and salt onto wax paper.
2. Combine butter, sugar and egg in large bowl. Beat with electric mixer at high speed until light and fluffy. Beat in the dry ingredients slowly at low speed until mixture is smooth. Divide dough into 3 portions; wrap each in foil or plastic wrap and chill at least 2 hours.
3. Roll dough, one portion at a time, between two sheets of wax paper to a ⅛-inch thickness. Cut with fancy Christmas cutters or a 2½-inch round cutter. Place cookies on large greased cookie sheets. Press in any decorations you wish.
4. Bake in a moderate oven (350°) for 12 minutes or until cookies are slightly brown at the edges. Cool on wire racks. Store up to 4 weeks. Decorate with Royal Frosting, if you wish (*recipe on page 211*).

4 cups *sifted* all-purpose **flour**
3 teaspoons baking **powder**
3 teaspoons ground **cinnamon**
1½ teaspoons ground ginger
1 teaspoon ground **cardamom**
½ teaspoon ground allspice
½ teaspoon ground anise **seed (pound with hammer to grind)**
¼ teaspoon salt
1 cup (2 sticks) unsalted **butter or margarine, softened**
1½ cups firmly packed dark **brown sugar, lump-free**
1 egg

MINCEMEAT HERMITS

Bake at 350° for 30 minutes.
Makes about 32.

A rich moist variation of an old American favorite. The flavors mellow as the bars age.

1. Sift flour, baking powder, baking soda and cinnamon onto wax paper.
2. Beat butter, sugar, egg and molasses in medium-size bowl with electric mixer until light and fluffy, about 2 minutes. Stir in mincemeat by hand, then add flour mixture and beat until well blended. Spread batter in a greased 13x9x2-inch baking pan.
3. Bake in a moderate oven (350°) for 30 minutes or until center springs back when lightly pressed with fingertip. Cool for 15 minutes in the pan on a wire rack, then cut into 32 rectangles and cool completely. Leave in pan and wrap tightly in foil or plastic wrap (or remove from pan and wrap in a single layer) and store up to

2 cups *sifted* all-purpose **flour**
½ teaspoon baking powder
½ teaspoon baking soda
½ teaspoon ground **cinnamon**
½ cup (1 stick) unsalted **butter or margarine, softened**
⅓ cup sugar
1 egg
⅓ cup molasses
1 cup prepared mincemeat

2 weeks. Drizzle confectioners' sugar glaze over cookies, if you wish.

MARZIPAN-FILLED GINGERBREAD BAR COOKIES

Bake at 350° for 45 minutes.
Makes about 2 dozen.

Soft, smooth and elegant.

1. Break up almond paste into large bowl; beat in egg white and almond extract with electric mixer. Slowly beat in 10X sugar until mixture is quite smooth. Turn out onto well-floured wax paper and pat to a 7½-inch square. Sprinkle with flour; cover with wax paper. Refrigerate until firm, 1 hour or more.
2. Sift flour, baking soda, cinnamon, ginger and salt onto wax paper.
3. Beat butter in medium-size bowl with electric mixer. While beating, sprinkle in the brown sugar with your fingers, removing lumps if any. Add the corn syrup, sour cream and egg yolk and continue to beat until mixture is fluffy.
4. Stir in the flour mixture until batter is smooth. Spread half the batter evenly in a greased 8x8x2-inch pan. Place the sheet of marzipan on top, then spread remaining batter over marzipan with a wet spatula.
5. Bake in a moderate oven (350°) for 45 minutes, or until firm in the center. Let cool 10 minutes in the pan. Turn out on wire rack and cool completely. Cut into bars; wrap tightly in a single layer and store 2 to 3 weeks.

To serve: Frost with your favorite butter-cream frosting, garnish with chopped almonds and chopped citron, if you wish.

½ pound almond paste
1 egg white
½ teaspoon almond extract
½ cup 10X (confectioners') sugar, sifted
1½ cups *sifted* all-purpose flour
¾ teaspoon baking soda
1 teaspoon ground cinnamon
1 teaspoon ground ginger
¼ teaspoon salt
6 tablespoons unsalted butter or margarine, softened
½ cup firmly packed light brown sugar
¼ cup dark corn syrup
⅓ cup dairy sour cream
1 egg yolk

GLAZED RYE-HONEY SQUARES

Bake at 325° for 35 minutes.
Makes 40.

Shiny golden morsels with a spicy Christmas fragrance.

1. Grease a 15x10x1-inch jelly-roll pan; line with wax paper to extend slightly over short ends; grease paper.
2. Combine the ¾ cup sugar, honey and butter in a medium-size saucepan. Cook and stir over moderate heat until mixture comes to boiling. Pour into a large bowl; cool. Beat in rum, egg and egg yolk.
3. Sift flour, baking powder, salt, cardamom, cinnamon, coriander and cloves onto wax paper.
4. Sprinkle 1 tablespoon rye flour over ⅓ cup of the orange peel on a chopping board; chop peel finely.
5. Add flour mixture, orange peel and remaining rye flour to cooled sugar-honey mixture. Stir until well blended. Spread the batter evenly in prepared pan. Dip hands in cold water and pat the batter smooth. Score the batter with a sharp knife to make 40 rectangles. Place a halved cherry and two pieces of the remaining orange peel on each rectangle.
6. Bake in a slow oven (325°) for 35 minutes or until center springs back when lightly pressed with finger.
7. Heat the remaining milk with the sugar in a small saucepan, stirring constantly just until sugar is dissolved. Brush on hot cake. Let cake cool 5 minutes in the pan on wire rack, then cut rectangles all the way
continued

¾ cup sugar
1 cup honey
6 tablespoons unsalted butter or margarine,
¼ cup dark rum
1 egg
1 egg yolk
3 cups *sifted* all-purpose flour
3 teaspoons baking powder
¼ teaspoon salt
1 teaspoon ground cardamom
1 teaspoon ground cinnamon
1 teaspoon ground coriander
¼ teaspoon ground cloves
1 cup rye flour
1 container (4 ounces) candied orange peel
20 candied red cherries, halved
2 tablespoons milk
2 tablespoons sugar

through at the score marks. Leave in pan and cover tightly with foil or plastic wrap, or remove from pan (leaving on wax paper), wrap and store up to 3 weeks.

SUGAR-CRUSTED CHOCOLATE PRETZELS

Bake at 350° for 12 minutes.
Makes about 6 dozen.

Cookies with a deep chocolate flavor and crunchy sugary surface—which gets crunchier with storage.

1. Sift flour, cocoa, baking powder and salt onto wax paper.
2. Beat butter, sugar, 1 egg and rum in a medium-size bowl with electric mixer at high speed until very light and fluffy. Stir in the dry ingredients, mixing well until soft dough forms. Wrap dough in foil or plastic and chill for at least 1 hour.
3. Divide dough in thirds. Work with 1 part; keep others refrigerated. Using 1 level tablespoonful of dough, roll to a 15-inch rope with palms of hands. Cut into three 5-inch pieces. Roll each piece to 7 inches, tapering ends. Twist into pretzel shape on baking sheet. Repeat with remaining dough.
4. Beat remaining egg with the water in a small bowl. Brush over the pretzels, then sprinkle on the decorating sugar.
5. Bake in a moderate oven (350°) for 12 minutes or until firm. Cool on wire racks. Pack in airtight containers with foil or plastic between layers. Store up to 1½ weeks.

1¾ cups *sifted* all-purpose flour
½ cup unsweetened cocoa powder
1 teaspoon baking powder
⅛ teaspoon salt
½ cup (1 stick) unsalted butter or margarine, softened
¾ cup sugar
2 eggs
1 tablespoon dark rum
1 teaspoon water
¼ cup large-crystal decorating sugar
OR: 12 sugar cubes crushed with a rolling pin

ALMOND-ORANGE CONFECTIONS

Bake at 350° for 15 minutes.
Makes 40 cookies.

Fragrant, heavy and rich, this unusual sweetmeat should be nibbled slowly and savored at leisure.

1. Combine almonds, the ½ cup sugar, flour and orange rind in a large bowl.
2. Beat egg, orange juice and the ¼ teaspoon almond extract in a small bowl until frothy and light. Add to the almond mixture and mix thoroughly. Knead lightly in bowl until mixture clings together and can be formed into a ball.
3. Divide dough in half; roll each half on floured surface with floured hands into a cylinder about 10 inches long. Cut each into 20 slices about ½ inch thick. Place slices on a foil-covered cookie sheet.
4. Bake in a moderate oven (350°) for 15 minutes or until cookies are lightly golden brown. Cool on wire racks.
5. Combine water and the ⅓ cup sugar in a small saucepan. Bring to boiling, lower heat and simmer for 15 minutes. Pour into a small bowl and cool until lukewarm. Stir in orange and almond extracts.
6. Dip the cookies into the syrup and place them on a wire rack set over wax paper to catch the drips. When all have been coated, roll in 10X sugar, then dry on rack for 30 minutes. Pack in airtight containers and store up to 2 weeks. Just before serving roll again in 10X sugar.

3 cans (4½ ounces each) blanched almonds, finely ground (3 cups)
½ cup granulated sugar
1 tablespoon flour
1 teaspoon grated orange rind
1 egg
4 teaspoons orange juice
¼ teaspoon almond extract
¾ cup water
⅓ cup granulated sugar
⅛ teaspoon orange extract
⅛ teaspoon almond extract
1 cup 10 X (confectioners') sugar

COCONUT GINGEROONS

Bake at 375° for 15 minutes.
Makes about 3½ dozen.

The crunchy surface of these cookies is like that of gingersnaps, while the rather soft centers suggest coconut macaroons.

1. Sift flour, baking soda, ginger, cinnamon, coriander and salt onto wax paper.
2. Beat the butter in a medium-size bowl with electric mixer. While beating, sprinkle in the brown sugar with your fingers, removing lumps if any. Add molasses and egg and continue to beat until mixture is fluffy.
3. Stir in the flour mixture until smooth; stir in the coconut. Chill several hours.
4. Roll dough by level tablespoonfuls between your palms to form balls. Quickly dip one side into water, then into the granulated sugar. Place sugar side up on a large foil-covered cookie sheet. Flatten slightly.
5. Bake in a moderate oven (375°) for 15 minutes or until cookies are lightly browned. Transfer to wire racks; cool completely. Pack into airtight containers and store up to 2 weeks.

2 cups *sifted* all-purpose flour
½ teaspoon baking soda
1½ teaspoons ground ginger
½ teaspoon ground cinnamon
½ teaspoon ground coriander
⅛ teaspoon salt
½ cup (1 stick) unsalted butter or margarine, softened
½ cup firmly packed light brown sugar
¼ cup molasses
1 egg
2 cans (4 ounces each) shredded coconut, chopped (2 cups)
½ cup granulated sugar

CANDY-MAKING TIPS

• Always test a candy thermometer, even a new one, in boiling water (212°). Any inaccuracies can then be recorded on the back of the thermometer and the temperature adjusted accordingly.
• To cook candy without a thermometer, use the cold water test. Directions are given in each of our recipes.
• Read recipe carefully and use size of saucepan recommended. (Candy mixtures usually triple in volume when boiling.)
• For high altitudes: Cook the candy to a temperature one degree lower than the recipe directs for each 500 feet of elevation.
• Sugar crystals should always be washed from side of pan to prevent premature crystallization. A wet pastry brush or a fork wrapped in cheesecloth will do the job.
• When a batch of fudge is overbeaten and hardens, it can always be turned out on a board and kneaded until it softens. It won't be as fine-grained and creamy, but it will still be good.
• Candies like fudge that require beating should not be disturbed until lukewarm. You can judge that by resting the saucepan on the palm of the hand—it will feel just comfortable.
• Never double a candy recipe. If a larger amount of candy is needed, make a second batch.

MOLASSES COCONUT CHEWS

Makes 2½ pounds with chocolate or 2¼ pounds without.

Tender little nuggets bursting with coconut. Try them dipped in sugar or chocolate.

1. Combine sugar, corn syrup, molasses and butter in a large saucepan. Cook, stirring constantly, until sugar dissolves. Cover pan for 1 minute to allow the steam to wash down the sugar crystals that cling to side of pan; or, wipe down the crystals with a damp cloth.
2. Uncover pan; insert candy thermometer. Cook without stirring until candy thermometer reaches 253° (hard ball stage, where syrup when dropped in very
continued

1¼ cups sugar
⅔ cup light corn syrup
⅓ cup molasses
2 tablespoons butter or margarine
3 cans (4 ounces each) shredded coconut (about 4 cups)

cold water forms a ball in the fingers that is hard enough to hold a shape, yet still plastic).

3. Remove from heat; stir in the coconut. Pour mixture into a well-buttered 13x9x2-inch pan. Cool until lukewarm or comfortable to handle.

4. Form candy into ½-inch balls, then cool completely before coating with granulated sugar or chocolate.
For sugar coating: Roll cooled balls in granulated sugar.
For chocolate coating: Melt 1 large package (12 ounces) semi-sweet chocolate pieces in top of double boiler over hot—not boiling—water. Dip each coconut ball in the chocolate. Lift out with a fork; tap off excess chocolate on edge of pan. Cool on wax paper until chocolate is firm. Store 2 to 3 weeks in refrigerator or in tightly covered container with foil or plastic wrap between layers in a cool dry place.

PEANUT BUTTER FUDGE

Makes about 2 pounds.

Creamy and divinely peanutty—a treat for the whole family.

1. Combine sugar, corn syrup, milk and salt in a medium-size saucepan. Cook over *low* heat, stirring constantly, until sugar dissolves. Cover pan for 1 minute to allow the steam to wash down the sugar crystals that cling to side of pan, or wipe down the crystals with a damp cloth.

2. Uncover pan; insert candy thermometer. Cook without stirring until candy thermometer reaches 236° (soft ball stage, where syrup when dropped into very cold water forms a soft ball that flattens on removal from water).

3. Remove from heat. Add butter. Cool syrup until lukewarm (110°). Add vanilla, peanut butter and nuts. Beat until candy begins to thicken and loses its high gloss. Turn immediately into a buttered 8x8x2-inch pan. Score with a sharp knife into small squares; cool. When completely cool, cut squares all the way through. Store 2 to 3 weeks in tightly covered container with foil or plastic wrap between layers.

2 cups sugar
¼ cup light corn syrup
½ cup milk
¼ teaspoon salt
2 tablespoons butter
   or margarine
1 teaspoon vanilla
1 cup crunchy or smooth
   peanut butter
½ cup finely chopped
   peanuts (*Optional*)

MOLASSES CHIPS

Makes about 1¾ pounds.

A taffy-like candy to dissolve slowly in the mouth for full flavor.

1. Combine ingredients in a large saucepan. Cook, stirring constantly, until sugar dissolves. Cover pan for 1 minute to allow the steam to wash down the sugar crystals that cling to side of pan, or wipe down the crystals with a damp cloth.

2. Uncover pan; insert candy thermometer. Cook without stirring until candy thermometer reaches 266° (hard ball stage, where syrup when dropped into very cold water forms a ball in the fingers that is hard enough to hold a shape, yet still plastic).

3. Remove from heat; pour syrup onto two well-buttered jelly-roll pans or a very large platter. Cool candy for about 5 minutes, then fold edges to center.

4. When candy is cool enough to handle, butter hands

2 cups sugar
¾ cup light corn syrup
¼ cup molasses
1 tablespoon butter or
   margarine
¾ cup water

and pull candy into a rope. Pull rope, folding it back on itself as you pull 25 times. When candy loses its transparent appearance but is still "plastic," knead it like bread dough on a well-buttered surface. Flatten candy, then stretch it from one side into a long ribbon-like strip. Cut the ribbon into 1½-inch pieces.

5. Wrap each piece of candy separately in foil or plastic wrap. Store 2 to 3 weeks in a tightly covered container.

ALMOND BRITTLE

Makes about ¾ pound.

One of the easiest candies to make, and one that deserves its popularity.

1. Combine sugar, corn syrup, water, salt and butter in a large saucepan. Cook, stirring constantly, until sugar dissolves. Cover pan for 1 minute to allow the steam to wash down the sugar crystals that cling to side of pan, or wipe down the crystals with a damp cloth.
2. Uncover pan; insert candy thermometer. Cook without stirring until candy thermometer reaches 270° (soft crack stage, where syrup, when dropped into very cold water, separates into hard but not brittle threads).
3. Remove from heat; stir in almonds; return to heat. Continue cooking until candy thermometer reaches 300° (hard crack stage, where syrup, when dropped into very cold water, separates into threads that are hard and brittle).
4. Remove from heat; stir in baking soda. Let foaming syrup settle just a bit, then quickly pour out onto a well-buttered large cookie sheet, and stretch out as thin as possible with the aid of two forks. Cool completely, then break in pieces. Store 2 to 3 weeks in tightly covered containers, separating the layers with foil or plastic wrap.

1 cup sugar
½ cup light corn syrup
½ cup water
¼ teaspoon salt
1 tablespoon butter or margarine
1 cup whole unblanched almonds (or peanuts)
1 teaspoon baking soda

OLD-FASHIONED SPONGE CANDY

Makes about 1 pound.

Crunchy and porous, like a big candy sponge—kids love it.

1. Combine sugar, corn syrup and vinegar in a large saucepan. Cook, stirring constantly, until sugar dissolves. Cover pan for 1 minute to allow the steam to wash down the sugar crystals that cling to side of pan, or wipe down the crystals with a damp cloth.
2. Uncover pan; insert candy thermometer. Cook without stirring until candy thermometer reaches 300° (hard crack stage, when syrup dropped in very cold water separates into hard and brittle threads).
3. Remove from heat; stir in baking soda. Pour into a buttered 9x9x2-inch pan. (It's not necessary to spread, as the mixture will bubble and spread itself); cool in pan on wire rack. Break cooled sponge into pieces. Store 2 to 3 weeks in a tightly covered container with foil or plastic wrap between layers.

1 cup sugar
1 cup dark corn syrup
1 tablespoon white vinegar
1 tablespoon baking soda

NO-BAKE "GINGERBREAD" HOUSES KIDS CAN MAKE

As every child knows, a gingerbread house is basic at Christmas! But sometimes it's hard to get a busy mom to bake all the gingerbread needed to build one. Here's an idea that makes building a "gingerbread" house so simple, children can have the fun of creating one—or a whole village—by themselves. All you need are lots of graham crackers, candies such as gumdrops, candy canes, licorice twists and peppermints, and some no-cook white frosting you just mix up in a bowl. A 12-year-old can make a house alone, while 6-year-olds may need a little help. A class of schoolchildren or a Brownie troop can do several in a few hours.

GENERAL DIRECTIONS

General Materials needed:
Quart-size milk cartons
9- to 12-inch-diameter heavy-
    weight paper plates
Masking or transparent tape
Wooden picks; Scissors; Ruler
Cake decorating set
Paper figures cut from magazines or Christmas cards:
Santa, trees, etc.

Foods needed:

Graham crackers
Royal Frosting
(*recipe on page 211*)
Green leaf gumdrops
Red licorice twists
Red licorice shoestrings

Candy canes
Cinnamon red hots
Round peppermints
Lemon drops
Pillow mints—assorted colors
Sugar-coated chocolate candies

General Construction Directions:

1. Cut top off milk carton, leaving a 5-inch-tall base for the Candy Cane, Stone, and Hansel & Gretel Houses, and for the lower section of the Candy House. Cut second carton, leaving a 7-inch-high base for the taller section of the Candy House. Secure 5-inch base and 7-inch base together for Candy House.
2. Mark 3 inches up from bottom of one of the carton's sides. Slit all four corners down to the mark. On two opposite sides, cut off both top corners on a slant upward from the 3-inch mark to the center of the side. These two pointed sides will make the roof supports.
3. Bend straight uncut sides of carton in to form the roof. (Graham crackers will cover opening on top.) Tape to pointed sections.
4. Secure bottom of milk carton to inverted heavyweight paper plate with Royal Frosting.
5. **Sides:** Cut two double graham crackers to fit tall, pointed ends of house, using a sawing motion with a serrated knife.
6. **Roof:** Cut one inch off ends of four double graham crackers. Attach two cut crackers firmly to each slanted side to form roof, using icing as "glue." (Roof should overhang on sides and front of house.) You may have to wait before adding each cracker in order to let the frosting set.
7. **Corners and edges:** Fit cake decorator with a small-size plain decorating tube; fill with icing. Pipe icing at corners and roof lines. Cut licorice twists or candy canes to size; fit onto corners over icing.
8. **Chimneys:** Cut one square graham cracker into quarters. Arrange pieces on roof at one end to make chimney, using Royal Frosting "glue." Cover crackers with icing and mints or cinnamon red hots. Spread icing on one end of house, in chimney design; arrange mints like "bricks."
9. **Doors and shutters:** Attach half or quarters of graham crackers with icing. Leave doors open and paste a Christmas interior picture cut from a Christmas card in the open doorway, if you wish. Make shutters from quarters of graham crackers and attach with icing.

Use any of the following decorating ideas or create your own:

1. **Roof:** (a) Spread icing over entire roof; place pillow mints in icing to resemble "shingles," or arrange pillow mints, cinnamon red hots and lemon drops in alternate rows. (b) Using a decorating bag fitted with a small decorating tube, pipe icing onto roof in a scallop design by bringing the points of the second line to the center of the curve on the previous line.
2. **Windows:** Using a narrow spatula, spread icing on window area on one side of house. Outline panes with licorice shoestrings, licorice twists, lemon drops or cinnamon red hots.
3. **Miscellaneous decorating ideas:** (a) Using the decorating bag, pipe icicles from the edge of the roof. (b) Spread icing over remainder of paper plate to make "snow-covered" ground. (c) Outline paths with licorice shoestrings or sugar-coated chocolate candies. Use broken graham cracker pieces to make "flagstone" walk. (d) Make bushes with green leaf gumdrops and wooden picks. Attach to paper plate with icing. (e) Make fences with curved or small straight pieces of candy with a round peppermint glued to the top.

Gourmet Food Gifts You'll Be Proud to Give

A gift of your own homemade food has many pleasures. For the food fancier, it is special—a treat made just for him by you. For you, a chance to give a gift at a fraction of the cost to buy in fancy gourmet shops. Starting at top *(page 195)*, center, and going clockwise: **Crêpes au Grand Marnier**—the most delicate of pancakes, served with an orange and honey sauce. **Glazed Walnuts** are candy-coated, delicious as nibbles or atop a sundae. Olives take on a new zest in **Olives Jerez**, packed with cocktail onions, almonds and sherry. **Chocolate Sauce Supreme** is flavored with a touch of crème de cacao; **Brandied Butterscotch Sauce**, naturally, with brandy. **Mustard Trio** is three great mustards flavored with tomato, tarragon or orange. **Carioca Pastries** are made with a piecrust mix, chocolate frosting and a sprinkling of pistachio nuts. **Ten-Minute Pâté** starts off with liverwurst, takes on flavor with a bacon-and-hoseradish dip, sherry and onion. **Vin Rosé Jelly** and **Vin Chablis Jelly**, really two recipes in one, can be jarred separately or parfait-style using the two. **Fruits aux Rhum**—pears, peaches, apricots and pineapple in a dark rum syrup. **Banana Bread** makes two moist loaves.

CRÊPES AU GRAND MARNIER
Makes 3 pint jars or 24 crêpes.

For special friends, a gift of delicate dessert crêpes.

1. Beat eggs until foamy in a large bowl; stir in milk and melted butter. Sift in flour, granulated sugar and salt; beat until smooth; cover bowl with plastic wrap; chill at least 2 hours.
2. Heat an 8-inch heavy skillet slowly, until drops of water bounce about on pan. Butter lightly.
3. Pour batter, a scant ¼ cup at a time, onto skillet, tilting to cover bottom completely. Cook over medium heat until top is set and underside is golden; turn; brown other side. Roll up; place on a cookie sheet. Repeat with remaining batter to make 24 crêpes.
4. Combine the 10X sugar and remaining butter in a small bowl until smooth. Unroll crêpes; spread with butter-sugar mixture; re-roll and pack 8 crêpes in each of 3 hot sterilized pint jars.
5. Combine honey and orange juice in a small skillet; bring to boiling; lower heat; add orange slices; simmer 5 minutes.
6. Pack orange slices into jars; stir Grand Marnier into skillet; pour syrup into jars to within ¼-inch of top; seal and refrigerate until gift-giving time.
   Note: To serve crêpes (put directions on your gift card) place crêpes with sauce in a small skillet and heat slowly, basting with sauce, until crêpes, are heated through. To flame crêpes, heat ¼ cup fruit flavor liqueur, brandy or rum in a small saucepan; pour over crêpes and light with a match held a distance from the pan.

6 eggs
2 cups milk
2 tablespoons butter or margarine, melted
1½ cups *sifted* all-purpose flour
2 tablespoons granulated sugar
½ teaspoon salt
½ cup (1 stick) butter or margarine
1 cup *sifted* 10X (confectioners') sugar
¾ cup honey
¾ cup orange juice
1 seedless orange, thinly sliced
½ cup Grand Marnier (an orange liqueur)

all recipes have been triple-tested in Family Circle's Test Kitchens

GLAZED WALNUTS

Makes 5 cups.

A thin crackly candy coats the nuts, making them such good nibbles.

1. Combine sugar and water in a small heavy saucepan. Heat slowly, stirring constantly, until sugar dissolves, then cook rapidly, without stirring, to 300° on a candy thermometer, or until a spoonful of syrup poured into a cup of cold water forms hard brittle threads that break when pressed.
2. Remove saucepan from heat. Add walnuts to syrup, ½ cup at a time, and toss to coat well. (If syrup begins to harden, return saucepan to a *very* low heat.)
3. Remove nuts from syrup with two forks and place on wire racks lined with wax paper or aluminum foil. Allow to cool until glaze is firm. Store in air-tight metal tins.

2 cups sugar
1 cup water
1 package (1 pound) shelled walnuts

OLIVES JEREZ

Makes 3 eight-ounce jars.

Sherry and oregano combine to add a delightfully different flavor to olives.

1. Drain olives, pimiento and cocktail onions. Layer ripe olives with almonds at the bottom of 3 hot sterilized 8-ounce jars.
2. Alternate layers of pimiento, green olives and cocktail onions with ripe olives and almonds until jars are packed.
3. Combine sherry, oil, oregano, salt and pepper in a jar with a screw top; cover jar and shake until well-blended; pour over packed jars to within ¼-inch of top; cover jars. Refrigerate at least 1 week for flavors to develop. Plan to give within a few days.

1 can (6 ounces) pitted ripe olives
1 jar (4 ounces) pitted green olives
1 jar (4 ounces) pimiento
1 jar (5 ounces) cocktail onions
Whole blanched almonds
¾ cup dry sherry
¼ cup olive or vegetable oil
2 teaspoons leaf oregano, crumbled
1½ teaspoons salt
¼ teaspoon freshly ground pepper

MUSTARD TRIO

Makes 3 six-ounce jars.

The French have known for years that there can be many varieties of mustards. Here are three—so good, so simple.

1. Combine wine, onion and garlic in a medium-size saucepan; bring to boiling; lower heat; simmer 5 minutes. Strain into a small bowl; cool to room temperature.
2. Empty dry mustard into medium-size saucepan; pour in cooled wine and stir until very smooth; blend in honey, oil, salt and pepper seasoning.
3. Cook over medium heat, stirring constantly, until mixture thickens; remove from heat and pour into 3 hot sterilized 6-ounce jars; stir tomato paste into one jar, tarragon into a second and orange rind into the third; seal and refrigerate at least 1 week to blend flavors.

2 cups dry white wine
1 large onion, chopped (1 cup)
2 cloves garlic, minced
1 can (4 ounces) dry mustard
2 tablespoons honey
1 tablespoon vegetable oil
2 teaspoons salt
Few drops liquid red-pepper seasoning
1 tablespoon tomato paste
1 tablespoon chopped fresh tarragon
OR: 1 teaspoon leaf tarragon, crumbled
1 tablespoon grated orange rind

VIN ROSÉ JELLY

Makes 4 eight-ounce jars.

Since the days of Victorian England, wine jellies have been considered a special treat for family and friends.

1. Combine sugar, grape juice, water and spice in a large heavy saucepan.
2. Place over high heat; bring to a full rolling boil; add wine; return to a full rolling boil and boil hard, stirring constantly, 1 minute. Remove from heat; stir in ½ bottle of liquid pectin; remove spice with a slotted spoon.
3. Ladle into 4 hot sterilized 8-ounce jars; seal, following manufacturer's directions. Cool on wire rack until room temperature, then refrigerate at least 1 week before gift-giving.
   For VIN CHABLIS JELLY: Substitute *white* grape juice for the red, 4 whole allspice for the cinnamon and white wine for the rosé. Proceed as for VIN ROSÉ.
   Note: For a two-tone effect, make up a batch of VIN ROSÉ and ladle into 8 hot sterilized jars, filling each half full. Allow to stand until room temperature, then make up a batch of VIN CHABLIS and ladle over VIN ROSÉ.

3½ cups sugar
1½ cups bottled red grape juice
½ cup water
1 three-inch piece stick cinnamon
¾ cup rosé wine
½ six-ounce bottle liquid pectin

CHOCOLATE SAUCE SUPREME

Makes 2 cups.

A super sauce—perfect for pouring over ice cream.

1. Melt chocolate in the top of a double boiler over simmering water; remove from water.
2. Stir in butter until melted; blend in 10X sugar, salt, corn syrup, hot water, crème de cacao and vanilla. Pour into hot, sterilized containers for your gift-giving. Serve it either warm or cold as a sundae topping, or pour it over cake à la mode.

1 package (6 ounces) semisweet chocolate pieces
¼ cup (½ stick) butter or margarine
1 cup *sifted* 10X (confectioners') sugar
Dash of salt
½ cup light corn syrup
¼ cup hot water
¼ cup crème de cacao liqueur
1 teaspoon vanilla

BRANDIED BUTTERSCOTCH SAUCE

Makes 2 cups.

So smooth, so rich, with a sophisticated flavor, who'd ever guess that it's ready in just minutes?

1. Combine sugar, salt and water in a small heavy saucepan; bring to boiling, stirring constantly. Cook to 230° on a candy thermometer, or until a spoonful of syrup poured into a cup of cold water spins a soft 3-inch thread.
2. Empty condensed milk into a medium-size bowl; stir in hot syrup until well-blended; stir in instant coffee, then brandy and vanilla. Pour into hot sterilized containers for gift-giving. Serve warm or cold over ice cream, pudding or sherbet.

¾ cup firmly packed dark brown sugar
Dash of salt
½ cup water
1 can (15 ounces) sweetened condensed milk
1 tablespoon instant coffee powder
¼ cup brandy
1 teaspoon vanilla

FRUITS AUX RHUM

You've seen them in the gourmet departments with fancy import labels and prices. Prepare them yourself in almost no time.

1. Empty canned fruits into a large shallow pan. Place a maraschino cherry inside each pear half.
2. Arrange pear halves, peach slices, whole apricots and pineapple pieces in hot sterilized jars.
3. Measure 2 cups of the fruit syrups remaining in the pan into a medium-size saucepan; add cinnamon stick, whole cloves and allspice. Bring to boiling; lower heat and simmer 5 minutes; add rum; remove spices with a slotted spoon.
4. Pour hot liquid over fruits in jars to within 1/4-inch of the top. Seal jars and refrigerate at least 1 week to develop flavors.

1 can (1 pound, 14 ounces) pear halves
1 can (1 pound, 14 ounces) cling peach halves
1 can (1 pound, 14 ounces) whole apricots
1 can (1 pound, 13 1/2 ounces) sliced pineapple, quartered
Red Maraschino cherries
1 three-inch piece stick cinnamon
1 teaspoon whole cloves
1 teaspoon whole allspice
1/2 cup dark rum

BANANA BREAD

Makes 2 medium-sized loaves.

Moist and flavorful, this special bread keeps well.
Bake at 350° for 45 minutes.

1. Beat sugar, shortening and eggs for 3 minutes at high speed in a large bowl with electric mixer. Blend in large, ripe bananas.
2. Sift in flour, baking soda, salt and baking powder; stir with a wooden spoon, just until well-blended; stir in chopped walnuts. Pour into two 7 3/8x3 5/8x2 1/4-inch greased loaf pans.
3. Bake in moderate oven (350°) 45 minutes, or until a wooden pick inserted near the center comes out clean. Cool in pans on wire racks 5 minutes; remove from pans and cool completely. Wrap in plastic wrap or aluminum foil and allow to mellow for several days.

3/4 cup sugar
1/2 cup vegetable shortening
2 eggs
3 large ripe bananas, mashed (1 1/2 cups)
2 1/4 cups *sifted* all-purpose flour
1/2 teaspoon baking soda
1/2 teaspoon salt
1/2 teaspoon baking powder
1/2 cup chopped walnuts

CARIOCA PASTRIES

Bake at 400° for 15 minutes.
Makes 18 pastries.

Simple—so very easy to make with pie-crust mix, preserves and ready prepared frosting.

1. Combine piecrust mix, cocoa and sugar in a medium-size bowl until well-blended. Beat egg and water together in a cup; stir, all at once, into dry mixture. Toss with a fork until pastry is blended.
2. Sprinkle flour on a large cookie sheet; roll out pastry on cookie sheet to a 13 1/2x10-inch rectangle.
3. Bake in hot oven (400°) 15 minutes, or until pastry is firm to the touch. Cut pastry, while still warm, into 1 1/2-inch-wide strips, lengthwise. Cool on cookie sheet.
4. Drizzle pastry strips with rum; spread first with raspberry preserves, then with frosting. Stack 3 strips together to make 2 stacks. Sprinkle chopped pistachio nuts on top layers. Chill at least 2 hours, or until firm. Cut each stack into 9 pastries. Store in an air-tight box and give within a few days.

1 package (11 ounces) piecrust mix
1/4 cup unsweetened cocoa powder
1/4 cup sugar
1 egg
2 tablespoons water
3 tablespoons rum
1/3 cup red raspberry preserves
1 can (1 pound, 1/2 ounce) dark chocolate frosting
Pistachio nuts

TEN-MINUTE PÂTÉ

Makes 2 eight-ounce containers.

Pâté in minutes? Of course, when you start with handy ready-to-go ingredients.

1. Break up liverwurst with a fork in a medium-size bowl; blend in bacon and horseradish dip, sherry and onion until smooth.
2. Arrange a ring of sliced olives around the bottom of 2 hot sterilized 8-ounce containers. Pack in half the pâté mixture. Arrange a second ring of olive slices and pack in remaining pâté; seal. Refrigerate and plan to give within a few days.

1 package (8 ounces) liverwurst
1 container (8 ounces) bacon and horseradish dip
3 tablespoons dry sherry
1 tablespoon grated onion
Stuffed green olives, sliced

A Treasure Box of Cookies

JEWELED COOKIE BOX *(see page 196)*

Makes one 8x6x2½-inch cookie box.

When the cookies are gone you can eat the box!
Bake at 350° for 10 minutes.

1. Prepare CHRISTMAS SUGAR COOKIES through Step 3.
2. Roll dough, one half at a time, to a ¼-inch thickness on a lightly floured pastry board. Cut an 8x6-inch rectangle for bottom of box. Cut an 8½x6½-inch rectangle for top of box.
3. Roll remaining dough to a ¼-inch thickness and cut out two 8x2½-inch pieces for long sides of box and two 6x2½-inch pieces for short sides. Place cookie pieces 1 inch apart on ungreased large cookie sheets.
4. Bake in moderate oven (350°) 10 minutes, or until cookies are firm but still light in color. If pieces have baked unevenly, trim with a sharp knife and a ruler to sizes specified while cookie pieces are still warm. Cool completely on wire racks.
5. Fit a pastry bag or cake-decorating cylinder with a notched tip; fill with ROYAL FROSTING. Place bottom of box on a small cookie sheet. Pipe frosting along one long edge of bottom. Press one of the long sides into frosting; hold in place for a minute or two. Brace with cans or food packages to hold upright while frosting sets. All four sides may be held in this manner.
6. Pipe frosting along one short edge of bottom; press a short side into frosting; hold in place. Pipe more frosting into corner joinings, inside and out, to secure. Repeat with remaining pieces.
7. To decorate: Pipe frosting in decorative pattern on edges and sides of box. Decorate with silver dragees, pastel candies and cinnamon red-hots, as pictured.
8. Place top of box on a bowl just a little smaller than top. This protects frosted edges until frosting dries. Pipe frosting along edges and on top in decorative pattern. Decorate with candies. Let frosting set about 1 hour, then place top on flat surface.
9. Allow box to dry for 1 day on cookie sheet, then carefully loosen box around edges with spatula and place on a tray, if you wish. Fill with Christmas cookies.

Christmas Sugar Cookies *(recipe follows)*
Royal Frosting *(recipe follows)*
Silver dragees
Tiny pastel mints
Peppermint candies
Cinnamon red-hots

210

ROYAL FROSTING

Makes about 2½ cups.

A no-smear frosting especially for decorating, it becomes candy-hard.

Beat egg whites and cream of tartar until foamy in a small bowl; slowly beat in 10X sugar until frosting stands in firm peaks and is stiff enough to hold a sharp line when cut through with a knife. Keep bowl of frosting covered with damp paper toweling while working, to keep frosting from drying out. Store any leftover frosting in a tightly covered jar in the refrigerator for another day's baking.

Note: For ½ recipe, use 2 egg whites, ½ teaspoon cream of tartar and 3 cups sifted 10X sugar.

3 egg whites
½ teaspoon cream of tartar
1 package (1 pound) 10X (confectioners') sugar, *sifted*

CHRISTMAS SUGAR COOKIES

Bake at 350° for 8 minutes.
Makes 3 dozen cookies.

A crispy vanilla cookie to cut out and decorate.

1. Sift flour and salt onto wax paper.
2. Beat butter or margarine, sugar and egg in large bowl of electric mixer at high speed 3 minutes, or until fluffy; blend in vanilla.
3. Stir in flour mixture to make a stiff dough; wrap in wax paper; chill 3 hours or until firm enough to roll.
4. Roll dough, one quarter at a time, to a ¼-inch thickness on a lightly floured pastry board. Cut into rounds with a 3-inch cutter.
5. Place, 1 inch apart, on ungreased cookie sheets. Sprinkle with colored sugars.
6. Bake in moderate oven (350°) 8 minutes, or until cookies are lightly browned at edges.
7. Remove to wire racks with spatula; cool.

2½ cups *sifted* all-purpose flour
½ teaspoon salt
¾ cup (1½ sticks) butter or margarine
1¼ cups sugar
1 egg
2 teaspoons vanilla
Colored decorating sugars

HOLLY SPRIGS

Bake at 350° for 10 minutes.
Makes about 3 dozen double cookies.

Tiny melt-in-the-mouth cookies are sandwiched with tart preserves and brightly decorated with a symbol of the season.

1. Cream butter or margarine and 10X sugar until well-blended in a large bowl; stir in flour, vanilla and nuts.
2. Roll dough, a level teaspoonful at a time, into balls between palms of hands. Place, 2 inches apart, on a greased cookie sheet. Lightly grease the bottom of a measuring cup and dip in 10X sugar; press over each ball to flatten to about a 1-inch round.
3. Bake in moderate oven (350°) 10 minutes, or until golden around edges. Remove carefully to wire racks with spatula; cool completely.
4. Spread bottoms of half of the cookies with raspberry preserves; top, sandwich style, with remaining cookies, flat side down.
5. Divide ROYAL FROSTING into 2 small cups, ¾ of the frosting in one and remaining in the other. Tint the larger amount green with green food coloring and the remaining red with the red food coloring. Decorate cookies with frosting to resemble holly.

1 cup (2 sticks) butter or margarine
½ cup *sifted* 10X (confectioners') sugar
1½ cups *sifted* all-purpose flour
1 teaspoon vanilla
½ cup walnuts or almonds, ground
Red and green food colorings
½ recipe Royal Frosting (*recipe above*)
1 cup red raspberry preserves

WINTER RAINBOWS

Bake at 350° for 8 minutes.
Makes 8 dozen cookies.

This multi-hued dough will keep in the refrigerator for several days—all ready to slice and bake at a moment's notice.

1. Sift flour, baking powder, salt and baking soda onto wax paper.
2. Beat butter or margarine with brown and granulated sugars until fluffy in a large bowl; beat in egg and vanilla. Stir in flour mixture, a third at a time, blending well to make a soft dough.
3. Divide dough into 3 equal portions; tint 1 portion yellow, 1 green and 1 pink, with food colorings.
4. Roll each portion of dough into a 9x5-inch rectangle between sheets of wax paper. Chill in freezer 10 minutes. Cut each piece of dough in half lengthwise, cutting through wax paper. Peel off top sheets. Brush top of one strip lightly with milk; place another strip, paper side up, on top. Peel off paper. Repeat procedure with remaining dough strips, alternating colors, to make 6 layers. Press lightly together; cut finished stack lengthwise to make 2 narrow stacks. Wrap in plastic wrap or foil; chill in refrigerator 3 hours or overnight.
5. Unwrap dough; cut into ⅛-inch slices with a sharp knife; place on greased cookie sheets.
6. Bake in moderate oven (350°) for 8 minutes, or until edges are golden. Remove to wire racks with spatula; cool.

2 cups *sifted* all-purpose flour
½ teaspoon baking powder
½ teaspoon salt
⅛ teaspoon baking soda
10 tablespoons (1¼ sticks) butter or margarine softened
½ cup firmly packed brown sugar
¼ cup granulated sugar
1 egg
1 teaspoon vanilla
Yellow, green and red food colorings
Milk

SPRITZ BONBONS

Bake at 375° for 8 minutes.
Makes 10 dozen cookies.

One of the easiest cookies to make, the cookie press does all the fanciful shaping.

1. Beat butter or margarine, sugar and egg yolks in large bowl of electric mixer at high speed 3 minutes, or until fluffy. Blend in vanilla, lemon extract and salt. Stir in flour gradually to make a soft dough.
2. Divide dough into 3 parts; tint one part pink with red food coloring and another with green.
3. Fit your favorite plate or disk onto cookie press; fill press with one color dough. Press dough out onto ungreased cookie sheets. Rinse out cookie press before filling with another color dough. Decorate some cookies with colored sugars or cinnamon red-hots before baking.
4. Bake in moderate oven (375°) 8 minutes, or until firm; remove to wire racks; cool completely.
5. Melt chocolate and shortening in top of a double boiler over hot water; spread on top of some of the cookies and sprinkle with chopped walnuts. Decorate other cookies with ROYAL FROSTING, colored sugars and cinnamon red-hots.

1½ cups (3 sticks) butter or margarine
1 cup sugar
3 egg yolks
1 teaspoon vanilla
1 teaspoon lemon extract
¼ teaspoon salt
3½ cups *sifted* all-purpose flour
Red and green food colorings
Colored sugars
Cinnamon red-hots
½ cup semisweet-chocolate pieces
1 teaspoon vegetable shortening
¼ cup chopped walnuts
Royal Frosting (*recipe on page 211*)

TOASTY CLUSTERS

Nutrition-packed and bound to be popular with the visiting milk-and-cookies set.

Bake at 325° for 15 minutes.
Makes 3 dozen cookies.

1. Combine granola, sweetened condensed milk, almond extract and ginger in a medium-size bowl. Stir mixture until well-blended.
2. Drop by teaspoonfuls onto foil-lined cookie sheets. Garnish each with a piece of candied cherry.
3. Bake in slow oven (325°) 15 minutes, or until cookies are firm. Cool on cookie sheets until cookies can be handled. Peel foil from cookies. Cool completely on wire racks.

2 cups honey-almond-flavor granola
⅔ cup sweetened condensed milk (from a 14-ounce can)
1 teaspoon almond extract
¼ teaspoon ground ginger
Red candied cherries, quartered

EVERGREENS

Sprightly little tree-shaped cookies, bright and colorful for the children.

Bake at 400° for 5 minutes.
Makes 8 dozen cookies.

1. Prepare and chill CHRISTMAS SUGAR COOKIE dough, through Step 3.
2. Roll out dough, one quarter at a time, to a ⅛-inch thickness on a lightly floured pastry board. Cut tree shapes with a floured 3½-inch cutter. Place trees, 1 inch apart, on ungreased cookie sheet.
3. Bake in hot oven (400°) 5 minutes, or until cookies are golden. Remove to wire racks with spatula; cool.
4. Tint ROYAL FROSTING pale green.
5. Drop frosting from tip of knife in a zigzag pattern on cookies (or use cake decorating set). Decorate with silver candies and/or candy sprinkles.

Christmas Sugar Cookies (*recipe on page 211*)
Royal Frosting (*recipe on page 211*)
Green food coloring
Silver candies
Multicolored candy sprinkles

ALMOND MACAROONS

Puffy, crunchy little cookies, chock-full of delicate almond flavor.

Bake at 325° for 20 minutes.
Makes about 3 dozen cookies.

1. Grease a large cookie sheet; dust with flour; tap off any excess.
2. Break up almond paste with fingers into bowl of electric mixer.
3. Add egg whites, salt and vanilla. Beat at low speed until mixture is smooth and well-blended.
4. Add confectioners' sugar slowly, continuing to beat at low speed, until a soft dough forms.
5. Fit a pastry bag with a round tip. Fill bag with dough.
6. Pipe dough out in small rounds, or drop by teaspoonfuls on prepared cookie sheet. (Macaroons will spread very little when they bake.)
7. For a crackly top: Dip fingertip into water; pat over tops; sprinkle with granulated sugar. Decorate tops with almonds and cherries.
8. Bake in slow oven (325°) for 20 minutes, or until golden-brown.
9. Remove to wire racks with a spatula; cool.

1 can (8 ounces) almond paste
2 egg whites
Dash of salt
1 teaspoon vanilla
1 cup *sifted* 10 X (confectioners') sugar
Granulated sugar
Sliced almonds
Red candied cherries, quartered

all recipes have been triple-tested in Family Circle's Test Kitchens

CANDY CANES

Bake at 350° for 10 minutes.
Makes 4 dozen cookies.

Simple to make, and a merry sight to see hanging on the Christmas tree.

1. Sift flour, baking powder and salt onto wax paper.
2. Beat butter or margarine and sugar until fluffy in a large bowl; beat in egg and peppermint extract. Stir in flour mixture alternately with milk.
3. Spoon half of dough into a medium-size bowl; tint pink with red food coloring. Leave remaining dough plain.
4. Pinch off about a teaspoonful of each dough; roll each into a pencil-thin strip 5 inches long. Place strips side by side, pressing ends together; twist. Place on ungreased cookie sheets, 1 inch apart, bending into cane shape.
5. Bake in moderate oven (350°) 10 minutes, or until firm. Cool a few minutes on cookie sheets. Carefully remove to wire racks with spatula; cool.

3¼ cups *sifted* all-purpose flour
4 teaspoons baking powder
1 teaspoon salt
½ cup (1 stick) butter or margarine, softened
1¼ cups sugar
1 egg
½ teaspoon peppermint extract
¼ cup milk
Red food coloring

MOLASSES COOKIE CUTOUTS

Bake at 350° for 8 minutes.
Makes 8 dozen cookies.

These spicy morsels, cut out in favorite animal shapes, are sure to catch the children's fancy.

1. Sift flour, baking soda, salt, cocoa, ginger, cinnamon and cloves onto wax paper.
2. Beat butter or margarine until fluffy; add sugar gradually, beating well after each addition. Add egg and molasses; beat well. Stir in flour mixture; blend well. Wrap in plastic wrap or foil; refrigerate several hours, or overnight.
3. Roll out small portions of dough on a floured pastry board; cut into animal or Christmas shapes with cookie cutters; brush excess flour off dough. Place on lightly greased cookie sheets.
4. Bake in moderate oven (350°) for 8 minutes, or until edges are browned. Let cookies cool a few minutes on cookie sheets. Remove to wire racks with spatula; cool.
5. Decorate the cookies with ROYAL FROSTING.

3¾ cups *sifted* all-purpose flour
1 teaspoon baking soda
½ teaspoon salt
2 tablespoons cocoa
2 teaspoons ground ginger
1 tablespoon ground cinnamon
2 teaspoons ground cloves
1 cup (2 sticks) butter or margarine, softened
1 cup sugar
1 egg
½ cup molasses
Royal Frosting (*recipe on page 211*)

TOASTY MACAROONS

Bake at 325° for 15 minutes.
Makes about 3 dozen cookies.

Easy-to-make coconut treats.

1. Combine coconut, sweetened condensed milk, rum extract, and ginger in a medium-size bowl. Stir mixture until well-blended.
2. Drop by teaspoonfuls onto foil-lined large cookie sheet. Garnish each cookie with a slice of candied cherry.
3. Bake in slow oven (325°) 15 minutes, or until macaroons are firm. Remove from cookie sheet to wire racks. Cool completely.

2 cans (4½ ounces each) toasted sweetened coconut
⅔ cup sweetened condensed milk (from a 14-ounce can)
1 teaspoon rum extract
¼ teaspoon ground ginger
Red and green candied cherries, sliced

CHAPTER 11

METHODS

This section contains the special information and illustrations required
when the DIRECTIONS for any item tell you to see METHODS Chapter.

HOW TO ENLARGE PATTERNS

Draw crisscross lines, vertically and horizontally, with a ruler, on brown wrapping
paper or lightweight cardboard, spacing the lines as indicated. Then copy our
pattern, one square at a time, using a ruler and/or compass if necessary. Cut out
the enlarged pattern if necessary, and use as directed.

KNIT AND CROCHET ABBREVIATIONS

beg—begin, beginning; **bet**—between; **bl**—block; **cc**—contrasting color; **ch**—chain;
dc—double crochet; **dec(s)**—decrease(s); **dp**—double-pointed; **dtr**—double treble
crochet; **gr**—gram; **hdc**—half double crochet; **in(s) or ″**—inch(es); **incl**—including;
inc—increase; **k**—knit; **lp(s)**—loop(s); **mc**—main color; **oz(s)**—ounce(s); **p**—purl;
pat(s)—pattern(s); **pc**—picot; **psso**—pass slip stitch over; **rpt**—repeat; **rem**—remaining; **rnd(s)**—round(s); **sc**—single crochet; **sk(s)**—skein(s); **sk**—skip; **sl**—slip; **sl st**—
slip stitch; **sp(s)**—space(s); **st(s)**—stitch(es); **st st**—stockinette stitch; **tog**—together;
tr—triple crochet; **work even**—work without inc or dec; **yo**—yarn over; **yd(s)**—
yard(s); *****—repeat whatever follows the * as many times as specified; **( )**—do what
is in parentheses the number of times indicated.

EMBROIDERY STITCHES

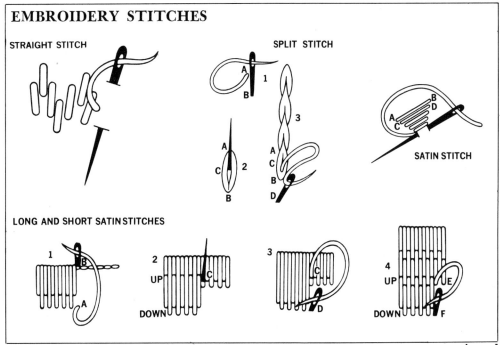

STRAIGHT STITCH

SPLIT STITCH

SATIN STITCH

LONG AND SHORT SATIN STITCHES

continued

Embroidery Stitches, continued

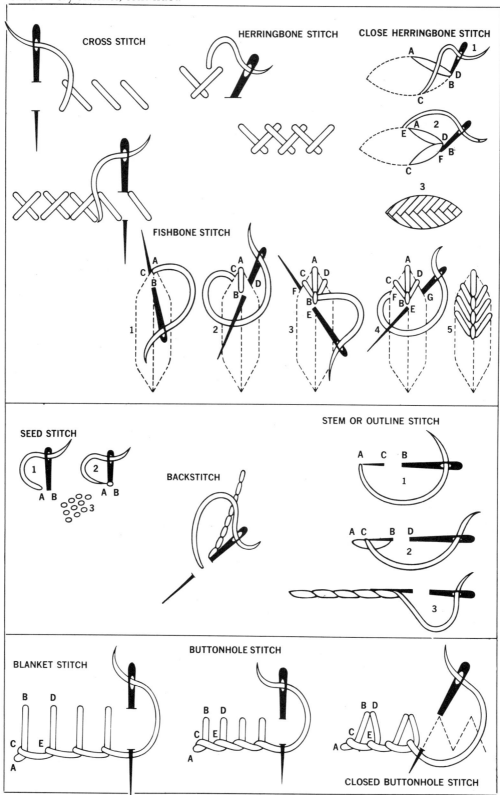

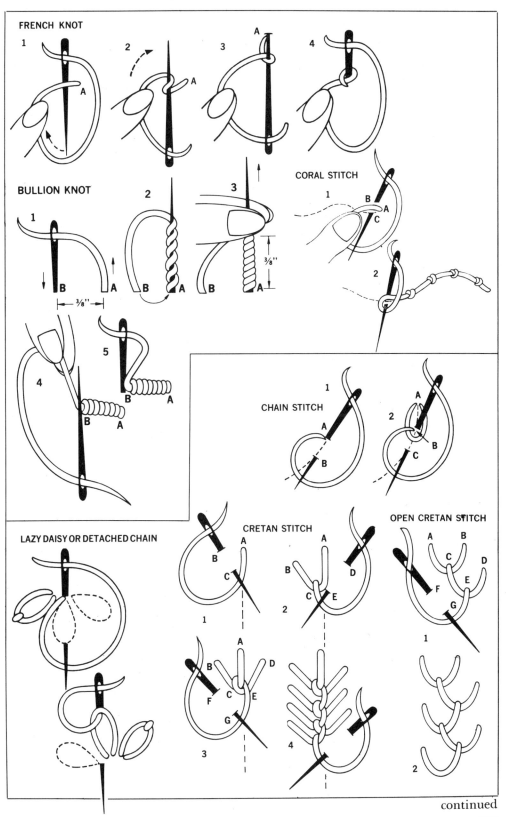

FRENCH KNOT

1 2 3 4

BULLION KNOT

1 2 3 A
3/8"

4 5

CORAL STITCH

1 2

CHAIN STITCH

1 2

LAZY DAISY OR DETACHED CHAIN

CRETAN STITCH

1 2 3 4

OPEN CRETAN STITCH

1 2

continued

Embroidery Stitches, continued

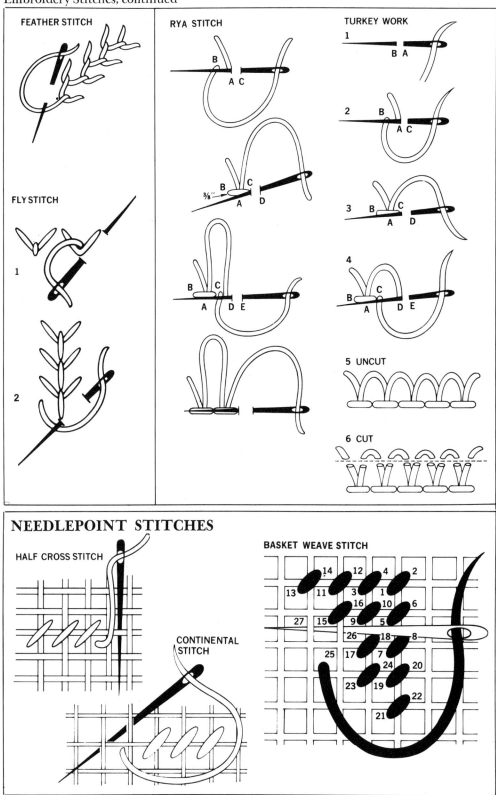

FEATHER STITCH

FLY STITCH

1

2

RYA STITCH

B
A C

³⁄₈″ B C
A D

B C
A D E

TURKEY WORK

1
B A

2
B
A C

3
B C
A D

4
B C
A D E

5 UNCUT

6 CUT

NEEDLEPOINT STITCHES

HALF CROSS STITCH

CONTINENTAL
STITCH

BASKET WEAVE STITCH

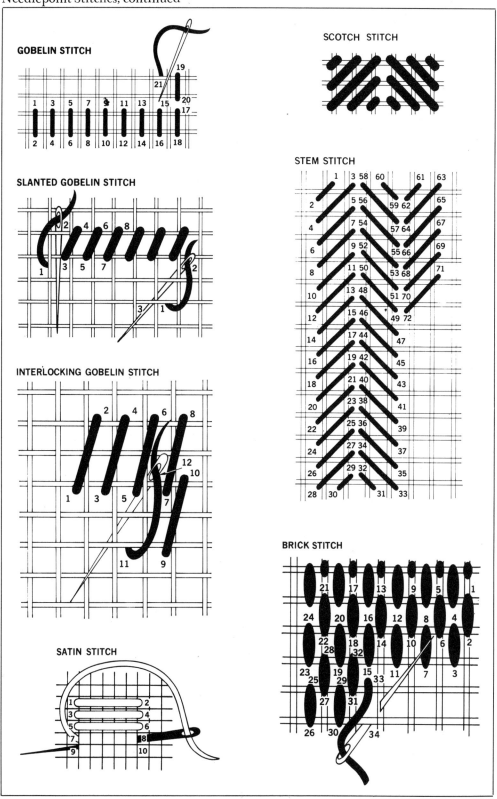

GOBELIN STITCH

SLANTED GOBELIN STITCH

INTERLOCKING GOBELIN STITCH

SATIN STITCH

SCOTCH STITCH

STEM STITCH

BRICK STITCH

EMBROIDERY STITCHES FOR THE LEFT-HANDED

For left-handed readers, we have chosen to illustrate the most frequently used embroidery stitches. Left-handed embroiderers can, in most cases, use all the right-handed diagrams by simply turning this book upside down and placing a mirror (with backstand) so that it reflects the left-handed version.

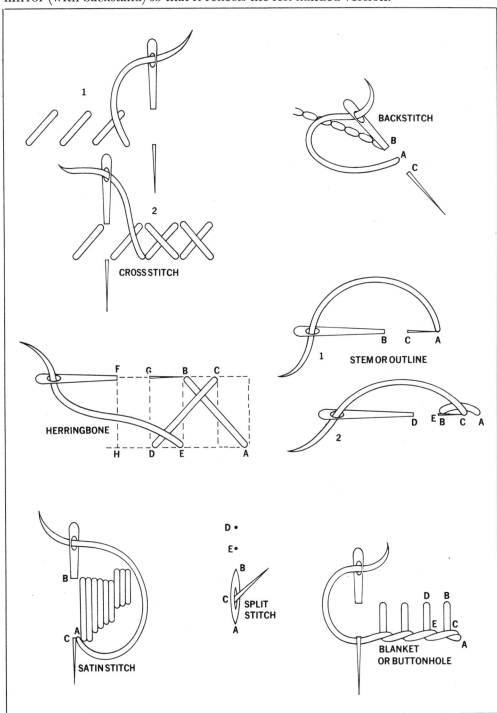

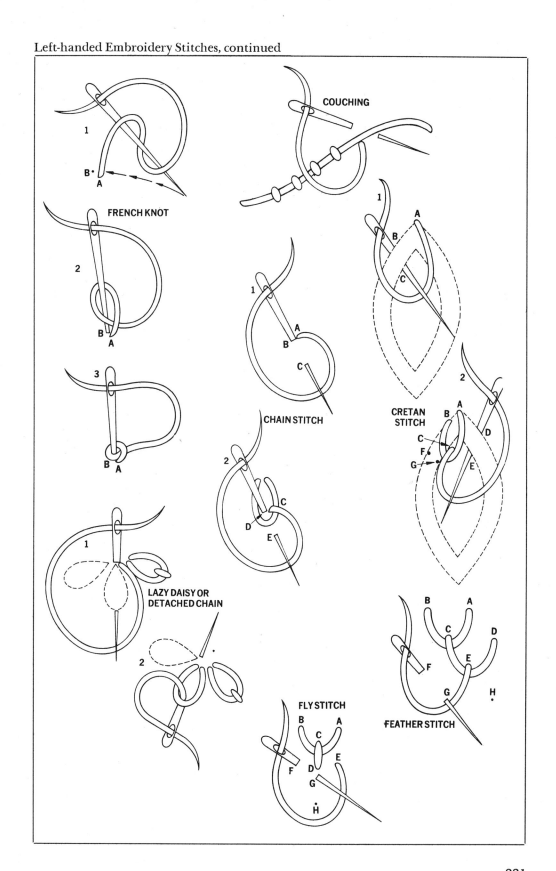

COUCHING

FRENCH KNOT

CHAIN STITCH

CRETAN STITCH

LAZY DAISY OR DETACHED CHAIN

FLY STITCH

FEATHER STITCH

index

INDEX

acknowledgements

We wish to acknowledge the following designers and photographers whose work appears in this book. Their excellence and creativity have helped FAMILY CIRCLE maintain its consistently high standards over the years.

PHOTOGRAPHERS

George Nordhausen	Alan Blumenthal	Gordon E. Smith
William McGinn	Alan Hicks	Bob Stoller
	Vincent Lisanti	Bob Strode
Adelio Bianchini	Mort Mace	Ben Swedowsky
Richard Blinkoff	Victor Skrebneski	Jack Ward

DESIGNERS

Marianne Ake	Jacqueline Heriteau	Charlotte Patera
Liza Andreas	Mr. and Mrs. Alfred Hilarski	Nina Pellegrini
Amy Bahrt	Millie Hines	Robert Pfreundschuh
Kristina Becker	ChrisJan	Gary Porcano
Joanne Beretta	Jacqueline Jewett	Ruth Potter
Linda Blood	Dale Joe	Toni Scott
Pat Boyle	Marilyn Judson	Mimi Shimmin
Marga Bremer	Dione King	Maida Silverman
John Burton Brimer	Donna Lang	Colleen Smith
Audrey Brown	Jean Ray Laury	Glenora Smith
Judy Copeland	Helen Maris	Constance Spates
Jackie Curry	Joan McElroy	Kathryn Stoll
Peter Davis	Jeff Millstein	Mary Lou Stribling
Gail Diven	Kathy Moore	Susan Toplitz
Kent Forrester	Gene Morin	David B. Traum, Inc.
Linda Giampa	Diane Moschillo	Rein Virkmaa
Donna Guardino	Offray and Sons	Carole Vizbara
Sara Gutierres	Ruth O'Mara	Les Walker
Mel Hammock	Sandy Paisley	Jean Wilkinson
Anni Hayum		Nancy Wykstra